Highway
to
Hell

John Geddes

Broadway Books, New York

Highway to Hell

Dispatches from
a Mercenary in Iraq

BROADWAY

PUBLISHED BY BROADWAY BOOKS

Copyright © 2008 by John Geddes and Alun Rees

All Rights Reserved

Published in the United States by Broadway Books, an imprint of the
Doubleday Publishing Group, a division of Random House, Inc., New York.
www.broadwaybooks.com

Originally published in a somewhat different form in the United Kingdom by
Century, London, in 2006. Copyright © 2006 by John Geddes and Alun Rees.
This edition published by arrangement with Century.

BROADWAY BOOKS and its logo, a letter B bisected on the diagonal, are
trademarks of Random House, Inc.

Book design by Ralph Fowler / rlf design

LIBRARY OF CONGRESS CATALOGING-IN-PUBLICATION DATA
Geddes, John.
  Highway to hell : dispatches from a mercenary in Iraq / John Geddes.
     p. cm.
  1. Iraq War, 2003—Personal narratives, British. 2. Geddes, John. 3. Mercenary
troops—Iraq—Biography. 4. Mercenary troops—Great Britain—Biography.
I. Title.

  DS79.76.G43 2008
  956.7044'3092—dc22
  [B]

                                                 2008002668

ISBN 978-0-7679-3025-3

PRINTED IN THE UNITED STATES OF AMERICA

10 9 8 7 6 5 4 3 2 1

First U.S. Edition

To all the PMCs
who have died in the name
of protection . . .

Contents

Foreword to U.S. Edition

Four years and a river of blood have run their course since the U.S.-led coalition pounded their way into Iraq on a wave of shock and awe and President George W. Bush was confident enough to claim a victory in a May Day speech on the deck of the USS *Abraham Lincoln.*

You wonder what Abe Lincoln would have made of it all if he had been alive to see the carnage and the descent into near civil war as Iraq, the ancient Babylon, descended into the pits of hell.

I arrived in Iraq shortly after that speech on the deck of the carrier, when the Iraqis were still stunned and paralyzed in the weeks immediately after the invasion, looking for big bucks. The false peace wasn't going to last long, and within a few weeks the insurgency kicked off big-time.

My name is John Geddes. I'm an ex-SAS warrant officer and I was there as a private military contractor (PMC), one of the first of the estimated forty to fifty thousand mercenary soldiers who swarmed over Iraq to take up big-bucks protection contracts ferrying engineers, financiers, diplomats, and the media across the ravaged country.

We call it "the Highway to Hell" and the tariff is counted in roadside improvised explosive devices (IEDs), suicide bombers, rocket attacks, and hammerings from machine guns. Most of all, it's counted in bodies. Men and women have died on both sides as the PMCs and the insurgents have fought out their own private war in the shadow of the flames of the coalition offensive. In the pages that follow, I tell of my own personal battles with the insurgency and my late-night boozing as endless trips riding as one-man shotgun to media crews got to me. I relate some of the fantastic gun battles that friends of mine engaged in, too, as they rode the Highway and I tell of the close relationships built up between PMCs and some of their courageous Arab drivers.

I show how different PMC companies use different tactics. The low-profile way preferred by British and Australian companies, whose PMCs will even use garbage trucks to blend into the background. That contrasts with the high-profile way preferred by many U.S. companies, whose PMCs travel in big convoys with an equally big firepower.

And I don't shy away from the Blackwater controversy, which has seen the issue of modern PMCs propelled center stage in U.S. politics as American citizens stand accused of indiscriminately shooting civilians across Iraq.

There's nothing new about hiring mercenaries. England's King George V paid thirty thousand blue-coated Hessian soldiers in his failed bid to crush the emerging independent Americans. But now it's the U.S. administration that's spending billions on a similar number of PMCs to service the coalition troops, protect the reconstruction effort, and even to guard high-ranking military officers and diplomats as they cross the Iraqi warscape.

Every dawn, PMCs emerge to take to the Highway in the world's most dangerous and mind-numbing job. They come from all over the world to ride the roller coaster. Hold on tight for your ride along the Highway to Hell.

—*J.G., December 2007*

Highway
to Hell

1. Contact!

IFIRST SAW THEM ON THE SLIP ROAD. THEY were trapped in a muddle of traffic, jostling to get through, eager, anxious, impatient; the mood of the driver transmitted down through the steering wheel and the throttle into the jerking, pushy movements of the car. I'd watched them as we drove past with that dawning of unease that comes from instinct, and now they were behind us, framed in my rearview mirror, kicking up a plume of road dust as they wove through the morning traffic on the highway through Fallujah. Pickups loaded with workers on the open backs, loose-fitting robes snapping in the milky warm slipstream, moved to let the black BMW 7 Series charge through. They were like members of a herd making way for a big predator that had earmarked its prey farther into the throng.

I knew what was coming now just as the herd, watching from their pickups and battered sedans, did. They simply watched the pursuit with relieved interest, glad not to be the one pursued and hoping, above all, not to be noticed. To be honest, I'd known what was coming from the moment I'd seen the BMW, with its blacked-out windows, stuck temporarily on the slip road. It was typical, too typical, of the vehicles used by gangs of insurgents in Iraq, and as they loomed up in my mirror, I knew with utter certainty they were about to strike. But the difference was that I'm not one of the herd.

I used to be a warrant officer in the British SAS and now I'm a soldier of fortune. I'm a hired gun, a mercenary if you like, and I'm the man who was trying to keep the other four guys in the car alive on the drive from Jordan to Baghdad along the most dangerous road in the world, down the Fallujah bypass and around the Ramadi Ring Road. It's a route they call "the Highway to Hell."

There were four others in the car, a TV crew from a major UK network and a Jordanian driver, and as I watched that BMW gaining on us, all my senses combined to help me stay focused on keeping my clients and myself alive. I barely took my eyes off the mirror, leaving my peripheral senses to tell me if other predators had joined the chase, but as events unfolded, it was to be just us and them. Ahmed, my driver, had seen them, too, and I didn't have to tell him who they were. He started to mutter and jabber under his breath and I couldn't tell whether he was praying or cursing, only that he was terrified. He never usually perspired, but within seconds beads of sweat were running down his forehead and the side of his neck.

The BMW was cruising behind us, closely matching our speed, and that's always a real giveaway. They call it a "combat indicator" in the military, but I didn't need any indicators; I'd had a shit feeling about them ever since I'd spotted the BMW on the slip road.

Then they began moving up on us with evident hostile intent and I weighed in my hands the AK-47 lying on my lap for a moment before resting it back there again. I had my window open, but I closed it to hide behind its tinted glass. The BMW came up alongside us and the black window in the front came down like a theater curtain, revealing the driver and a guy who had the air of a man in charge sitting alongside him.

They cruised past us at a good speed, nice and steady, though, since they had nothing to worry about—it was their backyard, they were the top predator in the chain, and they were going to take their time. I guess they were thinking that maybe we were rich Iraqis or Kuwaitis, or that Japanese tourists would be nice— and yes, believe it or not, they do come sightseeing from Tokyo. The crew in the BMW would have loved the three-man Western TV crew on board—all that hostage money—and whatever happened, they'd have the camera kit and three satellite phones to sell. A real steal, and just for good measure, Ahmed would be slotted like a dog.

Ahmed kept on muttering under his breath and they were still in no hurry to put him out of his suspense as I watched them come alongside us a second time. Again they drew back behind us, only to spurt forward and come back alongside us yet again. Maybe they were enjoying their game of cat and mouse. The clients were sleeping off a hangover on the backseat. No need to wake them, I thought, nothing they can do about it.

Anyway, I had one advantage because our big GMC four-wheel-drive SUV gave me a view down onto the gunmen, and as I looked into the car, their back windows were lowered and I saw three armed men on the rear passenger seat. In the front, the driver was wearing a sick smile behind a *shemag* that had partly fallen away from his face; the guy alongside him had his *shemag* wrapped around his features as he leaned halfway across the driver to wave and gesticulate out of the window with his AK-47. I've got one of them, too, I was thinking, but I'm not showing it. His eyes were burning with hatred and disdain and he obviously wanted us to pull over, but I couldn't believe it when I felt us slow down as Ahmed, the man with most to lose if you count his life, actually began to obey.

"Fucking drive, Ahmed," I snarled at him. His foot went down again and we temporarily spoiled the synchronized driving display of the scumbag in the 7 Series, but they were soon backing us.

Ahmed was gibbering out loud in Arabic in a constant flow of verbalized terror as I looked through my tinted window at the four armed men in the car. Years of experience told me that their demeanor and the way they were holding their weapons meant that the last thing they were expecting was a real fight. They must have believed they had all the cards and that much sooner than later we'd be pulling over to the side of the road to deliver them their prize. I decided to keep my ace well hidden under the table, on my lap and out of sight.

They forged ahead again and the boss leaned across once more, but this time he shoved the AK in front of the driver and out of the window and let a burst go across our hood to encourage us to pull over. I fought hard with any idea of dropping my window and lifting my AK off my lap and into sight. Ace under the table was my lifesaving mantra at that moment, ace under the table. I pushed everything else out of my mind but my sight of the gunmen and the thought of the ace I would play. I knew what I had to do, because the next time he fired, the burst would pour directly into our vehicle and that would be a very bad thing.

I stared through my tinted window across the three feet of door metal and swirling dusty air that separated us and I could clearly see that the scowling gunman next to the driver was trying to eyeball me. I lowered my window as I looked back at him. I looked straight through him and then I did it. I played my ace, but even then I didn't lay it on the table. They never saw my cards. I just pressed my finger onto the trigger of the Kalashnikov still resting on my lap and let go a long burst of fire.

The familiar metallic clattering of an AK was indiscernible inside the car as it filled with the most terrible, deafening cacophony of sound. *Clat! Clat! Clat!* It seemed to go on and on, filling my world with an awful fanfare of destruction. *Clat! Clat! Clat!*

The armor-piercing assault rounds tore through our door and their door, too, in a microsecond, ripping metal and flesh without discrimination in the 7 Series. I watched the driver's head explode as the height difference of the two vehicles laid it on the line. The gunman next to him screamed, openmouthed in horror, all hatred and disdain wiped clean from his eyes by disbelief, as the assault rounds sliced into him, too, and tracked through his body.

CLAT! CLAT! CLAT! My finger still pressed the trigger and rounds kept tearing across that tiny three-foot space for another couple of seconds, until the BMW suddenly faded and fell back. I followed it in the mirror and saw steam and black smoke billowing from under the hood, so that I knew the end of my burst had smashed their engine block.

I watched the BMW start to fishtail and skid as our previously close contact became a surreal disconnection. We were still in traffic, but cars and trucks were now evaporating from the scene of the high-speed shoot-out with practiced ease. But my imperative wasn't traffic flow, and the critical thing was my certainty that the driver was dead and his boss was probably dead in the seat alongside him, too. As for the three gunmen behind them, they hadn't even had time to spit, let alone respond, and they were left impotent as the BMW spun out of control.

"Drive, fucking drive," I screamed at Ahmed, and he floored it as I turned to the correspondent and his crew, who were now sitting transfixed and deafened by sound and fury after the rudest awakening of their lives.

"Okay, guys?" I asked, barely able to hear my own voice. They nodded rigidly through the haze of acrid cordite that filled the car. I watched as their eyes kept wandering away from mine toward the gun still resting on my lap and then to the door alongside me and then back again. They were trying to work out why I hadn't fired through the window, why the door wasn't a mangled mess, just pierced by a series of neat holes marked out by flash burns. They were trying to work out why they were still alive.

"Welcome to Fallujah," I said, but they looked very pale and not another word was spoken until we reached Baghdad.

OUR JOURNEY HAD BEGUN at dawn that day when light welled up over the city, still cooling from the heat of the day before like a giant concrete radiator, and the haunting wail of the call to prayer floated down from a mosque tower over downtown Amman.

That chant of the muezzin to the faithful, the clichéd sound track to every documentary ever made on the Middle East—you know exactly what to expect, but it still gets to you every time and never fails to raise the hairs on the back of your neck. These days, it never fails to set me on edge. It's become the theme song for episodes of death and mayhem and starts the day with an unwelcome reminder that a religion founded on a philosophy of order and mutual respect has been twisted into an alibi for murder and bombing.

I'd already showered and shaved and my kit had been checked, rechecked, and checked again; now it was ready to go, so there was nothing to do but get on with it. That constant checking of kit is an abiding theme in my life and it gets to be such a routine that I almost find myself looking into the mirror to check that I'm taking the right bloke on the job. I grabbed my small day sack with a survival kit in it, checked that I had my ID and passport, and then went downstairs to join the others in the hotel foyer.

The correspondent was seasoned, his cameraman an experienced guy who knew the ropes, and the soundman-cum-fixer was the third member of the crew. Ahmed was a veteran on the run.

I went through the drill with them. It always begins with the briefing—the "actions on," as the military call it—when I cover what they've got to do in the event of a road accident, an ambush, or a hijack. I stood there feeling like a member of the cabin crew going through the preflight emergency drill, while my clients, sprawled out on the hotel's leather sofas, looked just as bored as the average business passenger on a scheduled flight.

They smiled wanly when I got to the bit where I told them, "Remember, we don't stop at service areas; we piss on the side of the road. And we don't look at our dicks while we're doing it; we keep aware and look about us."

There were no women on that trip, but it would have been just the same for them, with a biological variation, of course, and the guys knew that I was serious when I told them, "There are service areas, but they're a no-no since a CNN crew stopped at one and got rumbled by insurgents. They were followed and a few rounds were fired through the back of the vehicle. The driver was killed and they were very lucky to get away."

It was time to go and they hauled themselves out of their seats and joined the pile of aluminum camera boxes stacked up under the front awning of the hotel, alongside the SUV.

"Hard cases up against the backseats, please," I told them, and the camera boxes were packed where they would afford at least some protection from any incoming rounds to our rear. The soft luggage—rucksacks and holdalls full of clothing—were piled in front of the hard boxes.

While the kit was being packed, the correspondent paced nervously up and down, as though he was rehearsing a piece to film. He'd been up drinking with the cameraman into the early hours and all they wanted to do was to get into the vehicle and go to sleep.

Meanwhile, Ahmed dragged on a foul-smelling cigarette, and I placed myself upwind of him, carefully watching the unfolding scene as the rising sun glinted off my mirrored shades. He's a nice guy, Ahmed, a family man who knows only too well that captured Jordanian drivers are always killed by insurgents. Why? Because they're not worth a bean on the hostage market, and anyway, they've betrayed Islam by chauffeuring the infidel invaders. Like all the Jordanians who daily risk their lives on the Baghdad run, Ahmed's either very broke or very brave, or, I suspect, probably both.

I pointed toward the hood of the SUV and he lifted it so that I could personally check the oil and the radiator levels. I even checked the windshield wash. Check and recheck—it's attention to detail that keeps you alive. I glanced at the tires, too, just to make sure they had some tread on them; then Ahmed turned the key in the ignition and I watched the needle on the fuel gauge rise to full.

"Thanks," I told him. "You happy with everything?" Ahmed smiled in reply and I turned to the TV crew. "All aboard, guys, time to roll. Just make sure you've got everything you need."

It takes three hours to get to the Iraqi border, and there wasn't a great deal of chat in the car once they'd discussed some details of their arrangements, whom they'd be meeting, and the first story they hoped to get in the can. The correspondent and the cameraman were obviously desperate to get some sleep and they soon nodded off, heads occasionally lolling from side to side with the unsynchronized rhythm of the car. It wasn't long before the soundman joined them.

That first leg of the journey is always unrelentingly boring, with mile after mile of yellowy gray rock and sand, and I knew that we wouldn't see a scrap of vegetation until we got to Iraq. The difference is quite dramatic then because the civil service mandarin in Britain who drew the lines on the map, laying out the boundaries of the two countries nearly a century ago, gave the

Jordanians the short straw. They got a lunar landscape with not a drop of oil beneath it, while the Iraqis got two rivers and a bit of greenery sitting on top of a gigantic oil well.

I spotted Iraq as that change in landscape came into view, just before I spotted the border post itself, a nondescript collection of buildings with a small U.S. Army stockade standing at arm's length from the local administration. It's a sight that galvanized me and pulled me out of the wheel-drumming monotony of the past three hours, and I knew that the mood over the next couple of hours would be very different.

The Jordanian checkpoint is always a flurry of activity—visas being stamped, waiting in a queue of fifty, and, of course, the obligatory payment to preclude any more border bureaucracy. The Iraqi border patrol just waves us through most of the time, only occasionally taking a look at credentials, but there's really never a lot of fuss.

We soon pulled up outside the U.S. guardhouse for the really important part of the proceedings. "You guys put your flak jackets on while I collect my tools," I told them, and then I vanished into the guardhouse.

When I first arrived in Iraq, I learned that a lot of the security teams bury their weapons in caches on the Iraqi side, take a GPS bearing on the spot, and just dig them up when they cross back over the frontier on their next run in. Well, I really didn't like the sound of that at all. What if there's a pair of unsympathetic eyes out there watching you as you make your cache? You might just find yourself digging into a booby trap or walking onto a small antipersonnel mine that's been laid as a welcome mat by insurgents.

No, I didn't think that was the way for me, so I pondered the problem for a while, until my natural affection and admiration for the Americans and their way of doing business led me to a direct approach. I visited the U.S. border detachment on my first run and spoke to the big Louisiana-born master sergeant in charge.

"Do you know those Westerns where the sheriff takes the weapons off the cowboys when they arrive in town?" I asked him when the introductions were over.

"Sure do," he said.

"Well, I'm not a cowboy and you're not the sheriff, but I wondered if you could do the same sort of thing for me, but in reverse, and take my guns off me when I leave town, so to speak, and go back to Jordan?"

"Why, hell yes, it'd be our pleasure," he told me, and that's the way it panned out. I just handed them in and got a receipt and they locked them up until I returned. No fear of land mines or a nasty ambush, no sweaty digging in the scrub. In fact, no burial party of any sort at all.

There was another key benefit from this more civilized transaction, and that was the chance to chat with the Yanks in the guardhouse and get any intelligence on insurgent activity that might have come back down the line to them. There were very few problems close to the Jordanian border, but the guys in the guardhouse always knew about anything going on farther up the road and they always liked to shoot the breeze and gossip with people passing through—and information can mean survival in Iraq.

The master sergeant and I sealed the deal that day with a case of beer, which the Yanks are always grateful to receive, as the poor suckers fight in a dry army, and then I showed them a couple of special-range drills with an AK. They were pleased, and I was happy to leave an infantry unit of the U.S. Army with a little bit of SAS polish on its troops.

So it was that I stepped into the guardhouse as usual and

handed over my gun chit, then waited for my weapons to be brought out from the armory and handed over to me.

"Here you go, sir," the young GI said, counting out my private arsenal. "One AK-47, serial number—"

"No need for the number, thanks. I'm sure it's the right one."

"Sure thing, sir. So that's one AK-47 assault rifle, plus six thirty-round mags; one Glock pistol, plus four twelve-round mags. Serial number?" He looked up inquiringly.

"No thanks."

"Okay, so here we go. Two NS. L2 grenades and one white phos' grenade. That's everything, sir, so if you just sign here, you can take your weapons. Anything else I can help you with, sir?"

"Not really. Thanks very much." I scrawl my name across the bottom of the chit. "Nothing going on up the road, is there?"

"All quiet, as far as we know, sir. Now you-all have a safe journey."

"Thanks, old son. See you on the way back."

I transferred the weapons to the vehicle, where the crew studiously avoided mentioning them at all because officially, as far as they were concerned, the guns, let alone the grenades, were not supposed to exist. You see, the problem about looking after TV crews tends to begin with their network's policy on war coverage. The British and the other European media mostly work on the principle that once weapons are involved, journalistic impartiality and neutrality are lost and their crews will then be open to hostage taking and the unthinkable possibility of execution.

Paradoxically, it's argued, the absence of weapons will protect correspondents and crews from those fates as they tangibly demonstrate their noncombatant status. If only. You can be fairly sure that people like the infamous Musab al-Zarqawi, who was Al Qaeda's man in Iraq at the time, hadn't taken the time to read the network editorial handbooks, but their actions spell out clearly any views they may have on the issues. It's quite simple. The word *neutrality* does not exist in their dictionary and all that matters to them is their own twisted interpretation of the word of the Almighty embodied in the Holy Koran. That boils down to a rule-of-thumb judgment that absolutely no one at all is offered safe passage through their hands, which in itself goes against the deeply ingrained traditions of hospitality in the Arab world. Rather, you're more likely to be exploited for your propaganda value on a few pleading video appeals, then have your head chopped off.

The U.S. networks have been quick to recognize the realities in the region and tend to have a robust "balls to neutrality" policy and travel with more than enough firepower to take on the average gang of insurgents. No one can legislate for sniper shots or a lucky hit with a rocket-propelled grenade and no one can insulate himself against a suicide bomber intent on hell, but if less than the worst happens, they reckon to have enough in reserve to protect and maintain the convoy until help arrives. There are certainly arguments for and against their strategy, which you might characterize as heavy-handed, but there are absolutely no sane arguments for moving around Iraq without any weapons at all. None.

Anyway, I'd already had a free and frank exchange of views with my clients about the issues and told them that they could certainly instruct me that they didn't want me to carry a weapon. I, on the other hand, would ignore their instruction and would be carrying a weapon unless they absolutely did not want me to, in which case they'd have to find someone else. Therein, of course, lies their dilemma, because finding someone willing to drive the Highway without a weapon is a bit like looking for a free beer in a brothel. Like quite a few others on the security circuit out there, I had been persuaded to drive along the Highway unarmed on a score or more of occasions, but the number of close shaves I'd had left me feeling like Kojak and I resolved to travel armed or not at all. If people didn't like it, they didn't have to travel with me.

"Look," I told the correspondent, "just tell the news desk that you're traveling with a bodyguard who has been told not to carry a weapon. When you've done that, just pretend you haven't seen the weapon I'm carrying. It's simple. You didn't see it, so if we end up in a shoot-out, then I'm the one to blame."

"That's all very well, John, but I could get the sack for traveling with an armed bodyguard," he replied.

"Of course you could and that would be terrible, but you could just as easily get yourself dead if I don't carry a weapon. Besides, the only way your bosses will find out that the rules have been broken is if we get captured, at which point it won't matter anyway."

"What you say is all very well, John, but what if—"

"No what-ifs, mate. I'll tell you what. If a band of insurgents decides to take us hostage because I'm carrying a weapon, it will be because I haven't used the weapon. Therefore, if we are taken then, either way, it's my fault, so you can sack me before they sack you. In the meantime, pretend I'm the man with the invisible gun. Agreed?"

"Okay, but—"

"No buts. Deal?"

"Deal."

That's the way it went, yet I know full well that he could still face the sack today if his highly scrupled colleagues at the news desk, who were sitting safely back in the London studio at the time, found out that he'd broken their standing orders on war coverage. Crazy.

Well, the deal was done and I had sealed it by retrieving my weapons from the U.S. armory, so I went back to organizing the trip. They'd put on their body armor, the bulky type you commonly see worn on TV reports, which provides maximum protection but is crap for moving about in. I use my own high-spec "restricted entry" body armor, designed for fighting in tight spots, which is very expensive but, in the words of the brochure, an effective compromise between total protection and mobility. Don't know about that, but I certainly feel more comfortable in one.

The mood had shifted up a couple of gears in the car by then and there was a tangible sense of increased tension, even though it would be another hour and a half before the really high-voltage ride began through Fallujah and Ramadi, and the start of the roller coaster is the point known as Feature 127.

It's just a stone way mark on the side of the road in the middle of nowhere, erected to tell the weary traveler that there are 127 kilometers to go before reaching Baghdad, but it has taken on great significance for those who ride the Highway. That's because for some reason nothing ever seems to happen on the western side of Feature 127 and all hell can, and often does, break loose on the other side of it. Now it's a recognized rendezvous point and a place to stop, consider, and compose oneself before the roller coaster begins.

I spotted the landscape around 127 before we reached the way mark itself and told Ahmed to pull in for a pit stop before we went on. There were a couple of reasons for that, and first I reminded everyone on board to have that "heads-up" piss before we continued, because there'd be no stopping on the road from then on unless we were absolutely forced to pull up. The correspondent yawned and looked a bit fed up at being woken from a sleep that might have left him untroubled by the stresses and dangers of the Highway until he arrived at his hotel in Baghdad.

Unscrewing the cap on a bottle of water, I took a swig, then set about arranging the cabin space for the rest of the run. At the same time, I was tuning myself up mentally for whatever might come with a routine that clearly signaled a watershed in the journey and the need for a new, more focused mind-set.

"Right, fellas, get your helmets on and keep them on for the rest of the trip, please. If there's anything you want out of your kit, get it now, if you would, and please don't mention it to me once we've set off again. I won't be interested. Whatever it is."

They strapped their helmets on and I looked at them carefully. They all had that same expression of incipient fear, just like someone who's going to go on a very big roller coaster. Their eyes were flat, almost glazed by a sheen of adrenaline waiting to be used. They didn't want to do it, but they were going to do it anyway, and they became increasingly aware of the thumping of their hearts and the dryness in their mouths as they fought the demons within to remain outwardly composed.

Ahmed fingered his worry beads and unconsciously chewed on his lip as he waited anxiously to take the wheel again. I was busy hanging spare body armor onto the door fixtures inside the car to make an effective and proven barrier between the passengers and small-arms fire. It's a precaution that has saved many lives. The check reflex kicked in again and I checked the oil, water, and the fuel. Just in case. When we were all loaded up, I cradled the AK in my lap, covering it with my green and black *shemag* headdress to hide it from any prying eyes and handed Ahmed the Glock pistol, knowing he could use it, because I'd shown him how. He stuffed it between his leg and the seat and nodded to me.

"Let's roll," I said, and Ahmed did just that, speeding down the road as if he were trying to lift a jet off a runway. He'd push the thing like that all the way to Baghdad, keeping the speedometer at a 100, as if a cartful of demons were tailing him, and perhaps they were.

The traffic began to thicken a little as we approached Fallujah, a town that straddles the Highway like a piece of malevolent lagging, bombed, battered, and shot up but largely unyielding, and that's when I spotted them jostling to find a way through the constipated traffic on the slip road. And then the black BMW 7 Series was framed in the side-view mirror as it charged up behind us.

2. From Drama into Crisis

IT SEEMS HARD TO BELIEVE NOW, BUT IT WAS the movie stars Lee Marvin and Steve McQueen who inspired me to join the army, and another star, Dirk Bogarde, became my recruiting captain.

It happened like this. I was brought up in a proud shipbuilding town called Newcastle upon Tyne on the northeast coast of England. Geographically, it faces straight across to Scandinavia, and in historical times the area was invaded and settled by Viking raiders. No surprise, then, that it's got a reputation for hard-fighting men. Come to think of it, the whole island of Britain is populated by a race that our neighbors on the European mainland consider to be violent and warlike. They may have a point.

I was a complete dud in school and never passed an exam, and that's because I preferred boxing to books and in those days I'd been a promising amateur fighter. But I did have an ambition. I was convinced that I was going to become a movie star.

So when the time came to leave school, I went to the careers adviser, who gave me a list of acting academies, and I left home to head off for the bright lights of the Birmingham School of Speech & Drama. At the audition for a place in the college, I was told that there were dogs and kangaroos with successful acting careers that had more talent than I did, but they gave me a place anyway because they said I had the right look.

To be honest, I was a complete disaster. When I sang, people scattered for cover, and when I attempted to act out scenes from a play, I sounded flatter than a witch's tit. I didn't care. Nothing was going to stop me from making it big on the silver screen. I just needed to change my tactics.

I came up with a bold plan. My hero Steve had served in the Merchant Marine and Lee in the U.S. Marine Corps and both had seen action, so I thought I'd leave BSSD and enlist in the army. That way, I'd get the front-line experience that would turn me into a convincing hero who could draw on his combat experience to make the action leap off the screen. I decided the army would become my drama school and I would rehearse for my movie career in battle.

The college term was nearly over, only a couple of weeks left and one more torment to endure. I was asked to recite a poem called "The Charge of the Light Brigade," written by Tennyson as a tribute to six hundred British cavalrymen who made a suicidal charge against a battery of Russian cannons during the Crimean War, in the days of Queen Victoria. It was for the end-of-semester show.

The principal of the school was a formidable lady named Mary Richards, who was a friend of Sir Laurence Olivier, and she'd persuaded another of her old acting chums to come to the show, and she grandly announced that the guest of honor would be the great Dirk Bogarde himself. It sent a shock wave of nerves through the college, but I kept cool. No sweat, I thought, I'll just give it my all on the night. I did just that, pouring heart and soul into my recitation, knowing that a real screen hero was out there among the silhouettes beyond the footlights, listening to me.

It was a real torture, worse than any interrogation I was ever to endure, but to be fair, it was the best thing I'd ever done at the college and I got my first and last spontaneous round of applause from an audience. Afterward, Dirk himself came up to me and gave me a critical accolade I'll never forget.

"Bloody good effort, that," he said. "Difficult to get that poem right; got to weigh and balance it properly."

"Thanks," I said lamely. "I just gave it my best shot."

Dirk had been a soldier himself during World War II, and he said to me, "I was in the Parachute Regiment. Fought in the Normandy landings; parachuted onto Plimsoll Bridge on D-day. Unforgettable experiences, you know."

That settled it. The military was the place to learn about acting, and if the Airborne was good enough for Dirk Bogarde, then it was good enough for me.

Term ended a couple of days later, and as soon as I got back to Newcastle, I was hammering at the door of the Army Recruiting Office to sign up for the Red Berets of the Parachute Regiment—the Paras, as they are popularly known in Britain—and begin the long journey from Birmingham to Baghdad in a military career unwittingly launched by the great Dirk Bogarde.

To be honest, I'm sure the army was in me; after all, my father had fought at the epic desert battle of El Alamein as a Desert Rat in World War II. The fact that I was actually born in Rhodesia, as Zimbabwe was then known, and taken from Africa to England at the age of three may also have given me a bit of a soldier's wanderlust. So a few weeks later, I found myself at the Para Depot in the English garrison town of Aldershot and enlisted with the Second

Battalion, Parachute Regiment—aka 2 Para—after successfully completing the grueling P Company selection process for the regiment. I was now in the drama school of my choice, but what a very different world it turned out to be.

I spent seven years in 2 Para and survived several tours of duty in Northern Ireland, but nothing could have prepared me for the bloodletting that followed when we got the call to liberate the Falkland Islands from an Argentine invasion. It's a war that's been written about in many books, and I've actually been mentioned in two or three of them, and it's a war that changed my life profoundly.

When we sailed to the South Atlantic, I was a corporal and patrol commander in C Company, which specialized in reconnaissance. We were charged with getting as close as possible to the enemy lines to report on their deployment in detail, a mission that's known in the jargon as CTR, or close target reconnaissance, and my patrol was tasked to do the CTRs on the enemy lines at a tiny settlement called Goose Green.

The Battle of Goose Green turned out to be the most fierce and dreadful struggle of the Falklands conflict, with the Paras outnumbered three to one, storming well-dug-in positions where the enemy lay in wait with a .50-cal machine gun in every trench. We took them without artillery, without any air support or helicopters, without vehicles to ferry in ammo or take wounded off the field of battle. We'd bitten off more than we could chew, but we chewed it anyway.

I suspect many people in the States think of the Falklands War as some weird hangover from Britain's colonial days, but the two issues for me are the nature of the Argentine military junta and the Cold War implications of the Falklands campaign.

That junta gave not only safe haven to fugitive Nazis but also jobs in the military infrastructure of the Argentine. Little wonder then that this regime would snatch college kids off the streets, torture them, and then drop them, alive and weighted down with chains, out of airplanes into the ocean. They'd also arrest women who were political opponents and take their babies away from them before killing the women in one of those notorious death flights. It's reckoned that over seven hundred infants were stolen from their families, then offered to childless officers in the army and police to adopt. Foul bastards.

There was no way that our prime minister, Maggie Thatcher, could leave that tiny population of islanders loyal to the queen in such hands. And anyway, the Argentine claim to the Falklands went back to the eighteenth and nineteenth centuries. They had about as much right to reclaim it as Mexico would have to lay claim to Texas.

The other thing you have to remember is that at this time, the Cold War with the Soviet Union was still running below zero, and when Britain's task force headed off for the South Atlantic, the Russians scrambled spy planes, deployed submarines, and positioned satellites to watch the action.

Why? Well, those guys in the Kremlin wanted to see just how well the forces of the USA's closest ally would perform. They wanted to see how our troops fought and how well our navy and air force performed. That was so important that years later, Secretary of State Madeleine Albright revealed that if a British troop ship had been sunk, the president would have made up our numbers with U.S. marines, who would have joined us in battle. Some great commitment!

Britain had to triumph in battle, but the real winners were the thirteen million people of the Argentine, who got rid of a murdering fascist dictatorship and had their first democratic elections in nearly thirty years, enabling them to take back a half-dead economy from the hands of the bungling military.

I don't expect a thank-you from the Argentinians, but that war taught me one thing. The army wasn't a rehearsal and I wasn't going to be a film star. I was a soldier.

T HIS IS THE TRACK you take, *mes enfants.*"
The Foreign Legion training sergeant pointed at a sweeping line on a classroom board. He was immaculate in his rigidly pressed uniform, his trademark kepi hat welded to his number-two haircut.

He was making an exception and instructing in English because he had a visitor from the UK in his course. I was at Pau, in southern France, at the French army's own parachuting school and I was the first British Para to go on a HALO (high-altitude, low-opening) course. In fact, I also completed our own UK Special Forces HALO parachute-jump course a bit later, and I think I'm right in saying I'm the only person to have done both.

Unlike many Brits, I really love the French, so apart from reveling in the adrenaline rush of the new skills I was learning, I loved the atmosphere of the French services. I was attached to the famous Deuxième REP of the Foreign Legion while I was there, and apart from free-falling, I acquired some new friends and a taste for decent red wine. The French serve it with their meals in the canteen and they even give their troops minibar bottles of the stuff in their combat ration packs! *Fantastique!*

I'd volunteered for the HALO course because my big ambition was to go on to do the ultimate challenge of SAS selection. However, there was a problem with that because I had what are known as "regimental entries" with the Paras. Basically, that's like having points on your license, and if you've got points, you can't apply for the Special Air Service. They don't want to consider guys who make trouble.

My points were for brawling with other NCOs and for insubordination to officers. I had always been a spirited lad, and in the discipline of service life, it had gotten me into trouble. With a year to go before the points were removed, I decided to fill in my time with all the courses and skill-learning efforts I could find. Anything but fighting and insubordination!

From then on, I became increasingly proficient and professional and I focused my every fiber on becoming a member of the SAS. I'd seen those guys operating in the Falklands; they were men apart, deadly wraiths who came and went in the mist and left the enemy smashed behind them. I wanted to be one of them, and eventually I was. I passed selection for the SAS, became a member of D Squadron, and specialized in HALO covert parachute entry into combat zones.

One of the great bonuses of serving with the SAS was the contact we had with the elite Special Forces groups of allied countries, and I met and worked with most of them, but undoubtedly the closest bond between the elite soldiers of any two countries in the world exists between the SAS and Delta Force.

Delta was born out of the U.S. Special Forces debacle surrounding the botched attempt to rescue the U.S. embassy hostages from Teheran. In a fine compliment to SAS methods, an American colonel named Charles Beckwith was dispatched to the UK to go through SAS training and selection. He went home and formed Delta, a force only about three times the size of the SAS, which in U.S. terms makes it highly elite. After a whirlwind of operations in Afghanistan and Iraq, Delta Force has well and truly buried the memory of the Teheran hostage mess and has become a formidable force, one matched only by the SAS itself.

Today, the bond between those two magnificent forces is stronger than ever, with Delta and the SAS working more closely and striking blows in the war against terrorism that the public may never hear about but that are vital to our global security.

I spent a great deal of time working with colleagues in Delta Force and number one or two of them among my closest friends, and I came to consider the USA as my adopted home for a while.

I'll never forget my first training foray with Delta. We were in some swampy scrubland on a huge military range; maybe it was in Louisiana—I can't quite remember. What I can remember is the scenario where we were meant to assault a building where hostages and a dirty nuclear device were being held. The whole thing was done up like a film set, with lots of pop-up cardboard commandos to shoot at and some stooges playing the hostages. The whole assault would involve live rounds.

At the pre-ops briefing, I met one of the resident helicopter pilots, a tall, rangy guy with a big twirled mustache who could have been Wyatt Earp's great-grandson. He was a colorful, eccentric character and he made it his business to tell the SAS guys, who were new on the range, what to do when he came streaking in to back up the assault in his Little Bird MH 6J helo.

"Don't bother with coordinates," he told us with a big smile. "Just hit this Starburst and anything in front of that sucker is fucking history."

We liked that and we liked him. We liked him even more when one of our Delta mates told us, "Yeah, he's something else. He gets in so close that he's shot himself down twice with ricochets from his own cannon."

Brilliant! And "Wyatt Earp" was right about the Starburst. He came in like a hooligan and blasted everything in front of us to smithereens. It was so close that we could almost feel the wind from his rounds. He really was something else!

We bugged out after the attack, with the hostages liberated and the dirty bomb safely exfiltrated by helicopter, but then they gave us a surprise by simulating our helicopter crashing. It was a *Black Hawk Down* scenario and we had the 101st Airborne as the "enemy" hunting us down. My call-sign group got through. Others weren't so lucky and found themselves being none too gently "processed" by the boys from the Band of Brothers.

On another training mission, we were hosts to Delta on an Arctic warfare exercise in Norway, on a peninsula overlooking the Russian submarine fleet's rat run to the Atlantic from its base in Kola, near Murmansk. We were living in snow holes or in snow-covered tents perched on the ice-gripped fjords. Out there, you make friends with the Arctic or you die, and when you've made a deal with the environment, you can begin to think about taking on the enemy.

At the time, the SAS was using the latest Norwegian army kit, which consisted of fleece-type garments that actually blotted water up when they got wet. We were carrying hundred-pound packs with spare clothing and sleeping bags, but when our friends from Delta came along, they left us standing in the kit stakes, as usual.

They were already wearing made-to-measure polypropylene suits, which meant they could come into a snow hole from an at-tack, brush the snow off their boots and clothing, then just settle down and sleep, as they were without the need for a bag. I don't mind admitting we were jealous, but fuck it; they were good blokes and there was a lot we could teach them, even if none of it was about the latest kit.

Anyway, one of the Delta guys was named Chuck and he was put in our call-sign group, under an SAS sergeant major who was known in the regiment as "Bobnoxious." Bob was a hard man, highly experienced and skilled, but he was very obnoxious, and on that tour of duty he decided his personal mission was to make Chuck's life a misery. Bobnoxious rode him like a mustang, but Chuck showed his mettle and refused to be bowed by the daily grind of orders and criticism.

Now, in the Arctic there are certain protocols, a set of rules that are followed as second nature just to make life in the freezer bearable. For instance, you always keep bars of chocolate close to your body. If you don't, they freeze into bars of iron, and when you absentmindedly take a bite, you can snap your teeth off! Similarly, you make it your business to brush all the snow off your kit before entering a tent or snow hole. If you don't, it simply melts and forms small puddles that enrage your mates, sometimes to the point where fights could start. Boots are often taken off before going into a tent or snow hole, but they're never left outside, because they'll just freeze harder than a garden ornament.

That's how Chuck got his revenge. He waited, sneaked around to Bobnoxious's tent, removed the major's boots, and placed them outside to cool down. The whole call-sign group watched, and at first light our reveille was the loud cursing from Bobnoxious's tent when he found his boots frozen to the ground and full of snow.

I loved it, and we took Chuck and his pals to our hearts. They were, and are, real comrades and we still exchange cards at Christmas and every now and then we meet up and talk through the night, with Jack Daniel's as the master of ceremonies.

So, DURING MY CAREER with the SAS, I served with a lot of brave and ballsy men and I was involved in many highly classified operations around the world. I fought terrorists in Northern Ireland; although I'd rather consign those memories to history, where I hope that conflict will remain forever. I operated against cocaine cartels in South America, too, in a secret war in the jungles and the foothills of the Andes, I went on top secret missions in Africa and Asia, and with other SAS soldiers I became the eyes and ears of NATO in the Balkans.

Then as a staff sergeant with 22 SAS, there was one last operation, when we evacuated a British embassy under threat in the Middle East. The operation itself was straightforward, but I was on what is called "gardening leave," the run-up to one's official retirement date from the army, when I got the call. I'd already handed my kit in and I thought I'd "beaten the clock," but the regiment was short of bodies and I had to go.

The names of those who die fighting in the SAS are inscribed around the base of a clock tower on the parade ground at our base, and those of us who survive our service in the regiment are said to have "beaten the clock." You can imagine the banter as I queued up to get some kit with some of the fresh-entry guys going on their first mission. Anyway, the job went smoothly and in the end I obviously did beat the clock, even if I'd been one of the few who'd had to undergo a rewind.

Around the world, the names of elite units like Special Air Service and Delta Force confer a very real exclusivity and military primacy on those who serve in them. These units are special in a very real sense and not just in terms of the skills, the knowledge, and the courage that are deployed by their members. I believe what's really special about the Special Forces are the friendships and comradeships that are found in its ranks. They are often born out of hardship and usually forged in the white heat of the dangers of covert operations, and that makes for strong and lasting loyalties.

It follows that most of my close friends are fellow "Blades"— that's the name we give ourselves, taken from the winged dagger of our regimental emblem. Perhaps it's a bit of a cliché, but sometimes it's only men who have endured those experiences and survived those dangers whom we can most easily relate to.

One of those lasting friendships I made is with a formidable warrior from Wales named Mike Curtis. We fought together at Goose Green and then served in the SAS, where Mike and I were on many operations together before we ran classified operations against the cocaine cartels in South America.

Since leaving the regiment, I've worked on many self-inflicted hairy-arsed capers in Africa and elsewhere as a security consultant, bodyguard, and mercenary fighter, often alongside Mike. But one of the most unusual experiences, and one that is strangely relevant to my story, is an incident that Mike and I call "the Near Death of a Princess."

It happened in the penthouse suite of a very smart London hotel, and the princess in question was a member of one of the most powerful royal families in the Middle East. We found her to be a charming and lovely person who was really easy to get on with and who relied on our advice quite closely.

Okay, Mike and I were the heavies in the entourage, but we tried to be as discreet as we could and make her feel comfortable and safe as she moved around London on a carousel of shopping expeditions, and she appreciated that. There was one other vital member of her staff who was always nearby, a private nurse, because our princess, and she was our princess while she was in our charge, suffered quite badly from diabetes and her doting parents could afford to have medical help at hand 24/7.

After a particularly grueling day trailing around the stores of London's famous West End on a seriously tactical shopping expedition, we got back to the hotel, where I was just settling down to the evening routine of meals and bed when Mike banged at my door. As I recall, he'd been to the gym—we'd take turns working out, one of us always on standby.

"John, we're needed! Room service found her in a coma! They've gone for the nurse! Let's go."

I can remember my heart pounding as I ran down the thickly carpeted corridor after Mike. I was praying she was going to be all right. We really liked the princess and I was truly worried about whether she'd be okay. But, to be honest, a part of me didn't want "Lost a princess" stamped across my CV.

We arrived at the princess's bedroom just after the nurse and the hotel manager, who'd been called, too. I'm a trained patrol medic and I could see that our princess was in bad shape and rapidly slipping away into a hypoglycemic coma.

Shit, that was bad enough, but things were actually much worse, because I could see the nurse was frozen to the spot. I didn't know where the family had found her, but I quickly realized the nurse had not experienced the life-or-death admissions at an emergency room for a very long time, and now she had a life-or-death situation right there in front of her. She had all the kit with her—the insulin jab, the adrenaline, everything she needed—but she'd frozen, petrified by the gravity of what was happening.

"For Christ sake, she's hypo. Do something," I hissed. No movement. I knew it was going to be down to me, so I grabbed the medical gear from her and got to work while giving Mike the strangest order he'd ever had.

"Get on the bed with her and keep her warm! Cuddle up to her!"

It was vital that we not let her body temperature drop if we could help it, but for a fraction of a second Mike's eyes met mine and I could read every word of his thoughts.

She's a princess. She's a devout Muslim. She's not allowed to have men anywhere near her. I'd get stoned to death for this in her country . . . if I was lucky. These were the thoughts zipping through his mind.

But he could see I meant it, so he shrugged, wrapped her in a cover, then dived onto the bed to hold her close to his body and give her brotherly warmth. The adrenaline I injected and Mike's body heat did the trick and we saved her life. We never saw the nurse again, but I swear I'll never forget the sight of one of the toughest men ever to serve in the SAS cuddling the life back into an Arabian princess.

There's a very eerie postscript to that incident, because on that very same night our own Princess Diana was killed in the Paris underpass while being driven in the very same model of Mercedes 500 that we were using to drive our princess around. Mike and I had some really spooky feelings about the lottery of fate that gave one princess life and took it from another on the same day. It overlaid our genuine sadness about Di's death.

N OW'S THE TIME for some straight talking. This is not a book about Special Forces' action. It's about my work as a private military contractor in Iraq and the huge mercenary army that has been employed to protect the civilians flooding into the country to work on multibillion-dollar projects to regenerate the country.

I profile the private military contractors and how they work, emphasizing the differences between American and British tactics on the Highway to Hell. The insurgents, too, come under my focus as I describe the roots and causes of the insurgency and the qualities of the men who fight for it. I chronicle the extraordinary exploits of some of the PMC heroes and my own firefights with the enemy during the eighteen months I worked in Iraq. There were some very low points for me personally after months of working the Fallujah road as a lone bodyguard, and stress and drunken nights with my clients nearly sent me over the edge. And I portray the women who have joined the mercenary army and the love affairs and marriages that take place in the midst of the nightmare insurgency.

I still visit Iraq and the Middle East, but in the spring of 2005 I stopped working the Highway as a security guard. Now I run a company that hires and trains other soldiers who want to work in

Iraq and elsewhere. They include my own son, Kurt, and a lot of his friends from the Paras who are still riding the Highway in Iraq. In this way, I've been able to keep up-to-date on the mercenary army and some of the extraordinary firefights with the insurgents that have happened since I left Iraq.

I've deliberately avoided telling of my operational experiences while I was actually in the SAS in any detail. I want to respect the secret nature of my service with the regiment and my operations with other countries' elite troops like Delta Force. And anyway, plenty has already been said and written about SAS and Delta Force operations.

But I'm giving away no secrets when I say that during my SAS service I was involved in operations that were designed to thwart the murderous activities of paramilitaries on all sides in the Bosnian conflict. In that conflict, I played a small role in preserving innocent, unarmed civilians from ethnic cleansing and murder, and most of them happened to be Bosnian Muslims. The fact that they were Muslims was neither here nor there to me. That's not the point. It doesn't make me a mujahideen fighting for Islam, nor does it make me a traitor to the Christian Serbs.

A good friend of mine in the SAS was observing a Serb column about to fall like wolves on a town full of unarmed Muslim men in Kosovo. He was hidden in an observation post just fifty meters away from the advancing Serbs when he called in an air strike to stop them. In a breathtakingly unselfish piece of heroism, he gave strike command the coordinates of his own position to make sure the air attack would hit the Serbian column with maximum impact. That cool, utterly courageous man later joked that he felt completely safe, because the air force never has direct hits on targets, especially with smart bombs, but I know he put his life on the line for total strangers of a different religious persuasion and a culture alien to his own. He did it out of a sense of humanity.

I've never heard a word of acknowledgment or thanks from the world of Islam for what was done for their brothers and sisters in the Balkans by me and my Christian comrades and I don't mind if I never do. But the fact that I was involved in saving Muslim lives meant that a few years later when I drove along the Highway to Hell, I could look anyone from the world of Islam in the eye and shrug off any bullshit about being part of an anti-Islamic invasion. The truth is that I believe I am no man's enemy unless he chooses to make me one. For me, it's humanity that counts, not the words written in the book of any religion.

3. The Breaking Storm

DESOLATE, TRAUMATIZED PEOPLE, THEIR eyes hollow with fatigue, their minds nearly broken after nights of bombing, were performing a ghastly mime of normal life. Many simply stood and watched as we drove through a desolate, broken landscape on the outskirts of Baghdad, where buildings reduced to rubble were the only milestones and the broken sticks of electricity poles, draped in a spaghetti of useless cable, pointed accusingly up to the sky. Bridges were buckled into the water like toys that had been stamped on, and a thin layer of bomb dust lay over the city, the freshly milled flour of modern warfare.

It had taken us a mind-numbing five-hour drive from Kuwait on a road that runs like a black ribbon through the barren, rock-strewn landscape, and most of us had dozed off for half the journey. "Highway Tampa," the Americans call it, and it's haunted by the ghosts of the Gulf War a decade or so earlier, when a convoy of thousands of

Iraqi conscripts fleeing from Desert Storm had been consigned to oblivion by U.S. Apache helicopters and A-10 Tankbuster aircraft.

There were thirty-five of us on the road, all ex–British Special Forces, mostly former SAS Blades, and we were at the vanguard of the mercenary force that would follow; we were the first private military contractors to go into Iraq at the end of a war that we were all told had been decisive.

Usual rules applied: We had a growth of stubble on our faces and maintained a steely indifference to the jet lag that comes from traveling halfway around the world to go to work. Official hostilities had ended just a few days earlier and we were traveling in a convoy of seven soft-skinned vehicles. We didn't have a solitary weapon between us, but we didn't feel threatened. Not then.

"Most of them are fucked-up, John," said Bungo, the guy sitting next to me. "They've had the shit kicked out of them."

"Hope so, mate," I replied, ever the practical man. "Let's face it: Life's going to be a lot easier if there's no fight left in them, that's for sure."

"Suppose you're right, but I can't help feeling sorry for them. There's nothing in their eyes; they're just empty. Thirty years of Saddam, then twenty-odd days of air strikes and an invasion. They didn't ask for any of it."

"True enough, Bungo, but they were here. They just happened to be in the way. You know how it works as well as I do. If you can't move out of the way, you get caught up in it, and this lot had nowhere to go. Anyway, it's early days yet. The people who might cause real problems are probably regrouping right now."

"Yeah, the next couple of months will tell which way it's going to go," he replied.

Bungo and I didn't like the feel of the place. We thought we were experiencing a phony peace and that sooner or later violence would come from soldiers who had dispersed from key units like the Republican Guard and Saddam's Fedayeens, who'd been in-doctrinated to lay down their lives for him. They'd be unleashed and directed by the political power brokers, those men whose faces featured on the U.S. Army's famous deck of cards, with the fugitive Saddam at the top of the pack, handing them wads of cash that he'd conned out of the UN in the oil for food program.

Yet most of the people we saw as we drove into Baghdad had simply been caught up in the squeeze. Fight or flight wasn't an op-tion for them, so they'd hunkered down and taken their chances. All around us we saw a shell-shocked population tired of it all. The euphoria they'd felt at the fall of Saddam and his hated Ba'ath party was short-lived as the reality of hour-by-hour living took hold again. They had children to feed and lives to salvage from the rubble. What did they care about elections? What use was democ-racy to them when they needed food, water, and power to keep their children alive?

I shook those thoughts aside and focused on what we needed. No matter how cowed and desolate the Iraqi people appeared, basic common sense told us that this was not a place to be British and unarmed. We were soldiers and the first thing we wanted to do was to get armed.

We'd been recruited by a big security corporation to carry out an "in-country survey" of Iraq, which basically meant we had to fan out into the key areas of the oil fields, the ports, and Baghdad on a fact-finding mission to assess the stability of those areas and any threat to the safety of the army of specialist engineers, survey-ors, and businessmen that would soon be pouring into Iraq to work on contracts for the multibillion-dollar reconstruction pro-gram of the country funded by the United States.

We weren't entirely on our own, because a team of Americans from the now-infamous U.S. corporation called Blackwater had arrived at about the same time on a similar task, but they were riding on the shirttails of the U.S. military. We, on the other hand, were flying by the seat of our pants in the finest British tradition. No sooner had we dumped our kit at the huddle of hastily erected cabins, grandly known as the "pioneer camp," which happened to be on the front lawn of the palace once owned by Saddam's son Uday, than we were out foraging for weapons.

Bungo had been in Iraq throughout the war, embedded as protection with a TV crew in Baghdad, and he'd spent only a couple of days at home before he'd signed up for this job and was back in-country. Naturally enough, he knew the lay of the land, and we were soon chatting to an ex–U.S. Ranger captain who was in an admin post with the office of the occupying authority. There's a kind of brotherhood of Special Forces soldiers, and we tuned in to him straightaway, so that within a few minutes he understood our needs completely and responded with the unique sympathy many Americans have for a bloke without a gun. To him, we appeared naked, and he wanted to see us properly clothed.

"No problem, guys," he said. "There's an arms dump in the compound at the airport and it just happens that a friend of mine is in charge of it. I'll call him and tell him to expect you."

We shook hands and left him with our heartfelt thanks and a case of beer, then wasted no time in driving out to Baghdad International along a route that is now a closely guarded corridor and the gruesome scene of many suicide car bombings. Then it was a free road, but we spotted the first hint of things to come in the shape of a wasted Humvee. There was nothing we could do. The vehicle was a burned-out shell and the incident was "post-op"—it was all over bar the cleanup—so we drove on to meet our man, feeling a little bit grimmer with every passing minute.

There were twelve thousand troops at the Baghdad airport in those early days, but we quickly found the officer we needed and he drove us out to a building on the airport's perimeter. It looked like an ordinary house from the outside, but inside it was packed to the rafters with weapons and explosives. Our scavenging was about to pay off big-time.

"Take what you like," the officer said with a beaming smile. So we did.

We were like kids in a sweet shop as we grabbed thirty AK-47s, which were all in good nick, and a similar number of G3 rifles and assorted pistols. We took boxes of grenades, boxes of ammunition, and a fair amount of demolition material in the form of explosives and mines, and finally we found several M79 grenade launchers in nice condition, then loaded the lot into our Tahoe 4 x 4, which sank onto its springs. When we got back to the pioneer camp, the other lads had found bits and pieces, but they knew we'd hit the jackpot when they saw the grins on our faces and the weight on our tires.

Around the same time, according to later intelligence reports, Saddam and a couple of the faces featured on the famous deck of cards were meeting in a Baghdad car park to play their own hand and activate the insurrection against the coalition. What none of us realized then was that the allies had overlooked a minor detail in the run-up to the invasion when someone, somewhere in the infrared glow of a computerized ops room, had forgotten to designate Saddam's huge arsenals as priority targets. Tragically, that left his supporters, and the chaotic insurgency of a hundred terrorist groups that followed, with the biggest free weapons arcade the world has ever seen. And though we expected trouble, we never dreamed how well armed it would be. In a strange irony, we'd just kit ourselves out with guns and explosives from basically the same source the insurgents were helping themselves to in unsecured locations. Soon we'd be turning those weapons on one another.

Each vehicle was allocated its own radio call-sign group, and

Bungo and I distributed the gear among the different vehicles so that every team we deployed would have enough weaponry and kit to mount anything from a surveillance operation to a hostage-release mission to a close-protection task. They would have everything they needed in the trunk of the car, because that was my old regiment's way of doing things.

I'll never forget leaving the camp the following day to go up to Mosul, when a young black U.S. Ranger—he was no more than eighteen—waved us down and put his head through the window to have a look inside. He saw two of us privateers armed to the teeth with AKs, pistols, and a grenade launcher, which were stashed around the compartment.

He gave a low whistle, put his hand out to shake mine, and said, "Man, you guys are truly rigged for combat!"

Well, I truly hope that young man got home safe and well to his family, because things were changing by the hour and more and more of his comrades were beginning to go home in body bags. We couldn't have been there for much more than a fortnight when Bungo and I started exchanging knowing glances as the U.S. body count quickly racked up from one a week to one a day.

Our sixth sense, developed in Northern Ireland, honed in the Falklands, and perfected in the Balkans, was telling us a shit storm was about to break. On the streets, there were more and more incidents with U.S. soldiers, who were still allowed downtown on a "semioperational" basis—in other words, they could go shopping and sightseeing as long as they carried their weapons. You'd see soldiers taking photos of one another at one of the toppled statues or against the backdrop of one of Saddam's palaces, but now the empty, vacuous looks of a shell-shocked population were being replaced with stares of open hostility. I imagine German soldiers got the same treatment from the citizens of Paris as they went sightseeing down the Champs-Elysèes. The isolated incidents culminated in one soldier being shot in the head when an insurgent stuck the barrel of his pistol under the back of the GI's helmet and fired. The sightseeing jaunts ended then.

The job was coming to an end for us, too, as our company lost the contract to the London-based ArmourGroup. It was all political, of course, and that's the way things are in the PMC business, shifting contracts and new bosses every few weeks or few days. After discussions with the ArmourGroup guy who'd arrived to organize a smooth changeover, the ex-officer handling our admin in the pioneer camp gave us our instructions.

"Right, men, the ArmourGroup team is going to arrive from Kuwait in the morning and then they'll be taking your weapons, vehicles, and call-sign groups. You'll be boarding a coach and they'll escort you out of Iraq and back into Kuwait. . . ."

He took one look at our faces and saw that his words had fallen on deaf ears. The rep from ArmourGroup, who looked a bit like Boss Hogg from *The Dukes of Hazzard,* tried to say something but was told to shut it. Who, exactly, did they think we were? They wanted us to hand over our much-cleaned weapons to a load of crow wanna-bes who were taking our jobs from us. By this time, we had gathered three times as much weaponry and had cached our spare guns and ammo safely away for a rainy day, but that wasn't the point.

"You're having a fucking laugh," said Bungo. "These aren't company weapons; they were honestly scrounged and we're not giving them to anyone. We might sell them to the company, but then again, we might not, and as for being escorted out of Iraq, you can forget it. At least eight of the blokes here drove out of Iraq in their desert Land Rovers after blowing up Scud missiles the last time they visited, and they aren't going home in a fucking bus."

The bosses knew that we had no intention of singing from any song sheet but our own, so they came up with a new plan, which was to do more or less exactly as we said. We drove halfway to Kuwait and met the incoming crows at an RV point in the desert. I don't know whether their company paid due diligence to people's CVs, but what we saw was a bunch of angels with dirty faces. They were mostly young adventurers moonlighting from various state National Guard units and teenage "soldier civvies," as we called them, looking for a thrill. There are a lot of them in Iraq. There were a few old ex-army has-beens with them, too, and most of them looked so pathetic that in the end we decided to take pity on them and hand over a couple of our weapons so they could defend themselves as they drove into the Wild East in their shiny new 4 x 4's.

We drove on to Kuwait City and got our flights home, knowing that we'd been in the vanguard of the PMCs who would follow, but as it panned out, I was back in Baghdad within a week, protecting a media team from a London TV network.

Bungo and I talked about it that day and we knew in our bones that the storm was about to break and that when it did, it would be a bastard. What we could never have guessed was the awesome size of the mercenary swarm that was already stirring and on the move to Iraq.

T O UNDERSTAND THE WAY the swarm gathers, you've got to leave the battlefield for the boardroom, because it's in the plush London and Washington offices of the security companies that the life-or-death deals of the mercenary business are done.

For the first half of the last century, during two world wars, and into the next quarter of the century, during the Cold War, there had been no room for private soldiers in a world of huge standing national armies. *Mercenary* was a dirty word in those days and still is, largely, but how things have changed. As the Cold War first thawed, then melted in a global warming of superpower politics, new challenges were presenting themselves and a new business took root in the UK and South Africa, where Special Forces officers from units like the SAS and the white Zimbabwean Selous Scouts saw opportunities to offer sophisticated security, military, and intelligence services to wealthy governments.

Jim Johnson, an SAS officer and onetime military attaché to the Queen Mother, had the foresight to see the way the wind was blowing and founded one of the first of them, setting up a company called KMS, an acronym for its cheeky name, Keeny Meeny Services. Jim is a real character; a posh ex-Guards officer, he was in one of the ops teams during the famous Iranian embassy siege bust in London.

When he left the regiment, his clients were oil-rich rulers, and KMS personnel were exclusively Blades employed to train local troops and to provide personal security for the heads of state and their families. Every now and then when a client had a particularly thorny problem, the lads would be asked to go out in full gear and do a "special," which, true to form, would be pulled off with the least-possible fuss.

Others eyed KMS and decided to cash in on this new business opportunity, and a succession of companies came and went as they were taken over by rivals in lucrative sellouts or simply vanished off the radar as their directors moved on to new adventures. All the while, they were growing both in number and size at a fairly steady rate as the oil-rich nations in particular began to use their highly specialized services to beef up their local forces and to watch their backs.

Given that a few energetic South African soldiers had entered the fray, it wasn't surprising that some of the companies were soon involved in African bushfire wars from Angola to the Congo to Zaire and that some less scrupulous outfits got in far too deep with a few very nasty sub-Saharan heads of state.

Watching all this unfolding were some U.S. Special Forces officers who had seen the potential, and while the European and South African companies were growing, they were growing, too. All the while, these companies were building up relationships with the British and U.S. intelligence services and, crucially, with the Pentagon. They were natural bedfellows and a quiet, unofficial understanding grew up among the spooks of MI5 and the CIA, the American top brass, and the new private military companies.

Over the years, there were complaints from the Left about the growth of these companies and their involvement in Third World conflicts, but there really wasn't a lot these individuals could say that had any resonance at a time when the Soviets, the Chinese, and the Cubans were up to their waists in the mire of African politics themselves. But suddenly and dramatically, the map of world politics changed with the implosion of the Warsaw Pact and the fall of the Wall in Berlin. Within the space of a few years, literally millions of soldiers were stood down and cashiered from armies around the world. Some estimates put the figure as high as six million troops discharged from military service around the globe.

The trouble then was that the new high-tech armies of the West, particularly the U.S. and British forces who'd been at the forefront of the forty-year stand-off in Germany, found themselves chronically short of manpower. Unlike "make do and mend" Britain, the five-star generals in the Pentagon simply got the checkbook out and picked up the phone to their old buddies in the private military companies, and that's when the PMC business really started to rock and roll. In 2005, it encompassed around nine hundred companies based in over one hundred countries on every continent but Antarctica, earning a global income of over $100 billion.

These companies offer three basic services. Some offer up front fighters, the hard-core ground troops. A few offer a gaggle of ex-generals as consultants to advise small states on strategy and long-term military planning. The third type are known as military support firms, MSFs, and they provide behind-the-lines logistics like transport, cooks, helicopter and aircraft maintenance, and whatever else the client army wants to pay for. They are huge, and at the last count there were thirty thousand of these noncombatant camp followers working in Iraq.

Do not confuse that figure with the estimated 45,000 combat-ready private military contractors like me who are employed on security details. They are different people. The MSFs employ cheap, unarmed labor in the area of conflict, people with low health and safety demands, to do the army's dirty work.

They also provide highly paid technicians to service the tanks and helicopters; they maintain B-2 bombers; and one company actually hires out the drone spy planes that fly on missions over the Sunni Triangle. They even forecast the weather for the military. Private military intelligence specialists were the people actually running the Abu Ghraib prison. Some were involved in the illegal humiliation and interrogation of prisoners, although, interestingly enough, it wasn't thought a good idea to arrest any PMCs, and thus it was the GIs who ended up taking the rap.

MSFs also hire out a huge number of low-skill workers to feed and water the troops, and a lot of them come from the Philippines, Pakistan, or Turkey, and some of them are killed in mortar attacks on military bases. But it's the truck drivers, known locally as *jundhis,* who take the most hits, and nearly a hundred of them have been bombed or pulled out of their cabs and summarily executed at the roadside by insurgents.

With the U.S. Army the biggest outsourcing force, it's U.S. private military companies like Blackwater and DynCorp that are the big providers, offering services across the whole spectrum, from combat contractors to behind-the-lines workers. During the Gulf War, private companies were making big bucks, and one in every one hundred members of the U.S. forces in Kuwait was a private contractor. They're earning a mountain now as a third of the entire U.S. fighting budget in Iraq, around thirty billion dollars, is paid out in private contracts, with one in ten of the U.S. presence in the country a civilian contractor.

UK companies haven't been left behind in this race, although they're almost exclusively in the business of providing trained fighters for up-front protection. They also do well from those crafty former generals who advise governments on the threats they face at home or from their neighbors, the strategy they should employ, and the kit they should buy. It's powerful stuff, with substantial and sometimes huge arms deals being brokered in the background on a commission basis.

It's largely the foreign adventures of British and South African companies like Executive Outcomes, Sandline International, and Gurkha Security Guards that brought the world of the dogs of war back into the public eye toward the end of the millennium. Simon Mann, one of the founders of Executive Outcomes, is presently incarcerated in a shit-pit African prison for trying to organize a coup in Equatorial Guinea, with a paper trail leading back to Mark Thatcher, the son of our former prime minister, Maggie.

But African adventures are glossy, high-profile scenarios, and for every one of them there are British private military companies discreetly supplying operatives to a score of countries in need of some military know-how and a corps of professional soldiers who can literally punch above their weight. The Brits weren't behind the door when it came to Iraq, either, and their efforts mean that

Britain's main export to the newly emerging Iraq has been an estimated billion pounds' worth of private military contracts a year.

It's ten in the morning at the post of the resettlement officer in Hereford and a long-serving permanent cadre SAS soldier has popped his head around the door to discuss his options on leaving the regiment. The guy in resettlement has heard it all in his time and seen the lads go into careers in the law, tree surgery, and, in one famous case, the Church of England as a vicar. Typically, though, the guys stick to what they know best, and this one's no different. He just hands the resettlement officer his CV and a form he's completed for a resettlement grant and asks, "Could you push my details around the security companies for me?"

This is routine, and soon twenty or thirty companies will have the details of a fresh ex-regiment face on their databases, and it's the database of former soldiers that is definitely the most valuable asset of any private military company.

Our soldier will use the grant money to go on a retraining and familiarization course for Iraq—I run one such course myself—and then he'll wait for the job offers to come in. He won't have to wait long, because the companies are gagging for operatives and a Blade will be snapped up in no time.

Of course, all those high-powered business deals I've talked about don't matter a lot to the guys on the ground. His own deal will be what's on the mind of each guy and his first question will be "How much?" There's nothing wrong with that. If a bloke is going to put his life on the line, he'd be mad not to ask how much he's going to be paid to do it.

The same process goes on throughout the rest of the army as more and more blokes tipping out of a wide range of units are deciding on the freelance route to maximize the cash potential from their hard-earned military skills. Not surprisingly, lots of ex-Paras are lining up for the big payday, but the rest come from a broad spectrum of regiments and corps.

Don't get the idea that the "ordinary" soldiers from regiments that the SAS and the Paras derisively call "crap hats" are not wanted. Far from it. Most such British soldiers are highly skilled, hard-fighting men by any world standard. So if you get a specialist guy coming from the motor pool, that's good news, because these days we like to balance the skills of a call-sign group. It's ideal if you can put a couple of hard shooters from, say, the Paras with the bloke from the motor pool who can mend the engine if it goes bang in the back of beyond while they're out on a risk assessment. The chances are he'll be quite handy with a rifle, too.

The pool of Special Forces men ran out pretty early on in the Iraq crisis and now these men usually find themselves in ops officers' jobs, running the show from Baghdad. So these days, relatively few SAS men go out on daily protection runs, but they're quite often leaping into their vehicles to race off and give some hard-edged support when there's a contact with the enemy.

Bungo is one exception. He still escorts clients around Iraq, clocking up hundreds of sorties, which, through his consummate skills in moving through a hostile environment, have attracted relatively few contacts. There've been enough contacts, though, and despite the fact that Bungo now runs his own company, he's a registered war junkie and insists on making the runs, saying his guys need an example on the ground.

Although ex-Blades like Bungo are relatively rare on the ground these days, we did leave a great legacy in those early days. What we left was a superb set of good working practices for the people who followed. We call them standard operating procedures, or SOPs. They include ways of moving through the country, ways of responding to attack, drills for regrouping—a whole set of lifesaving rules that have become a survival manual in a forest of terror.

I've described the way most British soldiers make the transition from national soldier to international freelance, but there are obviously as many stories as there are men in Iraq and as many variations on the theme as there are countries involved in the PMC industry.

But it's not just ex-soldiers who find their way into the privatized firing line. A surprising number of wanna-bes turn up in Iraq simply by applying for a job through one of the many PMC Web sites. They pluck a credible CV out of thin air and then con their way onto the flight. Some of the less scrupulous firms don't even bother to check the credentials of applicants; if they look the part, it seems, they're likely to get the job.

A few of them have done a dodgy bodyguard course; others have fed their egos on the right-wing survivalist magazines and on Web sites that glorify guns and knives in a very unhealthy way. I met a couple of them in Iraq, too, and thought they'd have been quite at home out on the town, having a beer with a campus killer.

But I've seen several men from that sort of background spin around and leave the country in a matter of days when reality gives them a terrifying kick in the crotch. Others stay on and present a very real threat to themselves and any clients entrusted to them, but the professionals can spot them from a hundred paces by the way they carry themselves, their obvious self-conscious weapons carriage, and the way they duck when a car backfires. They just stand out like the idiots they are, and once spotted, they are never worked with.

I t's the same story around the world: Web sites and resettlement officers in a host of armies directing men to Iraq. From 2003 to 2006, the number of PMCs had swollen to over twenty thousand. By the summer of 2007, it was estimated

there were an incredible 45,000 to 50,000 private military operatives in Iraq. They combined to form an unsung, unofficial army
in Iraq, one that dwarfed the 8,500 troops in the British contingent and was second only in size to the U.S. Army presence itself.

It's a huge and disparate army of men and a few extraordinary
women with guns for hire, each earning an average of one thousand dollars a day to provide security for the businessmen, surveyors, building contractors, oil experts, aid workers, and, of
course, the TV crews who have flocked to the country to pick over
the carcass of Saddam's regime and help Iraq rebuild.

Without doubt, it's the biggest mercenary army the world has
seen for over two centuries, since those distant days when the East
India Company used soldiers of fortune to depose the fabulously
wealthy maharajas and win India for Great Britain, or since King
George hired Hessian soldiers to fight against George Washington's
Continental Army in an attempt not to lose Britain's colonies in
North America.

Since military history has been recorded, men like these have
been called freelances, mercenaries, soldiers of fortune, or dogs of
war, but today they are known as PMCs the new, politically correct label that's been added to the lexicon of war.

Mingling among them are the so-called hard men from a score
of countries, the nightclub bouncers and bare-knuckle boxers,
who found their way to the action, foolishly believing that
courage would compensate for a lack of weapons training and
tactical awareness.

Many of the trained guys are "regulars" on the circuit, registered with big multinational private military companies, and take
to the road bristling with weaponry and armour-plated vehicles;
others come as one-man bands, equipped with little more than a
beaten-up 4 x 4 truck, an AK-47, and a holdall full of luck. But just
like professional soldiers through the ages, they come for one

thing—money—and in this case, that's a share of the estimated sixty million dollars a day being spent on private security in Iraq.

They come from across the globe—former Special Forces soldiers from Britain, the United States, Australia, Canada, New Zealand, and every country on the European mainland. There are Gurkhas, too, from the Himalayan foothills and Fijians from the South Sea Islands. There are men who learned their skills with the Japanese antiterrorist paramilitaries and men who have fought in the vicious bush wars in Zimbabwe. There was even one guy who'd served in the Chinese People's-Liberation Army before heading off to earn a dangerous fortune in Iraq. Chilean commandos and Sri Lankan antiterrorist experts, who'd fought the Tamil Tigers for years, joined the mercenary gold rush to Iraq, as well. They don't share a common ideology or a common loyalty, but what they do share is a thirst for adventure and a hunger for big bucks, and Iraq is the one place they are certain to find both.

Some of them pay the ultimate price for their appetite for adventure. As best I can tell, around three hundred PMCs have been killed in contacts with insurgents. There's no way of knowing exactly how many, because it's not in the interests of the companies who hire them to advertise a body-bag count, and back home dead men don't attract any political attention if they weren't killed in the uniform of their country.

4. Low Profile

NO ONE TOOK A BLIND BIT OF NOTICE as a battered old tipper truck loaded with tons of building rubble trundled out of Baghdad on the Mosul road, grinding through the gears. The driver was a lean, muscular young man dressed, insurgent-style, in a loose-fitting blue-and-gray robe over baggy Ali Baba trousers and a pair of Nike trainers. The fit-looking guy with his arm resting on the passenger window wore a cheap brown leather jacket and the same baggy trousers and had a *shemag* wrapped around his neck. Between the two of them, jammed on the occasional seat behind the gear lever, was an older guy in his fifties, heavily jowled and very nervous as he clutched a large leather holdall on his lap; his face was hidden by the hood of an old surplus Iraqi army parka he was wearing.

A suffocating hour later, the truck turned off the main road and drove for two or three miles through goat scrub, then turned into the gates of an oil-installation compound south of Kirkuk. The guard on gate duty looked at their load manifest. It was all properly signed by the manager, so he waved them on.

They pulled to a halt around the back of the site office with a hiss of air brakes, out of sight of the bored security guard on the front door, who'd watched their arrival. The driver dropped to the ground like a cat and walked around the back of the truck as if he was checking out the tires, but a closer look showed that he was carefully observing the scene around him. Then a flourish of warm desert wind snapped his robe against his side for a moment and briefly outlined the shape of the automatic rifle concealed beneath it. At that moment, the second young man jumped down from the passenger side of the truck and had a good look around, too, while the older guy stayed in the cab, still clinging to the holdall as if his life depended on it.

The driver quietly ordered him to get out of the car and he climbed ponderously to the ground, the holdall heavy and awkward; then he looked intently at the oil pipeline about thirty meters to his left. His bag could easily have been packed with explosives, but this was no insurgent attack on a vital installation. Far from it. In fact, it was a scheduled run by a British private military company, whose policy is to go deep undercover when ferrying clients around Iraq.

"All right, it's all clear." The driver had spoken English, not Arabic, and he quickly ushered the engineer with his bag full of blueprints and technical specifications through the back door of the building. It was vital that not even the local security guards witness him slipping into the building. Careless talk back in the village could see them under attack on their next run and a guard could easily be a spy for the insurgency.

This company uses old cars and pickups as well as trucks, sometimes traveling with a load of fruit or vegetables on board. Occasionally, a goat or a couple of sheep are tethered onto a flatbed as living camouflage. Attention to detail is everything, and the company is careful with its license plates, as each region in

Iraq has a distinctive plate. The plates are simply changed if the vehicle is leaving Baghdad for Basra, which exemplifies the meticulous emphasis on preparation that comes from the ex-Blade leadership of the company. I know these PMCs well; I trained most of them on my course. Like me, they never wear shades when they're on a job. Why? Because the Iraqis simply don't wear sunglasses; or at least very few of them do. If you do wear them, it's a dead giveaway that you're a "white eyes," so called because of the pale, untanned ring left by the shades.

While I usually go low profile, or jingly jangly, as we call it, these guys go deeply covert, and I admire them for that. The guy who runs the company is an ex–D Squadron SAS warrant officer and one of an increasing number of ex-NCOs who are putting the noses of former officers out of joint by setting up successful companies and, as the officers see it, taking their turf. But his way of doing things mirrors my own philosophy, which is: If you can't be seen, you can't be hit.

I asked one of the guys if he felt vulnerable in a slow, ponderous vehicle like a tipper truck, bumping along the highways and byways of Iraq.

"Not really," he said with a broad grin. "The bodywork's crap, but the engine's really sound, and we've got a strategy if we're rumbled."

"Which is?"

"If we're in town, we head for a narrow road between houses and tip the load to block the way. If we're on the Highway, we still tip the load; then one of us gets in the back with some heavy kit and we give them all we've got as we head off. It'll do seventy when it's empty, you know, but the thing is, we never get sussed."

In fact, they're so good at going covert that it's proved to be a double-edged sword, as a totally unexpected enemy has emerged in the form of our Americans friends, and those guys who look for all the world like Iraqis going about their business are more likely to get whacked by the Yanks than by insurgents.

Now don't get me wrong. I love the Americans and, as I said, I've spent a lot of time in the States over the years, training with soldiers in Delta Force whom I admire and like immensely. I think they are a wonderful people, but they do have a couple of serious attitude problems that come out like a rash when they're in a conflict. And the biggest problem is communication with anyone who doesn't speak English. Outside the USA, a lot of Americans can be quite insular, arrogant, and very paranoid, relaxing only when accosted by a familiar language, especially if the accent is British. The trouble is that the USA is the New Empire, but they just don't know how to deal with it. The Brits, on the other hand, with hundreds of years of imperial and colonial experience behind them, have learned that you might be able to conquer a people but that you'll never suppress them; instead, you just get on with it and do business with them.

You see, while the British PMC philosophy in Iraq roughly follows my theory of "No one shoots you if no one sees you" a lot of the American PMCs go for something more like "Here's my head; my arse will follow."

And that's the way they move their clients across the warscape in Iraq, headfirst in large convoys with as many as twenty armed guards, an armored scout car front and back, and sometimes top cover in the form of a helicopter gunship above them. They treat all Iraqis as potential insurgents, and I've seen their PMC convoys strafe junctions with machine-gun fire if they don't like the look of the vehicles on the road ahead.

Some British companies involved with U.S. clients are contractually obliged to move in high profile and, like their American counterparts, they regularly get whacked by insurgents because an offensive posture while engaged in an essentially defensive role is playing right into the hands of the enemy. Tactically, it's a crock of shit and inevitably draws the Americans into a wagon train situation when they're attacked, where all they can do is form a circle and fire like fuck. The helicopter cover doesn't really help because the helo is hanging there like a buzzard, vulnerable to a malleting itself if it gets too close.

Tragically, a chopper leased by Blackwater was shot down by a ground-to-air missile fired by the Islamic Army in Iraq in May 2003. It wasn't guarding a convoy; the Russian-built Mi-8 was apparently being used to transport U.S. officials from Baghdad to Tikrit when it was hit over a deserted piece of countryside. Six Americans died, along with the three-man Bulgarian crew and two Fijian security contractors hired by Blackwater.

In a cold-blooded and typically filthy piece of work, the insurgents found one of the crew, who'd been thrown clear on impact, and made the shocked middle-aged man stand and walk away so that they could shoot him in the back. True to form, they videotaped the whole thing, from the downing of the helicopter to the execution of the crewman in blue overalls.

But you've got to ask yourself why a team of insurgents armed with Stinger missiles and video cameras just happened to find themselves under the flight line of a helicopter in the middle of nowhere. I refuse to believe it was an accident. Either they'd been tipped off by a supporter at the air base with access to flight plans or the contractors had been too complacent. Avoid routine is the number-one rule in any secure movement operation. It was most likely an established flight route that was compromised by followers of the cause at a high level. Maybe it could have been an opportunistic attack, but that strikes me as being just too lucky to be feasible. We'll probably never know the truth of it.

The much-publicized murder of four Blackwater operators in Fallujah was another example of what happens when it all goes wrong. Blackwater took over a contract from British rival Control Risks, which gave the people at Blackwater a full rundown of the safest operational routes. In other words, they were told precisely where to go and where not to go. But soon afterward, four Blackwater operatives—one ex–Delta Force member and three former U.S. Rangers—were tasked to go up the Fallujah road toward a forward operating base, a FOB, all of which are always at covert locations. They were on a route I know well, traveling in two soft-skinned 4 x 4's with two men mounted up in each vehicle. I'm told they were actually carrying kitchen utilities in flat packs, apparently to furnish the base. They weren't even on a hard-core protection run.

For some inexplicable reason, they went down a road that took them into town and onto a street near the Euphrates River, where they were ambushed by half a dozen insurgents with AKs and machine guns. Then grenades were posted through the windows to finish the job and the men were dragged through the street, burning and dismembered, before being hung off a bridge over the Euphrates. It was videotaped, of course, and the film records grim scenes of crowds mutilating the corpses.

Some say they had gotten off the route and were orientating themselves Special Forces–style and ended up in the wrong place at the wrong time—hard to believe, considering that these operatives were formerly with Delta Force and the Rangers. I think they were just dicked, spotted, and set up, then malleted; that's how it works on the Highway.

That incident has been portrayed as being the catalyst for the huge Marine Corps assault on Fallujah that followed, but I think it unlikely that the United States would risk the political shit storm that would follow dozens of regular marines being sacrificed because a few PMCs carrying kitchen flat packs were slaughtered in the city. I also think it unlikely that the Marine Corps would get the go-ahead to attack in such a short time. No, it doesn't wash with me. I believe that Marine Corps assault was already calculated, already planned in advance, and executed perfectly. Maybe the military top brass just thought those four deaths were as good a starter flag for the assault on Fallujah as any.

So the American way is not my way. I don't mind a scrap, but I do draw the line at mooning my backside at the enemy, inviting him to shoot at it, and that's virtually what the U.S. contractors are doing. It's a difficult subject, this, but I'm convinced that many Americans hate the Iraqis, not just the insurgents but all Iraqis, and I've had conversations with many PMCs and regular U.S. soldiers who are essentially evangelical Christians and see themselves in a very serious crusade against the Moslem hordes. Let's be frank about it: From that point of view, they're not much different from the Iraqi militiamen and foreign fighters who see themselves at the heart of a jihad against Christian crusaders. What a mess.

The American PMCs feel no unease at all about infuriating ordinary Iraqis by setting up road blocks to give their convoys priority. It's not just the roadblocks, either, as they make a habit of forcing other vehicles off the road by ramming them from behind or forcing them over from the side. This is especially true in Baghdad, where they will actually fire at any vehicle that they feel is in the least bit suspicious. I know it's Suicide Bomb City, but I believe that this show of appalling manners has alienated the moderate Iraqi citizens, who aren't interested in jihad and just want to get on with their lives.

To be fair to the U.S. military, it does not behave in the same way and has tried to introduce some really good hearts and minds stuff into daily operations, being careful whenever possible not to get up the noses of ordinary Iraqis. It's got a lot of top professional troops who have been on the world's steepest learning curve and have adapted well. That's not true of too many of the American

PMCs, who seemed to have watched too many movies and think that intimidating the locals is the way to make your mark. The U.S. PMCs have alienated a lot of their international colleagues, too. Like me, my son, Kurt, works as a security contractor in Iraq and he and his colleagues are in constant scrapes with American columns and convoys. More than once I've heard him mutter, "I hate those bastards more than the scumbag insurgents!"

Now if a Brit, who's had several vicious contacts with insurgents, can say something like that, how much more galling must it be for the Iraqis, who feel dumped on in their own country? I find the Iraqis quite charming and open people, but they are a very proud people and live in a country where weapons are freely available. I'm certain that a fair percentage of attacks on the Yank contractors in Baghdad have been made by locals suffering from road rage. They may not be insurgents, in that they're not part of an armed cell or network, but they're certainly rising up against having their cars bashed by some idiot from another country, and if they're angry enough, they've got guns to make their point.

I've been very pissed off by the behavior of American PMCs myself when I've been operating low profile and have found myself bounced off the road by a big "fuck off" U.S. armored car driven by a contractor with too much attitude.

Once, an American contractor's scout car scraped half the paint off the wing of my car, which was really annoying, until I realized they'd done a good job of improving my camouflage. On another occasion, I even had my car forced into a ditch by a British PMC armored vehicle. But that was nothing compared to Bungo's experience when he was traveling high profile on the outskirts of Baghdad, escorting an American client with all his call-sign group flying Union Jacks on their vehicles to clearly identify themselves against friendly fire.

"You wouldn't believe it, John," he told me. "We spotted a big column of Yank PMC vehicles coming toward us, when suddenly they were firing at us out of the blue. About a dozen rounds hit the back end of my vehicle, too close to the fuel tank for comfort, and I swerved off the road and pulled up. We all piled out of the car, including our American client, who was terrified and well hacked off after watching his tax dollars incoming in the form of the machine-gun rounds that had nearly killed him.

"As they got closer, we showed ourselves, arms outstretched, to clearly show them we weren't carrying. I can tell you, I was crapping myself because they were so thick, I thought they might let us have another burst. Anyway, they pulled up when they realized we were all white eyes. I was furious and I strode up to them and had a real dingdong.

"I was yelling, 'Don't you know the British flag when you fucking see it?' And do you know what the bloody hillbilly in the turret said? Unbelievable, John. He said, 'Gee, I'm sorry, I thought they were Iraqi flags.' "

"*Iraqi flags?* I tried to explain to this muppet that, in any event, he was supposed to be on the side of the Iraqis, who actually flew their flag, and that the insurgents are the only fuckers who don't have any flags. I might as well have been talking to the wall. Some of those rednecks live in a parallel universe."

Bungo was lucky to survive that encounter, and even though he's a veteran SAS "Scud buster" from the Gulf War and a man not prone to nerves, I know the needless stupidity of that encounter left him quite shaken. He flies the Stars and Stripes now but still reckons the Americans are more dangerous than the insurgents.

Between these two extremes of very high profile and deeply covert, a lot of the British and Commonwealth blokes travel low profile or jingly jangly. The general idea is to make yourself look as unappetizing a target as possible to the big predators. You set your car up to look like a local vehicle. The bodywork should preferably be a bit beaten up, but the engine and the working parts should be in top condition and souped up for a chicken run.

Most of the guys will add their own individual touches—worry beads hanging off the rearview mirror, stickers with Islamic slogans stuck on the back windshield, anything that will give it the authentic Iraqi touch. The idea is not to become invisible like the deeply covert boys, but to avoid being offensive and confrontational; it's to match the wallpaper for a few seconds, even if you're going to be sussed on a second glance, because those few seconds get you down the street and on to the next hazard.

You can travel in a fairly loose convoy in this way, and nine times out of ten it'll get you through the day without a shot being fired in your direction, but beneath the rough exterior of the battered vehicles, there has to be a tight tactical deployment in the event of an attack.

Typically, we'd have four vehicles running low profile, and obviously we wouldn't have a lineup of the same make of vehicle so that we looked like a queue of ducks in a shooting gallery. We'd mix and match some distinctly different-type vehicles while trying to achieve the authentic Baghdad look. Front and back we'd have more heavily armed cars kitted out with machine guns, RPGs (rocket-propelled grenades), and any other sizable ordnance we could get our hands on, and they would be there to cover the protection vehicle in the middle, which would be carrying the client. Loosely shadowing these cars would be the gun vehicle or counterattack team (CAT), and the task of the guys in that callsign group would be to take the fight to the enemy the moment anything went down, allowing the others to deploy and get the client away.

While the convoy was on the road, the CAT would wander up and down the convoy, looking for trouble, which obviously could come from any direction. The moment it kicked off, they would aim to take the fight straight back into the enemy's face and seize the initiative away from him so that he was put on his back foot. Believe me, it works.

You can't fight bombs—only luck can help you there—but all the call-sign group vehicles would be ready to change roles and transfer personnel or clients from one vehicle to another in an instant if there was an explosion. If a vehicle was disabled by a bomb or by heavy gunfire, then the others would deploy for the transfer and extraction of the call-sign group vehicle that had been whacked and begin any first aid that was needed.

The moment an attack began, the CAT would start the fight while we'd simultaneously call for the cavalry in a radio contact to the coalition. If the CAT team's vehicle was hit and disabled, then it would be time for a big boy's decision, and you might have to leave them to fight and make their own way out. Nothing is cut-and-dried out there on the Highway to Hell.

IRAQ HAS BEEN KNOWN for millennia as Mesopotamia, the Land of Two Rivers, but now a third river flows. It's a river of blood, so it follows that firepower is everything out there. I'll now take some time to explain the weapons of choice that the private military contractor will carry.

Basically, it cuts two ways. As I've said, the American companies are usually closely linked to the U.S. military and so they use standard weaponry. They use the M4 rifle, which is a short-barreled 5.56-caliber piece and is compact and very accurate. On the vehicles, they carry Minimis or .50-caliber heavy machine guns.

The average British contractor, and here again I include the Commonwealth blokes, had to scrounge their weapons when we first got to Iraq, just as Bungo and I did, but later a lot of the guys exchanged those weapons for properly imported kit.

Personally, I like the shooting kit we cadged and foraged in those early days. A lot of it was Soviet gear. Such gear is immensely robust and durable, with an inbuilt serviceability, which means the mechanism of an AK-47 will still fire if you fill it with sand and leave a cleaning rag inside it. The AK is quite simply the best assault rifle in the world; it's accurate, it doesn't break, and it doesn't stop. It's just what you need if you're going against the same weapon systems, and remember, the AK is universal among insurgents. Some operators carry MP5 carbines, which are lightweight, pretty, and perfectly engineered, but an MP5's got no punch outside a room, so you may as well stand there and throw the rounds at someone trying to shoot you up with an AK; that's about as effective as its firepower is.

Perhaps more importantly in the context of Iraq is the fact that the Warsaw Pact kit generally packs a heavier punch because the preferred Russian approach to warfare, developed in hellish campaigns against the Nazis, is not just to kill your enemy but to blow a hole through him so that you can see his comrade behind him.

So I've remained fond of my Kalashnikov and have stayed loyal to the PKM machine gun. I'm keen on the Soviet-built RPK light machine gun, too. It comes with a bipod stand and is essentially an AK with a longer, stronger barrel and uses the same magazines. I also like to stash a Dragunov sniper rifle in the vehicle simply because you never know when you're going to have to take a long shot.

But it's the Soviet PSS machine gun that we used for a really heavy punch. It's the one with a big drum magazine underneath that you always see in those World War II films. That big magazine holds seventy rounds, and if you come under attack, you can just hose your enemy with a drumful of heavy hitting rounds. At times, we also had a huge .50-caliber Dushka mounted on a tripod at the end of hotel corridors, just in case we got disturbed at night.

In the early days, I carried a Walther PPK for personal protection or an Iraqi Tariq pistol, which is good at close quarters, although the safety catches are dodgy and it has an overcooked poundage pressure on the trigger. Still, it was better than nothing until we could get some superior Berettas, Glocks, and Czech-made CZ pistols.

More recently, most British contractors have a U.S.- or Belgian-made Minimi in their lineup of weapons because it really can pour out a tremendous weight of fire and, well directed, it will make most opponents think twice about standing their ground.

Weapons aside, PMCs have developed a dress code that suits the environment and the job at hand. They tend to wear lightweight shirts that have an element of UV proofing to protect the skin from sunlight, along with lightweight body armor, and a kit vest worn over it. Most of the guys wear lightweight, fairly loose-fitting cargo pants with four or five patch pockets where they can stash a small survival kit, important ID documents, and field dressings. I prefer blue jeans, and they became my piece of signature kit, as I tend to stash my survival kit and medical stuff in my vest. Desert boots or lightweight climbing boots are the favorite footwear.

In-country, we tend to eat a lot of U.S. military rations, officially designated as meals ready to eat, but known universally as MREs. These rations became famous during the first Gulf War, when they first made their appearance on the stage of world cuisine. They come in a thick brown plastic wrapping and they contain enough food for a day, with dishes like beef stew and macaroni. The main reason for scoffing MREs is that you need to be careful about what you eat in a situation where, for obvious reasons, an upset stomach and a nasty case of the squits are not really the way forward if you're caught in an ambush.

Water is vital in a hot, testing climate like the one that generally prevails in Iraq, although you shouldn't forget winter in the uplands, and parts of the desert at night can be absolutely freezing.

Generally, though, it's hot and humid, so we have mineral water stashed in liter bottles all over the vehicles and everyone makes sure they get at least two bottles down their throats every day. Again, most people avoid drinking local water for the simple reason that the public supply in Iraq is not safe or potable and no one wants to get a bug if they can avoid it. The dangers of dehydration are very real, and if you neglect to drink plenty of water, you'll quickly know that things are going wrong when your urine becomes dark in color and it stings when you piss. Believe me, that soon gets you reaching for the water bottle.

When it comes down to the wire, weapons and water are two of your best friends in the uncertain world of Iraq, but there's a third, one that's equally important. You may only call upon it for relatively short, frantic, and intense periods of time, but it may save your life. It's called situation awareness.

A PAIR OF BLACK KITES wheeled and circled in the sky over the half-eaten corpse of a dead dog on the waste ground between Highway 6 heading north out of Baghdad and the main railway line to Mosul. As the convoy passed, the sun was rising quickly, giving off heat, which stirred the air into tired breaths of wind that picked up scraps of paper from the heaps of rubbish, then threw them down again. Ahead of them was the North Gate out of Baghdad. Beyond it lay the open road.

There were three vehicles in the line, with three men in the first two and four in the gun truck bringing up the rear. It was a routine run with no clients on board—just a recce for a regular trip they'd be making with a paying customer over the next two or three weeks. That made things easier. Shepherding an unarmed civilian is a big responsibility, one that the guys take extremely seriously; after all, the client's life and theirs may depend on their actions. Life's a lot simpler when you've got only yourself and your mates to look after.

The 4 x 4's picked up speed as the open road beckoned. Only the gate to drive through, then they'd really turn up the speed. The twin turrets of the gate, holding a classical upended tulip-shaped arch between them, loomed ahead. As they got closer, random patches of ceramics glinted in the sun. They were once part of a mosaic portrait of Saddam, the rest of which had been etched away by machine-gun fire, so that now the face of the towers resembled a map of some distant archipelago.

Hal, the driver of the first vehicle, scanned the road ahead. Brad, the navigator and team leader, was distracted by a movement near the railway line, but Hal was getting edgy and he wasn't sure why.

"This doesn't look right, mate," he said, calling Brad's eyes back to the road ahead.

Brad took the scene in and immediately caught the vibe. No one about. No one at all. No street vendors, no rubbish scroungers, no people carriers lined up and waiting to pick up relatives who'd gotten a lift in from the country on a truck. No cabbies and, the big giveaway, no police.

"Stand by, here we fucking go?" Brad had spotted the tiniest movement on the rampart over the arch and called it on the radio. "Heads up. Keep an eye on the fucking gate arch!"

Hal was about to turn the wheel and start weaving, but their lives were saved because he didn't have time to do it.

BANG! BANG! BANG! A burst of .50-caliber rounds slammed into the engine block of the lead vehicle. It stopped abruptly, as if a huge invisible hand had slapped the radiator grille. The engine screamed and whined as bits of it flew around one another. Flashes and smoke erupted on the North Gate as the big gun poured out its venom.

More horrific bangs. The hood of the car was torn apart. The windshield exploded as the big-caliber rounds slammed into the cabin of the 4 x 4, whistling right between Hal and Brad and perforating the interior of the vehicle like a demented staple gun. The other call-sign group vehicles reacted instinctively as Hal and Brad abandoned their now-burning hulk.

"Come on! Come on!" The guys in the second truck screamed urgent encouragement as they rolled out of the doors with weapons and radios intact. The driver of the gun wagon was pulling on the hand brake, leaving half the vehicle's tire on the road, in order to give the rear gunner a clear field on the gate with the wicked Minimi he had poking out of the back. Whining like an angry hornet, the Minimi ripped more of Saddam's portrait off the wall of the gate, and the ceramic map was redrawn. As the team laid down covering fire, Brad and Hal climbed into the middle wagon as the guys recovered them and left their vehicle for scrap.

Then silence. The .50-cal gun was gone. No more metal-rending rounds. The would-be assassins had been one-burst wonders and they'd carted their prized weapon off and out of the tower as soon as they'd had their fairground shot at the lads. No way were they going to risk losing their weapon or their lives, and they'd fled in a car hidden behind the right-hand tower of the gate. Pursuit would be pointless and possibly fatal, as those guys were probably covered by a second ambush team waiting to mallet anyone who followed them.

It was luck that had sent those big rounds slamming down the middle of the car between Brad and Hal like a hot lead cheese wire from hell, but it was situation awareness that had made them suss that something was about to go down. It was the hairs on the back of Brad's neck that had given them the split-second edge, allowing them to give the other call-sign group vehicles a heads-up. That had allowed them to deploy in an instant, and if they hadn't put that suppressing fire on the North Gate, the .50-caliber gun would have kept up its murderous rant and claimed one of the team.

Then suddenly, the battle had ended without resolution and the adrenaline the guys pumped around their bodies had nowhere to go, driving them to action when there was none. The guys stood for a moment and scanned the urban horizon around them, half-hoping another terrorist would come along and have a go at them.

Brad and Hal felt a liberating sense of relief after surviving the burst of cannon fire that had cut the thin layer of air between them. The gun wagon guys felt cheated because the bastards hadn't stood their ground and fought it out. They all felt that way. It was an impotent, unresolved rage, one that's common on the Highway as time and again guys watch hit-and-run killers evaporate back into the community without standing for a fight.

Brad spoke for them all as he kicked the tire of the burning truck and said, "What the fuck was all that about?"

5. The Sheik of the Beheaders

I'M LYING IN THE CORNER OF A BRIGHTLY lit room, dressed in an orange boiler suit that's too small and pulls at my arms and chest. Not that it matters, because I'm trussed up like a turkey anyway, hands and feet tied together by nylon rope. I'm struggling, Christ, I'm struggling, but I can't get free, and across the room a small bearded figure with a false leg is leering at me with his black shark eyes while he strokes the blade of a wicked-looking scimitar-shaped knife. I know who he is. I know his face. He calls himself "the Sheik of the Beheaders." I scream with fury, but my defiance comes through the gag in my mouth as a muffled gurgle. He's laughing. Someone standing next to him with a video camera in his hand has made a joke about me. Then the beheader starts to walk toward me with the knife. I know he wants to sever my head off, but I'm going to live. I'm fucking well going to live. I brace myself and pull at the ropes that hold me with all my strength, and suddenly I'm free.

With a single bound, I leap across the room to meet my executioner full on and punch him as hard as I can. He falls to the floor, and now he's the one gurgling as I leap on him, pulling the gag from my mouth. Then I bite at his nose and tear it off with my teeth before spitting it in his face.

"John, John, it's time to go."

As I swam to the surface of consciousness through my retreating sleep, I recognized the voice of the person calling me. It was Ian, one of the cover team who was going with me to the meeting point that night.

"You all right, mate? You were thrashing around a bit."

"Yeah, yeah. Fine thanks," I said. "Just a bad dream."

I didn't tell him what I'd dreamed. There was no need; after all, everyone in Iraq had nightmares about Abu Musab al-Zarqawi, head of Al Qaeda in Iraq and the very same self-styled Sheik of the Beheaders.

Al-Zarqawi, a Jordanian psychopath under sentence of death in his own country, was responsible for organizing most of the suicide bombings in Iraq. It is the Al Qaeda network that brainwashed young men in the religious schools, called *madrassas,* around the world, then delivered them to al-Zarqawi along underground routes leading eventually through to Syria and across the Iraqi border. Then al-Zarqawi armed the human warheads and sent them on their one-way mission into the streets and marketplaces of Iraq.

But he was also the evil inspiration behind the tactic that has most terrorized Westerners in Iraq, and that is the kidnapping and beheading of hostages. He made his victims wear a signature orange boiler suit, mimicking the dress of prisoners in Guantánamo Bay; then he executed them by beheading them with a knife and transformed these horrifying murders into public executions simply by videotaping them and posting them on Islamic Web sites.

He was one of Osama bin Laden's most loyal lieutenants and no act was too savage or barbaric for al-Zarqawi if it furthered the cause of their twisted concept of a great world religion. In short, he was a nightmare, but in the upside-down world of Iraq, al-Zarqawi inspired other dreams as well among the thousands of private military contractors. They were dreams of great wealth and they stemmed from the fact that the Americans posted a $25 million reward on his head. We have all dreamed of collecting it and buying the harborside house in the Caribbean with a yacht tied up to the private jetty.

As soon as the reward became public, the whole PMC community got very interested in al-Zarqawi, and there were quite a number of serious-minded people putting a lot of their mental resources into dreaming up ways of getting him. I seem to remember it was a ten-million-dollar reward on his head at first, but he became such a huge pain in the arse that the State Department raised it to match the bounty on bin Laden himself. With $25 million on the table, most people in the PMC trade had memorized every feature on the wanted poster, just in case they might be lucky enough to come across him in the street, and for a few of us, hunting him down became a very serious, if potentially dangerous, ambition.

You'd be in the crowded lounge of a hotel when the CNN news came on the television and no one would take a blind bit of notice of a report on the latest suicide bombing. But the moment al-Zarqawi was mentioned, a hush would descend over the room and some seriously steely eyes would focus their undivided attention on the screen. No one admitted it of course—well, not publicly anyway—but they were all scheming away quietly and everyone kept an eye open for that unexpected opportunity that might present itself to capture al-Zarqawi, and they didn't mind if it was dead or alive.

That's what I was doing that night. I was out to get al-Zarqawi. Dead or alive. Things are never that simple, though, and this was to be my first step on the trail. I'd asked around discreetly while I was on a visit to Dubai and I'd been introduced to a Kurdish businessman. We beat around the bush a bit and then I said, "Everyone wants to find al-Zarqawi. I wonder how that might be done."

It would be very difficult indeed, he confided, but it so happened he had a sister who was married to a Sunni who happened to be a former Ba'ath party member. It's always this way in the Middle East: There's always a relative, a sister's husband, or "someone from my village you can trust." It's an endless game of family trees and complicated loyalties.

"So," I said, "your sister's husband. He knows what goes on in the Triangle?"

"Yes, of course. He is a very well-connected person."

"How so?"

"Well," he said, "when my sister met him and fell in love with him, he was running a small business in the Kurdish no-fly area, but I think he was a spy for Saddam. It was obvious to me that he was a spy for Saddam."

"If he was an agent for the regime, why was he tolerated?" I sort of knew the answer as I posed the question.

"You understand—of course you do—it is not impossible that one man's spy can be a different man's spy, too. This is not a great problem."

"Where is he now?"

"He is in the Triangle. He is helping those who want to fight the Americans. He has to do this, or some of his family will be put into a very difficult position."

"What about your sister? Is she with him?"

"No, of course not. We would not allow that. He comes and

goes; his children are safe with her in Kurdistan. They would not come there; they would be killed very quickly."

"So you think he might have information about the man I'm interested in?"

"The Sheik? Maybe not today. But he did before, and that was not long ago. Maybe he will again another day soon. I think you should meet him and make a good arrangement to have the information you need quickly when it is available."

"Fine, but why would he do this?" Again I knew the answer.

"For money, of course. He will have enough money to take his family out of Iraq and take my sister and their children to a safe country. Maybe Sweden or maybe America. There's enough money for everyone."

"Including you?"

"Of course, including me. I am a businessman. I make my living by trading and by charging commissions. But we could not do this thing ourselves. It must be someone like you. They would know he had been sold by someone, but you would be between us and them and you would never be named."

"Too bloody right I wouldn't! Okay, can you arrange a meeting?"

It had taken nearly a month, but my Kurdish friend had done just that. Now, the meeting was scheduled for the next morning, but just in case of problems, I and the lads would be at the meeting place a long time before the appointment. Just in case. That's why I'd been sleeping in the early evening; it was going to be a long night.

I checked my kit. Rechecked it, took a look in the mirror, then slipped my personal security card into my top pocket. Interesting thing, the card: It's the same dimensions as an ordinary credit card but twice as thick and is hinged so that it falls open into two flat sections. You never open it unless you're in real, al-

Zarqawi–style trouble and you're about to be captured. When you do, it transmits a GPS signal, which can be tracked from about a thousand meters. Not very far in the middle of a desert, but in the middle of a city, a radius of a thousand meters covers two or three suburbs and hundreds of thousands of people. In other words, it could perform the vital task of finding a human needle in a terrorist haystack. The hope is that even if you can't open it then, an inquisitive captor will do it as he's searching you, because once it's opened, it can't be resealed and the signal keeps pulsing out.

We set off from our safe house with some friends just inside the Kurdish area and headed out in two vehicles to an RV—army jargon for a meeting point—in a remote area on the edge of the Sunni Triangle, where we were to meet this guy, whom I'll call "Zuhair."

You might think this all seems a bit barmy, going to these lengths; after all, this bloke Zuhair could have been anyone at all. I agree. Of course, the fact is that he could have been completely dodgy on a number of counts. He might have been a con man. Well, so what? He wasn't going to get a penny from me until the target was in the bag. My real concern was that he was on a fishing expedition to reel me in and that I was meant to become the trussed turkey in the orange boiler suit of my nightmare. That's why I was taking some of the lads with me and that's why I had my card in my top pocket and that's why we were going to look over the RV very carefully a good six hours before the meeting. And I'll remind you why we were bothering to go to all this trouble, and that was the small matter of a $25 million reward on al-Zarqawi's head. Even a thousand-to-one chance that I could meet anyone who'd been anywhere near the Beheader of Baghdad and who might give me an angle to get a share of that sort of reward money was worth a punt, and the lads thought so, too.

We'd had a really good look at the area on maps and we'd seen

some aerial photography, too; then we'd had a drive-past recce ourselves earlier in the day, but this time we were going to carefully
check out the ruined house where the RV was to take place and
stake it out for the night. When we got close enough, we killed the
car lights and moved slowly into LUPs—laying-up positions—
we'd looked at earlier in the day with the two drivers, who now
went to precision night guidance headgear, ready for the drop-off.
They tucked the vehicles out of sight, rigged up the tracking devices
for the card, set up the radios, then settled down to wait. I walked
off into the night toward the house.

About thirty meters away, I stopped and settled down behind a
boulder to view the place through a light-intensifying monocu-
lar—I had one tucked in a pocket of my kit vest. I watched the
half-collapsed walls glowing a ghostly green through the lens for a
few minutes, then moved around to look at it from another angle.
Only when I'd viewed the RV carefully from all sides did I move in
for a closer look, and I discovered after a thorough viewing that
the property was clean. It was going to be a long night and I hid
myself away in a spot with a good view of most approaches to the
house. The others were covering any spots that were blind to me.

Five hours later, dawn rose after a night of mind-numbing bore-
dom, during which nothing had moved except a few scurrying ro-
dents and some sort of fox. Then half an hour later, a 4 x 4 came up
the track that led from the reasonably busy trunk route two miles
away. It was covered in dust, but it was quite a new vehicle. A short,
slightly built Iraqi got out of the car and moved nervously around
the building. He was a good-looking sort of bloke, and when I saw
his face clearly, I recognized him from the family snaps my Kurdish
friend had shown me. It was Zuhair, and the cheeky bugger had arrived two hours early for the meeting!

He had only a cursory look, though, and although he came
close to my hiding place, he didn't spot me, so I just stayed put

while he stood near his vehicle, listening to Arab music on the radio and occasionally answering calls on his mobile phone. He smoked a few cigarettes as the hours dragged by; then, when the meeting time was getting closer, he took a small pair of binoculars out of the car and began scanning the track back down to the road, obviously expecting to see my vehicle turn off the main drag.

He nearly crapped himself when I walked lightly up behind him right on time and said, "Morning, Zuhair."

His face was ashen and his knees nearly buckled as he spun around. His hand seemed to move toward the inside of his jacket, but if he was carrying, he thought better of it and composed himself quickly when he saw my hands were empty.

"Hello, Mac," he said. I'd not given him or his brother-in-law my real name. "You surprised me."

"Sorry about that. Just being careful."

"I think we should be quick about this," he said, getting straight down to business.

I nodded in agreement and we cut to the chase. "Can you help me and how much do you want?"

"Yes, I can help you and I want half," he replied.

"You have only to point me in the right direction," I said, "but I have a great many things to do after that. There'll be a lot to arrange and other people to pay. Fifteen percent for you."

He shook his head, muttering, "No, no." Then he said, "Twenty-five."

"Agreed. Okay, so where do I find him?"

"When I know, I will contact you with the details."

"Fair enough. I'll wait to hear from you."

We made some contact arrangements, using a system that for various reasons I'm not going to describe here. The meeting ended. He got into his car and drove back down the track toward the main drag. When he'd gone, Ian and the others moved in to collect me.

"What d'ya think, Johnny? Is it a runner?" asked Ian.

"Tell you what I think, mate. I think my arse in a sling would mean cash in the bank for that little bastard. I'll bet he'll be wanting another meeting in a couple of weeks' time just to clear up a few details of the deal and I bet he'll want to meet quite close to Al Qaeda's backyard and I also bet you a few of his mates will try to lift me, then sell me to al-Zarqawi or someone similar."

"Well, we thought it could be dodgy all along. The list of people who know where al-Zarqawi's going to be at any given moment must be shorter than your Christmas card list, John, and I can't see a Kurdish double agent being on it."

I was wrong about one thing, though. It was only a week, not two, before Zuhair contacted me. He said he needed to talk to me about the arrangements, he had to have assurances about his safety, he needed more money because so many of his family would have to be moved out of Iraq, and he wanted to explain some details to me. Could I meet him in . . .

I cut him off mid-flow and my reply was direct and to the point. I simply told him, "Zuhair, if I ever see you again, I will kill you."

This was not an absolutely literal threat, more of a clear message that I believed he was trying to line me up for a hostage taking and that if I did see him, I would assume that was about to happen. He knew he'd been rumbled and that he would have to deal with the consequences. My mission to get al-Zarqawi hadn't even gotten off the runway and visions of making myself a wealthy man on the reward money were just dreams again, but as they say, if you don't try, you don't get.

I know that variations of my particular experience are still going on as the size of the bounty on offer continues to challenge the ingenuity of soldiers of fortune in Iraq, but in November 2004, I had a call from another old regiment boy, whose name was Danny.

After catching up on old times, he said, "John, I'm trying to put a team together for a special job. It's got to be all ex-Blades, ex-Delta guys, or similar and I reckon I'll need five or six teams. Trying to muster many of the guys when Iraq's giving everyone full employment is a hell of a job, but I know you're in the swim and you may know who's available. I'm also hoping you'll want to get in on it yourself."

"What's the job, Dan?" I asked.

He told me straight off, because ex-SAS men don't go into all that need-to-know bullshit with one another. If an old Blade takes you into his loop, you keep your mouth shut and that's that. It's an accepted fact of life.

It turned out that Danny was trying to cook up his own scheme to get al-Zarqawi, and his daring vision made my attempt to track down the Al Qaeda chief look pretty lame. Danny's idea came after a bit of light reading in one of the science magazines. He's always looking through journals like *New Scientist, Scientific American,* and *Nature* just to keep up on the latest technological advances, obviously hoping that he'll spot some new development or a piece of kit that can be used in our trade.

One day, he found a short article about the development of microchips that can be implanted under the skin and that can hold an individual's medical history and other personal details on file so that they can be read in case of death or injury. Apparently, some scientists in the United States and Britain are working toward a small chip that holds all this info on it but also has a tiny integral GPS capability not unlike my card's and they've produced prototypes.

"It can be implanted with a simple medical procedure, John, and it's virtually undetectable," he told me.

"So, you put a chip under your skin. My dog's got a chip under his skin in case he runs off," I said.

"Precisely, mate. Your dog's got a chip so that you can identify him if he's found. Our chip has got GPS so we can find our lost or stolen human ourselves. I'm thinking of having our clients chipped for additional security, but the big idea is to chip one of the lads and stake him out for capture like a tethered goat for a tiger."

"You're having a fucking laugh," I said.

"No. One of the boys says he'll do it for ten million bucks, which is fair enough, but we'd have to have a big backup operation as well and that would take a lot of blokes. In a nutshell, we get him kidnapped and then we follow the signal, burst in on the Beheader and his team, and waste them, rescuing our bloke as we go."

"Well, I suppose it could work in principle, Danny, but there are so many variables involved, it's bound to end in a fuckup."

"Obviously, we'll have to make sure the chip is up to scratch— no one's going to literally put their head on the block with dodgy kit—but there's one thing that's no variable in this equation, John."

"What's that?"

"The twenty-five-million-dollar reward."

"Fair point, mate. It's definitely worth a go."

Danny and I agreed that he'd come back to me when he'd investigated the feasibility of the microchip system, but he later dropped the venture because of technical difficulties, not, you'll note, because he couldn't find a lad with balls enough to do it.

Anyway, we've since learned that around the time Danny was planning Operation Tethered Goat, al-Zarqawi had actually been arrested by the Iraqi police and held overnight in a cell. Despite the fact that he had only one leg, following a U.S. air strike on his chemical-warfare training camp in Afghanistan during the war against the Taliban, the police failed to identify al-Zarqawi and released him. This was only revealed when one of his team was arrested in the summer of 2005 and told U.S. intelligence officers the story. They made inquiries, but the IP, the Iraqi Police, just shrugged and claimed they knew nothing. It's generally believed that the IP involved in the nick that night weighed up the reward money against the almost certain slaughter of all of their families and opted to let him go after a good breakfast. What a nightmare!

The night of June 7, 2005, was clear and the pilot of the U.S. Air Force F-16 could see every detail of his target as he dropped a big "fuck off" five-hundred-pound bomb onto the farmhouse thirty miles north of Baghdad. Just in case that hadn't done the trick, his wingman dropped another five-hundred-pounder right on the nose, as well.

The next day, the Yanks called a press conference in Baghdad and announced that the Sheik of the Beheaders had been JDAMed to hell, swatted like the bug that he was. The U.S. military exhibited before and after pictures of the most wanted man in Iraq. Before—the smirking, arrogant psychopath, certain in the power that his terror endowed on him; after—a bloated cadaver with plugs of blood in his nose from the massive brain hemorrhage caused by the blast.

There's no doubt he was betrayed for the $25 million bounty on his head and I'm pretty certain that it was an inside job. I don't believe that any PMC was lucky enough to get onto his case, but even so, we were all looking for signs of anyone who'd left Iraq to live a lottery-win lifestyle.

Someone from inside Al Qaeda's own Iraq operation put the Americans onto al-Zarqawi's spiritual adviser, the Muslim equivalent of a father confessor, and tracked him with everything from surveillance teams to drone aircraft to satellites until he led them to the man himself.

The bogeyman is dead, but his nightmare continues as the sectarian holocaust he brewed develops into a full-blown civil war. And there are still rewards to be earned for catching insurgents on the U.S. wanted list, and as long as there are, we'll be looking for them.

I'LL NEVER FORGET the words of a Kuwaiti businessman at the beginning of the Iraq War when he told me, "Yes, the Iraqis have been liberated from Saddam, but now they're free to kill one another and that's just what they'll do."

Well, he was bang-on, and in my view his statement gets to the nub of the problem. I'm not a historian and I don't pretend to be a political analyst, but I'm a soldier, and fighting men have their own commonsense approach to working out why all hell has broken loose. I'm going to try to give you a practical, down-to-earth soldier's briefing on the roots and causes of the insurgency in Iraq.

One thing I can't emphasize too strongly is just how violent and bloody the insurgency is. It's a hundred times worse than in Northern Ireland. In my view, it's significantly worse than the ethnic cleansing in the former Yugoslavia, although that's not a subjective judgment, because in that war we weren't the ones being directly shot, at least not most of the time.

Another thing you've got to get your head around is that there was always going to be chaos in Iraq; it just took a long time to happen. The truth is, it didn't matter whether it was the U.S.-led coalition or an internal revolution that got rid of the late, unlamented Saddam Hussein; the ingredients for mayhem already existed in the country and mayhem was bound to follow as Iraq cracked along racial, tribal, and religious fracture lines that were there long before his madcap political adventures forced the United States to bring him down.

When the strongman falls, then the rest will scrap for power in the vacuum, and there are some very telling parallels and comparisons between Iraq and the former Yugoslavia. Marshal Tito was a strongman who was able to hold a handful of little countries like Croatia, Macedonia, Bosnia-Herzegovina, and Serbia together, but when he died, the artificial boundaries of Yugoslavia lasted only months after his state funeral and then issues of nationality, tribe, and religion exploded to the surface and years of civil war followed.

In Iraq, the arithmetic says it all, where a Sunni minority of 20 percent of the population sitting on zero precent of the oil wealth was able to suppress and rule 60 percent of the Shias sitting on lots of oil for over forty years. It was also able to dominate another 20 percent of the population, consisting of the Kurds in the north, who also sit on wells full of black gold. This minority did it through a dynamic and quite ruthless instrument of power called the Ba'ath party, which held to some notion of an Arab brotherhood, as long, that is, as the Arabs in question were Sunni.

Saddam took the party over nearly thirty years ago and held it in a viselike grip through repeated and ruthless culls of all who opposed him. He crushed the Shias and declared war on the Shia Muslim state of Iran, resulting in a conflict that killed a million men. In between times, he would turn his attention to the Kurds in the north, destroying whole villages and dropping nerve agent on innocent communities. Bullying and full of bravado, he then invaded Kuwait and got booted out by the first coalition put together by the first President Bush, but he was able to claim a phony victory because he still held power in his own country.

Then, encouraged by George Bush, the Shias and especially the

Marsh Arabs rose against Saddam and his regime, fully expecting U.S. military help. None came and the Marsh Arabs were brutally crushed and practically wiped out before Saddam built a canal to drain their homeland in a terrible ethnic and environmental rape that alone should have condemned him in any court.

Against this backdrop, the coalition invaded Iraq; the legitimacy of that invasion has been endlessly and futilely debated ever since. Did Saddam have weapons of mass destruction or didn't he? Everything I've heard on the intelligence grapevine in Iraq suggests that he actually did, but in the nick of time he moved them across the border and handed them all over to the Syrians before the invasion. There are stories of long convoys of Scud missiles being driven to President Assad, which may have marked the end of a falling-out between the Ba'athists of Iraq and those of Syria, where a version of the party also holds power.

Justified or not, the invasion is a fact, and once Saddam was ousted, the insurgency was a given. Nothing could stop this preplanned resistance movement and it happened very quickly. In the Sunni Triangle and Baghdad, the remnants of the old regime activated a plan they'd made long ago to rise up against the invader, and the basically unreligious Ba'ath party members of Saddam's rump joined with the zealots of Al Qaeda in a most unholy alliance.

It's highly likely that the man who helped forge this alliance was Izzat Ibrahim al-Douri, who was vice chairman of Saddam's Revolutionary Command Council and the only deeply religious Sunni in the regime. In November 2005, he died of the leukemia he'd been suffering from for years. But in the early days after the invasion, he was on the run, with a ten-million-dollar price on his head, and he's said to be one of the men who met Saddam in a car at a Baghdad park to trigger the uprising.

The point at which it turned from a murderous nuisance to a

full-blown insurgency came with the bomb attacks in the summer of 2003, when the Jordanian embassy and the United Nations headquarters were both subjected to devastating explosions, courtesy of al-Zarqawi.

Then in the summer of 2005, after the elections and just before a referendum on the constitution, Al Qaeda stopped beating around the bush and openly declared war on the Shiite majority, whom they see as heretics who don't follow mainstream Muslim beliefs. The truth was out and an embryonic civil war became a reality.

At the same time, the Shiites in the Basra region became increasingly active against British troops in a separate insurgency fomented by Iran and aimed at beefing up the power of the Mahdi Army run by the militant cleric Muqtuda al-Sadr. Iran is itself a Shiite state, and as soon as their new militant president, Mahmoud Ahmadinejad, was sworn into power in August 2005, he upped the ante. His aim was obviously to destabilize southern Iraq so that when a full-on civil war broke out in Iraq, the Iranian government could take control of the strategic Shatt al-Arab waterway on the Gulf for its own, together with the Marshes and whole of Basra province. Remember, the Iran-Iraq War was a border dispute fought over these very regions.

So you have the Sunni minority, backed by Al Qaeda and supported by Syria, fighting to regain control of the whole country in a fight that is essentially a battle for control of the oil fields and you have Iranian-backed Shiites squared up against them, with the coalition piggy in the middle, trying to rebuild a country that is filled with armed men desperate to tear it to pieces.

But it's not over yet, and I'll bet a barrelful of oil that before this is over Al Qaeda and Saddam's Ba'ath insurgents will be at one another's throats. Al Qaeda wants to convert the entire world to the Muslim religion and impose what they call a "global caliphate" on us all. The Ba'ath party fighters simply want to regain total power in their own land and don't give a fig about religion. They deserve each other and I'm certain treachery will break out between them.

Only in the new Kurdistan homeland in the north of the country is there any real sort of stability. Here the hard-grafting, business-minded Kurds have set up a decent semiautonomous state after years living in the jaws of a nutcracker between Turkey and Iraq, where their language and culture has been suppressed and they have been pitilessly slaughtered over generations. At the end of the Gulf War, they fled from Saddam's pursuing avengers into the snow-covered hills, but then the British Royal Marines piled in on the ground to stand between them and the bully of Baghdad. Together with a no-fly zone imposed by the mighty U.S. Air Force and the RAF above them, that has allowed the Kurds to flourish for a decade.

The geography of the insurgency is simple, then. The entire country outside of Kurdistan and the heavily fortified Green Zone in Baghdad is known as the Red Zone. And it's here that coalition troops and foreigners move around at their peril. Some areas are more dangerous than others. Ramadi, Fallujah, Mosul, Tikrit, and the notorious town of Tal Afar on the Syrian border are virtual suicide runs, but even beyond these hellholes, nowhere in the Red Zone can genuinely be called safe.

In Baghdad, the road from the Green Zone to the International Airport is supposed to be heavily protected, but in practice it's a honey pot for suicide bombers and IEDs. The city suburbs of al-Dourah, Aahamiya, and Gazaliya are hotbeds of the insurgency and the Ba'ath party housing projects in Amiriyah and al-Jihad are also fertile recruiting grounds for the insurgency.

The reason no road is safe is because the insurgency was unwittingly accelerated by decisions that the coalition must now bitterly regret. The first of these was over a decade ago, at the end of the Gulf War, when, as I've mentioned, the United States encouraged a Shia uprising, then allowed them to be slaughtered by Saddam's regime.

I wonder how you would feel if that had happened to your family, to your people? And how would you then react when a few years later the same characters fetched up and demanded respect and your total cooperation in something called "a road map to democracy"? Remember that your society has no history of democracy but has a strong tradition of tribal and clan loyalties instead, along with, of course, an even stronger religious underpinning. I think if you're an Iraqi, you're going to have a very sickly view of the foreign governments telling you that they are your new best friends.

Remember that's only the Shia majority I'm talking about. The Sunni minority hate your guts anyway because they had the best seats at the show until the Americans and British came along; they'd ruled the roost and it was their man Saddam who was crowing on the top of the muck heap when the coalition blew him off.

The second mistake came with the total waste of intelligence effort in the run-up to the war in looking for weapons of mass destruction (WMD) to justify the fact we were invading at all. It's pretty obvious they were going to mallet Saddam and his boys whatever, so once they'd decided to do that, the intelligence effort should have been going into discovering what his long-term plans for retaliation were. If they'd just taken the time to look under the mattress, Western intelligence would have found an insurgency long planned and waiting for activation. Instead of that, they were looking for political excuses and a weapons program that may never have existed.

It's difficult to paint the picture of your average, everyday insurgent. It doesn't work like that. They come from all sorts of backgrounds and they come in all shapes, sizes, and different age groups, too. The leadership is no doubt made up of men loyal to Saddam, possibly from the same Tikriti background, trained and then sent into society as sleepers to be activated after an invasion or a coup against their master. Many of the foot soldiers come from the ranks of the defeated army, whose units were obliterated or disbanded without pay at the end of the war. The police force was disbanded, too, in another shortsighted move by the coalition and many of them joined the insurgency, merely to be ordered by their terrorist bosses to rejoin and infiltrate the police force.

Ironically, many of the thousands of criminal, as opposed to political, prisoners released from jails like Abu Ghraib by Saddam then joined the policemen who had originally nicked them in the ranks of the insurgency. I've no doubt that even as they walked out of the prison gates they were given a number to call if they wanted to earn some dollars fighting for the insurgency.

The motives for men joining the insurgency are complex, but there is an X factor in all this and it's the war chests full of U.S. dollars paid to the regime in the scandalous food for oil deal brokered by a corrupt United Nations. Literally, billions of dollars meant for the hungry and sick children of Iraq are now fueling the Sunni insurgency and paying for Al Qaeda's support, too. Whatever a man's political or tribal loyalties, there's nothing that makes him feel more like fighting than a wad of cash to take home to the wife and kids, and in that respect the insurgents are just as mercenary as the PMCs.

The business of the Iraqi Police is a nasty one. We know that the IP is riddled from top to bottom with insurgents, and I believe the insurgents cynically and in cold blood used police recruitment as a way of culling out decent Iraqis who wanted to join up to make a difference to society. I don't believe for a second that the queues of police recruits targeted by suicide bombers contained insurgents wanting to join up and infiltrate the force. They would have been told by their masters exactly which recruitment queues to join and which ones not to join. The rest are blown to hell.

In the south of the country, the only essential difference is that the insurgents are Shia and the paymasters are the Iranian government and their agents. Again the coalition is playing piggy in the middle.

It might be useful if I explain as best I can the difference between Shia and Sunni Muslims. It's something I made it my business to bone up on when I got out there, as it's so central to much of the mayhem in Iraq. I'm not an Islamic scholar, so I'll apologize in advance for any offense I might cause through errors of fact or emphasis.

As the story goes, Husayn bin Ali was the honored grandson of the Prophet Muhammad and it was felt that he should be the Prophet's successor on his death. However, when Muhammad died, the majority of his followers decided to follow Abu Bakr, who became the first great caliph of the Muslim world. Ali was martyred and the women and children of his household forced on a march into exile, which saw many of the children die of thirst in the desert.

But many stayed loyal to Ali's memory and his martyrdom became the focus of a split in the Muslim religion, which gave us the Shia, or followers of Imam Ali, and the Sunni. Ali was buried at Najaf, in southern Iraq, which is the spiritual home of the Shiite world. So there we have the roots of the insurrection, some of them running deep into Iraq's history.

However, for a PMC like me, the insurgency spells work. It's precisely why the businessmen, engineers, surveyors, and media teams need armed security guards to shepherd them around the country.

There are two more things about the insurgents that you should understand. The first is that they are courageous and tenacious fighters who are worthy of respect. The second is that they can't shoot for shit and inevitably fall when sustained and accurate fire is brought to bear on them. The specialty of a British or U.S.-trained soldier is sustained and accurate fire, but sometimes a situation comes along that turns all the conventions on their head, and that happens quite often in the upside-down world of Iraq.

MAY 2005. Another long black snake of tarmac twisting through yet another anonymous rock-strewn, sun-grilled landscape. This time, it's just south of Mosul, yet another city that's a suppurating abscess on the arse of the coalition. A trio of 4 x 4's carrying eight British PMCs hurries back to a forward operating base on the edge of the city. They're hurrying, but they're doing it slowly because one of the vehicles in the convoy has broken down and is being towed by another, with the gun vehicle in the rear.

Ex-Para Chris was in the lead vehicle, towing the one that had broken down, and he told me what happened. He was twitchy. Let's face it, they were all twitchy, and who wouldn't have been in a limping wagon train deep in Indian country when the road was about to pass a low hill to their right that looked as though God had laid it out with ambushes in mind. Chris was about to say something, when a huge eruption lifted the side of the road into the air and said it for him.

The blast swatted the car and nearly rolled it, but his mate Jim, an Australian, I think, gripped the wheel, steadied it, and kept the car on the road. Thank Christ, whoever had set the IED (improvised explosive device) hadn't packed it properly and had placed it just a bit too far off the road.

"Fuck," said Chris, knowing what was coming next, and right on cue a burst of machine-gun fire raked the side of the car. Then as they pulled in to take cover and return fire, a second IED showered them in earth and rock, but that had been a shit job, too.

The RAV (rear-attack vehicle) team in the third car had reacted instantly, jinking and swerving off the road, maneuvering to position for a best-effect retaliation. Chris heard them through his earpiece as they spotted the insurgent. They'd pinged his position and they began firing furiously at him.

"Right at the base of that top feature rock." The voice was urgent and precise.

"Roger that! Roger that!" Other voices joined in as they spotted the enemy firing position among the rocks. Then as they poured considerable and accurate fire on the position, a young man in his late twenties, wearing the standard baggy trousers and a leather jacket, broke cover and doubled to a new piece of cover to return fire, his RPK whipping steel-cased rounds into the gun vehicle.

"Cheeky fucker!" The voice of the man who had first pinged the insurgent was frustrated now.

Eight weapons rained lead on the insurgent's new position, the shooters expecting to mallet him; then without warning, he was off again.

"He's like a fucking rabbit," snarled Chris into his mouthpiece.

A few seconds passed before the guy got his wind back and rattled more machine-gun rounds at them, and they were close enough that everyone kept their heads down. So it went on: bobbing and weaving, taking cover, breaking cover, demonstrating that the seemingly flat backdrop of the hill had a third dimension in among the rocks.

He was up again, the bastard, as he leaped like a goat from one rock onto another, the machine gun balanced over his shoulder. Then for the briefest moment, he turned to look down at them on the road below, total defiance implicit in that moment's pause.

Chris looked at him up there on that crag and wondered why he was taking them on alone. He knew instinctively that this young man must have sworn a blood oath to kill an infidel or die in the attempt. Perhaps his brother or his father had been killed by the coalition and he was here to avenge his family, but Chris knew for sure that this was one insurgent who was running from no one. Far from it. He was calling on death to follow him into those rocks if it dared.

It was then that Chris heard the hornet buzz of two Apache helicopter gunships charging down onto the scene. There'd been no call to them, but evidently they'd been passing nearby on patrol and had come to see what all the flash-bang was about. It didn't take the helo crews long to work out what was happening, and Chris and the lads watched their thermal-imaging devices moving like sinister robot eyes, probing the rocks below, an alien technology bringing the war of the worlds to this barren corner of the desert.

Inevitably, they found their target, just flesh and blood with the heart of a desert lion. They locked onto him and the big Gatling cannon slung under the nose of the nearest Apache streamed out rounds like a sawmill and vaporized the lone rebel. Later, an American army ground force examined the area and found three more IEDs laid alongside the road. All this set by one man whose heart had been filled with hate and revenge.

Chris and the others stepped out of their cover and just looked up into the rocks where they'd witnessed that display of raw courage. They took no pride in his death, as their respect for his valor led them to reflect on the waste of a young life. Chris told me, "I sort of wanted to salute him. I just didn't know how."

In a way, though, this remarkable lone warrior summed up both the attributes and the inadequacies of the insurgents. If I were asked to write his epitaph, it would go like this: "He was as brave as fuck, but he couldn't shoot for shit."

6. Unusual Business

I
T WAS A SCORCHER OF A DAY IN THE CONGO
jungle and I was acting as bodyguard for an Arab
businessman from Qatar. It wasn't just the weather
that was steaming, either, but also the four hundred miners at his
diamond concession. They hadn't been paid for six months.

The mine was owned in part by my boss, the government of the
Congo, and another company, which appeared to be run by the
Zimbabwe military command. In short, the mine was producing
blood diamonds, which I believe paid for the civil war in the
Congo and the support of the Zimbabwe army for the govern-
ment side in that war.

We'd flown up from the boss's luxury home on a big estate in
Zimbabwe because there are no unions on the diamond field and
the negotiations were being carried on Congo-style. That involved taking one of the British site managers as a hostage and
giving him a good kicking. The boss was rattled and he'd brought
the cash for the back payments with him. I put the money in the
safe at the site office as soon as we arrived.

Then we took a deep breath and went off to negotiate with the mob of very pissed-off miners. Our bargaining stance was that obviously no cash was going to be handed out till the manager was released without further harm.

I'd expected to have to go and meet the miners alone, but, to be fair to him, the boss had some mettle and he went into the lion's den with me. We drove from the office down to the site of the opencast mine. It was a huge mud bath of diamond-bearing alluvial deposits with millions of pounds' worth of processing machinery designed to gorge great loads of riverbed soil, then spit out the precious stones.

Waiting for us was the crowd of very angry workers. The place was buzzing like a wasps' nest that had been poked with a stick and they were all armed with spears, machetes, broken bottles, and big hammers. In fact, they were carrying anything at all that would inflict a savage wound on those who'd failed to hand over their beer and whore money.

As we pulled up in our Toyota flatbed, those in the mob were chanting rhythmically and stamping their feet on the ground in time as they tried to intimidate us. I say "tried," but actually they weren't making a bad job of the intimidation. They were a frightening sight.

I knew it was going to be an explosive situation, so I'd already arranged the deployment of a platoon of soldiers from the federal army of the Congo on the hill behind us. They were garrisoned at the mine to protect its perimeter from rebels, but at that moment at least, the rebels were inside the wire. The troops were dressed in vests, shorts, and flip-flops, and as far as I could make out, they had never been paid, either, but for some reason they were still up for a bit of pay bargaining on the bosses' behalf. Under the leadership of two fierce and fearless Nepalese Gurkhas I'd hired, they spread out with a GPMG, or general-purpose machine gun, on the flank.

So there we were: a crowd of angry men baying for money or blood, a platoon of "knickers, handbag, and trumpet" troops and, standing between them, me and a millionaire Arab businessman. Oh, and of course I mustn't forget the British mining engineer trussed up like the last chicken on a supermarket shelf.

The self-appointed union leaders stepped forward and some very tense negotiations began while I stood next to the boss, AK-47 at the ready, watching tensely, scanning the crowd for the one hothead who'd kick it all off. There was a palpable sense of fear and I knew that if something did go down, there was a strong possibility that we'd be hacked to death quite quickly. At that moment, it's fair to say, I had some perception of how General Custer must have felt just before the Battle of Little Bighorn went bottoms up.

Eventually, the deal was done and they brought our man to us while I radioed for the money to be taken out of the safe and brought down to them. Perfect. Get the engineer to a medic, watch the miners set off on the seven-mile walk to town, where they'd sink a few beers, and then everything back to normal in a day or so. Not quite. A disembodied voice crackled down the radio; it was one of my Brit security staff responding to my message.

"Sorry, John. Bit of a problem—Bob's forgotten the combination to the safe."

"He's fucking what?" I asked, trying to keep the hint of alarm out of my voice as a crowd of wound-up miners watched me.

"He can't remember the combination!"

Bob was the other engineer and site manager. That's not his real name, but he was known to one and all as "Bob the Builder" because of his civil engineering expertise. One thing's for sure, though: Bob wasn't as modern as his cartoon namesake. Bob might have stepped straight off the pages of a Graham Greene novel. He was a holdover from colonial times, an Englishman with Land of Hope and Glory stamped all over him. I liked Bob but wondered how he'd survived in Africa, a small dapper man with a head like a beach ball, who belonged in another era and who lived on-site, miles from anywhere, in the strife-torn Congo with his wife and their two pet dogs.

Anyway, in the excitement of it all, Bob had forgotten the combination to the safe and a lot of impatient men waving meat cleavers were waiting for their money. What were we going to do? I managed to get the boss's attention for a moment and quietly told him about our little problem with the safe. He looked as though he'd been informed of a death, possibly his own. Then it came to me.

"I've got an idea," I said. "Keep these lads talking while I phone a friend."

I took his satellite phone from him and dialed a number in England, hoping the phone would be picked up by Jim, an old SAS mate, who in his time had been the best demolitions man and safecracker in the regiment. Thank fuck he answered. You can just imagine the conversation as I explained the predicament I was in.

"Nice one, John," he said. "Tell me, is the safe fixed to the wall?"

I had my gun on the back of the flatbed now—useless if the shit hit the fan—as I used the radio to communicate with the office and the SAT phone to talk to Jim. I was surrounded by the mob of workers, all of whom had fallen silent and wide-eyed, barely able to believe what was happening and curious as to the outcome and, obviously, the part they were going to play in it.

"Yeah, it's bolted onto the wall."

"Right, rip it off the wall. The only way to attack a safe is from the rear."

I passed the instructions along through the radio and then explained blow by blow through the two handsets how they should crack the safe. Jim's instructions worked perfectly—so I'd best not upset any lawmen by revealing all the details—and within twenty minutes the cash was with its rightful owners and the battered engineer was untrussed and safe.

So, you might ask, what the hell's all this diamond mine in the Congo shit got to do with the war in Iraq? I would have asked the same question myself until November 2004, when I saw Bob the Builder striding toward me across the lobby of the Sheraton Hotel in Baghdad with his hand outstretched.

"John, how marvelous to see you." He grasped my hand.

"Jesus, what the hell are you doing here, Bob?" I could barely believe my eyes.

"Well, pastures new and all that. I'm going to sell refrigeration and air-conditioning equipment to the Americans. We've heard that they're short of that sort of stuff and the boss has got a good supply lined up in Qatar. We can have it here for them in double-quick time. Lot of money to be made."

"Yeah, well, that's great, mate. When do you start?" I think I was shaking my head in disbelief.

"Tomorrow, actually. I've got an appointment with an American buyer up at Camp Anaconda. I'm pretty confident I'll get a deal."

"Camp Anaconda? You know the road to Anaconda is crawling with insurgents? Have you got some protection?"

"No. I'll be fine, old boy. Piece of cake. In fact, when I get this business going, I was thinking of getting an apartment here in Baghdad and moving the memsahib and the dogs over, too."

I couldn't believe what he was saying. The idea was so mad that at first I couldn't think of anything sensible to say. He was actually thinking of bringing his wife, his memsahib, into this anarchy. But it was the dogs that was the craziest idea.

"Are you mad, Bob? Muslims can't stand dogs. In their culture, dogs are vermin."

"Really," he replied sniffily. "Well, I'm sure it'll be fine."

"No, Bob, it really won't be fine. The whole place is alive with fucking terrorists and they're falling over one another they're so desperate to find Westerners to mallet. They'll have your balls for cuff links before you know it. Believe me, Bob, you can't do it."

He gave me one of his tight upper-class "I know best" smiles and said, "Don't worry, John. It'll all settle down. Believe me."

Don't worry, John! I wasn't the one who had to worry. "Bollocks! It's never going to settle down, Bob. Sell your fridges and fuck off home, that's my advice."

I didn't see Bob in Iraq again and I haven't bumped into him since, but I know he did heed my warning and worked safely out of Qatar. I hope he stays safe.

Bob's not typical of the businessmen who head for Iraq, though. Most of them are not anywhere near as eccentric and they're not out there looking for speculative sales. They are mostly men from big corporations with contracts already in the bag. They come from all over the world, as the huge sums of money on offer act like a magnet to business.

The risks are huge, but so are the rewards. In my experience, only men with balls of steel head for Iraq to fulfill the obligations of the contracts. Most of them are levelheaded, quiet, and thoughtful. A lot of them are dedicated family men with children in expensive schools and wives they want to provide for. Some of them run their own small specialist engineering or electronic companies and see a lucrative contract in Iraq as worth the risk to establish the firm's future. Others are vice presidents of big multinational companies and are the centurions of the corporate world, prepared to go most places and take big risks for the sake of the business empire they serve, but they do it for huge rewards.

Diplomats need protection, too, and the U.S. and British governments both entrust that job to PMCs rather than to regular troops. Twenty years ago in Beirut, it was a special unit of the Royal Military Police, trained by the SAS, that was given the job of close protection of ambassadorial staff on assignment there, but not anymore. The Foreign Office contracted the work out to a PMC in Iraq and it looks as though that will be the trend in future hot spots.

Some of the most important security assignments are for the protection of economists and bankers from the International Monetary Fund and the World Bank who are pivotal to the financial future of the country. Their protection, too, is entrusted to PMCs, and a few of the people assigned to them are among the most unusual contractors working in Iraq. I'll be describing them in another chapter.

So, on any given day, there are thousands of businessmen, engineers, bankers, and diplomats on the move around Iraq, and it's a real credit to the mercenary army that protects them that relatively few of the clients, or principals, as they're known, have lost their lives. I reckon that it would be in the region of thirty or forty who have, and of those, only a couple were UK citizens, including, tragically, a man named Ken Bigley.

Ken was a sixty-two-year-old engineer from Liverpool, who by all accounts was a decent bloke. In contrast, his fate and the fate of two U.S. colleagues in October 2004 was particularly indecent. He'd been held hostage for three weeks and been forced to make several video appeals to Tony Blair and the coalition to convey his captors' demands that all women prisoners held by them should be released. Only two women, both WMD scientists, were being held by the United States, which made the appeal a bit of a red herring. Ken's captors were just playing games.

In the end, it seems that at least one of the Tawhid and Jihad Group holding Ken had some humanity and helped him escape, but he was soon picked up again after half an hour's liberty in the back streets of the town of Latifiya, located to the southwest of Baghdad.

That must have sealed his fate and probably the fate of the guy who sympathized with him, because they forced Ken to make another video appeal. I've watched this disgusting film and it seems to me that from his dignified demeanor, Ken was a man of more courage than the cowardly bastards who held him.

This final video shows six armed and hooded men standing behind Ken, who was being made to kneel in front of them. After his appeal for help, he uttered his last words: "I have a very short time left." The man behind him then made a minute-long speech in Arabic before taking a wicked blade out of its sheath and falling on Ken from behind like a dog. Three of the others grabbed him and held him as he was beheaded with the knife while the pack screamed, "God is great" time and time again.

Good protection is a lifesaver, and it is the presence of highly trained PMCs that gives these brave men, who want to give Iraq the lifeblood of trade, the confidence to keep doing business there.

I always point to the case of two Finnish businessmen, part of a trade delegation, who were murdered on the infamous Baghdad airport highway in March 2004. Seppo Haapanen and Jorma Törönen were hoping to revive old business contacts in Iraq and represented high-tech firms. But their protection certainly wasn't high-tech as they drove to the Ministry of Electricity offices near the airport. A large black car, probably one of the insurgents' favorite BMWs, drove alongside their vehicle and the gunmen inside it opened fire with automatic weapons. The Finns were shot to shit.

Those two Finnish guys didn't have any close protection, but their Iraqi driver was carrying a pistol. Great! Even if the driver could have gotten his pistol out in time, assuming that he would have wanted to have a shoot-out with a couple of machine guns, he wouldn't have been able to drive and fight effectively. A couple of trained PMCs alert and on the lookout for just that sort of attack would probably have seen the two Finns come out of it alive. I don't know who advised their delegation on security, but they should never have been in that car without a couple of armed men protecting them. It really makes me angry when I hear of wasted lives.

Of course Ken's death and the death of other hostages in similar circumstances has had a sobering effect on the men and women who travel to Iraq to help rebuild the country, but it hasn't stopped them coming.

Some of the people I've met in Iraq have been quite extraordinary. I'll never forget the two Israeli Jews who somehow found their way into the country, determined to make a fortune from the oil trade. Those guys looked typically Jewish, and when I met them, they'd already spent weeks traveling around the country without protection. I cannot imagine how they survived, but they did, and they play a part in my story later on.

I T WAS MARCH 2004 and I was in Baghdad doing the usual. I came back to the Sheraton after a day out on the ground with a client and the receptionist handed me a message with my key from the pigeon hole. My friend Adeeb had called. He'd been a mate for nearly ten years or more. He was a Palestinian guy whom I had very good reason to trust. I went to my room, showered, then called him.

"How are you, old friend?" I asked.

"I'm very good, Johnny, very good, and my family are good, too, but I wanted to get hold of you about some business," he said.

"Okay, sounds good. How can I help?"

"I have a friend who does business out of Dubai. He's got hold of some oil concessions in Iraq, but he wants to organize security. At the moment, the facilities are not working, but they are expensive, as you can imagine, and he wants to make sure they will not be damaged when they are working again. I mentioned you and he would like a meeting."

"Where?"

"In Baghdad, Johnny."

"Okay, well, he could come here and meet me at the hotel."

"I don't think so, my friend. There are people in all the hotels who report back to the Ba'ath party and the Al Qaeda people, too. Believe me, Baghdad is spy city these days and he will not want to be seen in a hotel full of Westerners. Not a good thing."

"Well, it's not a good idea for a Westerner to be wandering around Baghdad, either."

"I know, I know, but if you could see him, I would consider it a great favor," said Adeeb.

Well, I owed him a great favor, so I agreed to do it. And anyway, I trusted Adeeb and he'd given me his word the bloke was sound. The arrangements were made and I met Mr. X two days later, but when I did, I broke the only rule in the hitchhiker's guide to Iraq. I accepted a ride in his car.

It was early evening, but darkness was falling as we entered the twilight zone and drove away from the center and across the river, me sitting on the backseat with Mr. X. I was getting more than a little bit uneasy and the fact that we were heading in the general direction of the insurgency slums of Sadr City wasn't making me feel any easier. Neither did the fact that he wasn't from Dubai at all, but an Iraqi. What did make me feel slightly easier was the pistol in a concealed holster under my jacket—slightly, but not a lot.

We turned off before Sadr City, which was good, but then the car started winding around back streets in an alarming way, and it wasn't more than five minutes before I had no idea where I was. I felt in my pocket to make sure my security card was there. I did that a couple of times. It wasn't long then before the car pulled up and I was invited into a building that seemed to be some sort of office.

Mr. X, who was very courteous and spoke good English, took me into a room filled with about five of his associates, as he called them. To me, it was just a room full of Saddam look-alikes. When I sat down across a desk from him, I didn't make any pretense of it; I just put my hand inside my jacket and gripped my pistol. Just in case.

The conversation wandered around a bit, but to be honest, I wasn't thinking as much about what was being said as I was about leaving the place and whether I'd get back to the hotel in one piece.

He asked a bit about prices of security, but he seemed more interested in whom else I'd worked for, not a subject I was willing to discuss with him. In the end, I just bluntly asked to be returned to the hotel and said I'd wait to hear from him. I never did, but I do know that his business was none of mine.

What I'd done was foolish, even on the good word of an old friend, and I resolved never to break the only rule of the hitchhiker's guide, which is never to hitch a lift in Iraq.

P ERHAPS THE MOST ECCENTRIC and downright charming of all the businessmen I met in Iraq during eighteen months of protection work were two ex–British Army NCOs looking for oil contracts in Basra. If Bob the Builder could easily have stepped off the pages of a Graham Greene novel, then central casting would have replaced Sean Connery and Michael Caine with these other two in *The Man Who Would Be King*. I'll call them Doug and Mick.

When they first arrived in Iraq, they had a South African team serving as bodyguards while they went about the Basra area doing recces and building relationships in the oil business for a Qatar-based company. But after a couple of weeks, the PMCs looking after them told the two old sergeant majors that the contract was over and dumped them at the Basra airport. They were on their own.

They managed to get a cab back to Basra, and they were a striking sight when I first met them as they walked into the Mirbad Hotel dressed in old 1980s army camo jackets and olive green trousers. Each of them proudly wore their old berets, one that of the Irish Guards, the other that of the Parachute Regiment, but they had no other rank or insignia on their uniforms.

They told me their story and I was fascinated by the two old soldiers and, like everyone they came into contact with, thought they were great. Doug and Mick were charming old military rogues in the best traditions of the British Army. They were brave as lions and had probably known the *Queen's Regulations* back to front and every way of getting around them, too.

Doug had been living in Texas and working in the oil industry for years, but when the official war ended, he fancied his chances and thought he'd head for the gold rush in Iraq. He'd flown to England as a staging post first and met up with his old mate over a few pints in the British Legion club in a famous cathedral city.

"It was just plain good fortune, John," Doug told me at that first meeting. "Mick was at a loose end and he was up for it. You know yourself the value of a partner you can trust, and I'd trust Mick with my life."

"You may have to out here, old son," I told him; then I asked, "Where are you going to go now? You can't stay here without any minders, or you'll get chopped."

"Oh no, we're not leaving yet," said his mate Mick. "There's money to be made and we're going to make it."

"For fuck sake, Mick, get a grip. I'll make sure you two get safely down to Kuwait; then you can get a flight home. You'll be back on the piss in the Legion in a couple of days' time."

"Not a chance, John," said Doug. "Fortune favors the brave and we're going to strike oil one bloody way or another."

I didn't see them for a couple of weeks; then they pulled up in the hotel courtyard in a beaten-up old Range Rover they'd obtained somewhere on the Basra black market.

"Where are you two staying?" I asked.

"We're camped down at the Mitsubishi oil jetty on the docks," said Doug. "It's lovely down there, sea breezes and a view across the docks, couldn't be better."

Mick nodded in agreement as I pointed at their old shed of a 4 x 4. "You been driving around in that thing with your berets on?"

"Yup," replied Doug.

"And you haven't had any trouble?"

"No not a bit of it. We wouldn't mind getting hold of a couple of rifles just in case, though."

I shook my head, unable to credit that anyone could be so seemingly bonkers; then I made the only contribution I could to ensuring their survival: I gunned them up.

"I should be able to fix you up with a couple of AKs," I offered. "I'll give you a quick rundown on their works. I think we'd better get that done sooner than later."

"Thanks, John, much appreciated. Why don't you come down to our place with them; then we could try them out over the water," said Doug.

"I'll do that. See you there later."

I was amazed when I got to the jetty. There was their camp like an outpost of Empire, an old khaki brown tent pitched on the jetty at Al Subia with a Union Jack flapping lazily in the bright sunshine on a pole next to it. Hats off to them: They had it all set up military-style—shaving mirror on the upright tent pole, water cans in the shade—and the two old soldiers were obviously quite happy with their lot.

Again they'd huffed and puffed their way to a position of advantage and the IPA (Iraqi Petroleum Authority) had allowed them to set up on the jetty, which before the war had been a key oil-exporting point. They'd even let them use a hut as a temporary office.

I knew that they'd endeared themselves to one and all with their almost theatrical, parade-ground mannerisms, but the extent to which Doug and Mick were admired and welcomed precisely because of their old-style British Army ways was unbelievable.

I was to witness their hypnotic powers firsthand that afternoon. About five hundred meters away, a unit of Royal Engineers was set up, and before I'd had a chance to get the AKs out and put them through their paces, the 2 IC, the second in command, of the unit came striding down the jetty toward us. He'd only just arrived and he was obviously going about like a dervish, whipping the place into shape, and wanted to investigate this satellite British camp that had been set up under the walls of his castle.

"What the hell's going on here?" he asked.

The "boys" snapped to attention, chins up and out, big mustaches bristling forward. "SAH!"

Doug stamped one pace forward, then did a bit more parade-ground stamping and snapping to attention. Mick was doing a bit behind him, too.

"Sorry to inconvenience you, sir! We were about to come and make ourselves known!"

They explained their situation, which was, of course, entirely civilian, as though it were completely military. "No money. No provisions. Irish Guards. Parachute Regiment"—Those were the key words I heard Doug rattle out, and within ten minutes the Royal Engineers officer was completely won over.

"We can't have you out here exposed and without rations," said the officer. He turned to the sergeant who'd been glued hard onto his right shoulder and ordered, "Get these men inside the base. They can have the empty cabin on the east edge of the perimeter. While you're at it, put them on the ration roll and they can have a NAAFI card, and I expect they'll probably need some fuel, as well."

All the while he was talking, Doug and Mick were feebly uttering, "Don't want to put anyone out, sir."

They were trying to make out that they didn't want to be any trouble, but he wasn't listening. He was determined to make sure his new charges were well looked after and he brushed their feigned objections aside. "Nonsense, nonsense. See to it, Sergeant."

"He seems to be a good bloke, that young officer," said Mick as the Royal Engineer strode back to his duties.

"Salt of the earth," said Doug. "Salt of the earth."

I slipped them the guns and left them to get their feet well and truly under the table, which of course they did with charming ease. A couple of days later, I bumped into them in the hotel. They looked cheerful and spent five minutes telling me what a wonderful outfit the Royal Engineers was.

The charming old bastards hoodwinked me, too. On the

strength of promised contracts and some work they actually got, I advanced them a fair amount of cash to get them "started" in their words. Sure enough, they went on the lash with the cash and drank most of it in smart bars on business trips to Qatar. I was left twenty thousand dollars light and I vowed to stick to the day job from then on.

I haven't heard of them since, but maybe one day I'll roll down to that beautiful cathedral city, take a look in the British Legion club, and see if they'll buy me a pint or two. They owe me.

THE AIR-CONDITIONING had broken down, so my friend Joe, his Jordanian driver, and a three-man TV crew were sitting in a seventy-mile-per-hour sauna as they thundered down the Fallujah bypass in an ex–police issue GMC 4 x 4.

Usual rules. Joe's gut feelings about the trip were giving him gripes, when he saw a Toyota truck kicking up plumes of grit and dust as it headed down a desert track on a collision course with their own vehicle.

Two bandits/insurgents were in the front, two in the back, and one of them had a wicked RPG launcher over his shoulder, pointing it menacingly at the GMC. They'd obviously been patrolling the roads, looking for some white eyes, and it was their lucky day because, guess what, they had all the weapons and the GMC had none. That's because the correspondent in charge of this particular crew had little common sense and he was being a hard arse and sticking rigidly to the station policy of no weapons. Joe didn't like it, but he's a man with an acute belief in his abilities, and one of those was the ability to negotiate a triple fee for the job. No gun means lots of money; that's a basic principle in PMC work.

Anyway, that was the situation they found themselves in. Joe told me his only fleeting moment of satisfaction in the seconds before they were forced to pull up was the correspondent's chalk white face as the awful truth hit him.

Close-up and personal, the TV journalist could see that the insurgents were not people who would be easily impressed by his station's logo or his international press pass. Guns, on the other hand, did impress them and they had a monopoly on weapons. He was crapping himself.

They were hauled out of the vehicle within seconds of pulling over and with practiced ease the leader of the insurgent team quickly ran his eye over them and worked out who was who in the group they'd captured.

Joe reckoned their leader looked pleased with his bag as he snapped out an order to one of his men; there was no mistaking what was going on, even though the order had been too quick-fire for Joe's basic Arabic. It was simple: His appearance and demeanor spelled out bodyguard and he was going to be chopped before he could make trouble. They had three prime hostages and they would keep the driver until he'd delivered the captives and the GMC, then kill him. Why keep the one most likely to cause them problems in the meantime?

Sure enough, Joe was grabbed roughly by the shoulder and pushed in the direction of a high bank of sand alongside the road, with endless desert scrub stretching away behind it. A jab with an AK reinforced the order and Joe set off on what was meant to be his last walk.

They went over the top of the bank and that's when Joe moved. He's an ex-Blade and he knows the first rule of survival and escape after capture is a simple one: You make your move as soon as you possibly can.

The young Sunni terrorist came too close. It was enough. Joe grabbed him and spun him around like a top. Shots were fired and one badly grazed Joe's hand before he was able to drop the gunman with two blows, which left the man nearly dead. Joe was about to grab the weapon and sort the situation out once and for all, but the others were coming after him and firing furiously at him, so he legged it into the scrub.

One of the insurgents jumped into the driver's seat of the Toyota and tore into the desert to give chase, too. Joe managed to keep running parallel with the road for a while as the insurgents fired wildly after him. But now, the Jordanian driver was on the case and, with heroic courage, he decided he couldn't leave Joe to his fate, despite knowing he was on the menu, as well. He could have torn off down the Highway with the TV crew still intact, but he didn't. Instead, he raced down the road after him, then jolted across the desert to collect Joe, who leaped gratefully into the vehicle. Bullets were still whining around them as he cursed the day he'd agreed to come down the Highway without a weapon.

They thumped and bumped through the desert scrub, but by now the Toyota driver had picked up his mates and they were crashing over the terrain in hot pursuit. It was only a matter of time before they would be able to get a shot off with the RPG or, more likely, riddle the GMC with their AKs.

That's when it happened. It was one of those off-the-wall, tell-the-grandchildren situations that you just couldn't make up. Remember that I mentioned the GMC was a former police vehicle? Well, among the equipment that had been left in it was a public-address system with a microphone in the cab and loud-speakers back and front. It was meant for ordering motorists to pull over, that sort of thing, and Joe and the driver had messed around with it a bit themselves.

For some reason, the driver got it into his head that he would pray and he decided to make his prayers public, so he did it over the PA system. He picked up the mike and started praying, reciting passages from the Holy Koran and urging mercy on the pursuers. He quoted sections from the holy book on peace and justice and as he chanted them his voice broadcast the verses across the desert in the strange metallic voice of the loudspeakers.

And it worked. Suddenly and for no possible reason except the exhortations for peace and harmony from the Koran, the driver of the Toyota braked to a halt and the gunmen just watched Joe and his clients drive away to safety.

Needless to say, Joe never traveled on a bodyguard job without a gun again; that was his personal lesson from the incident. But I've told you the story because I believe it's a parable of modern Babylon that teaches those who want to survive in Iraq some vital lessons.

First, it illustrates the central truth that underlies all conflicts, not just the one in Iraq but those throughout the world. It's commonly known as the fog of war, but I call it the "fuck knows factor," and the main principle to bear in mind is that you should never be taken aback by what war and mayhem can throw up.

All conflicts take on a life of their own. Sometimes it involves violence so intense that only fate can steer you through it; sometimes quirky things happen like those stories of Bibles and cigarette cases tucked into soldiers' tunics that saved them from bullets in World War I. In this case, it was prayers on a public-address system that saved our heroes' lives. The point is that they didn't stand around gawking at their good fate; they grasped the opportunity and escaped.

Who knows what's going to happen when you walk into the casino called war and find the only game at the tables is Russian roulette. If you don't like the game, don't go into that casino, because there are no guarantees that you'll come out alive, and those that give such guarantees are liars.

The second lesson is one that Joe didn't need to read in the manual. It's simply this: The sooner you act, the more likely you are to survive. With typical understatement, the British military call this life-or-death rule "conduct after capture."

Joe knew that the edge he had when the insurgents got him out of the car would erode rapidly. In his case, that was on a steep downward curve leading to a point, after a few minutes, when he would be shot dead in the sand dunes. He knew that; he knew, too, that he had to act, and he did. In other circumstances, the erosion of your initiative might take longer, but it begins from the moment you are captured.

As time in captivity goes on, you lose kit, even down to the bootlaces that you might be able to use to throttle a guard. Crucially, you also lose the will to make a move. Joe seized the initiative when his adrenaline rush was in full drive, and it was his resolve to act and some very loud prayers on a PA system that saved his life. You have to go for it.

The third lesson is an important one. Joe's situation underscores the fact that you should know something about the culture you're immersing yourself in before you go to a country ravaged by war and insurrection. He'd obviously made a connection with the driver that made his Arab friend want to act to save him. I reckon those prayers must have been from the heart.

I already spoke some Arabic from my days in the regiment, but I also made it my business to learn about the Muslim culture and its local and regional variants in Iraq. You simply never know when that will come in useful. It can help you to build bridges in small but significant ways when you do business with locals. But in another situation, it could also help you to make crucial, life-saving bonds with captors, building an invisible shield around you if just one of them feels some sympathy for your plight.

This isn't pie in the sky. Shrinks call it "Stockholm syndrome" and it's named after a bank robbery in that city that turned into a police siege. The hostages were bank staff and trapped customers. They began to empathize with their captors and even spoke out for them when they were released.

It happened at the Iranian embassy siege in London, too, the one so famously broken by the SAS. When the regiment stormed the place, killing all but one of the terrorists, the one bad guy who lived was smuggled out of the building by female secretaries who sympathized with him because he'd shown them some small kindnesses.

Obviously, people at the mercy of robbers or terrorists instinctively think that being liked might save their lives, but Stockholm syndrome works both ways. When a bond has been made, individual captors will sometimes go a long way to save their captives.

It nearly worked for Ken Bigley, who evidently befriended one of his guards, who then helped him get out of his terrorist jail. He nearly escaped, but he was picked up again by the rest of the Al Qaeda gang and infamously beheaded in a videotaped execution. We don't know what happened to the man who showed him mercy, but there's little doubt that he paid with his life for his glimmer of humanity.

A wonderful Yank hostage, Thomas Hamill, made it work for him, too. I'd like to meet Tom Hamill, because from everything I've heard about him, he must be one hell of a man. Tom was a truck driver working for the giant Halliburton company when his convoy was attacked and he was taken captive by insurgents. It was April 2004 and the insurgents were on the warpath because of the assault on Fallujah by U.S. forces following the infamous murder and mutilation of the four Blackwater contractors a few days earlier.

Four other people taken with him were later found murdered,

but Tom Hamill was a valuable prize and he was quickly taken to a remote farmhouse ninety miles north of the ambush near Tikrit. He was there for a month, and during that time Tom wove his own peculiar brand of magic on his captors. He was a handy sort of guy and he showed them a few ways of filtering and purifying their domestic water supply—ways they were able to use back in their homes to benefit their families. They were grateful.

Tom used that advantage to create a more relaxed regime for himself and in the end persuaded them that he wouldn't try to escape. Where would he go? He was in the middle of the desert, and anyway, if he did happen to be seen, he would be handed in again.

They didn't want to be hanging about guarding him all day and Tom was a good guy, wasn't he? So they took him at his word and left him for days at a time locked in a room at the farm with water and supplies. Tom had turned the situation into one where he became his own jailer and soon found a way out. He actually tried to wave down some coalition helicopters, but they didn't spot him, so he returned to his cell for the next visit by his guards. Out again when they'd gone, he found the main oil pipeline through the region and reasoned correctly that this would be heavily patrolled. Soon enough, he was found by U.S. troops and returned to his home in Macon, Missouri.

It was a fantastic outcome and Tom Hamill did it all on his own, because when it came down to it, he used the only weapons he had at his disposal: his huge personality and his humanity. Top marks for survival.

I want to mention a couple more things that I believe are vital. First, anyone going to Iraq or Afghanistan to work would be crazy not to go on a hostile-environment course before setting off. You'll be put into simulations of engagements, complete with live rounds, and that will prepare you for the real thing better than any number of sleepless nights wondering what may lie in store.

More than that, you'll learn how to act, how to help, and how to give yourself the best chance of surviving.

Escape driving techniques and four-wheel driving skills should be part of the course. If someone in your security party is injured, you would then be in a position to use those skills to fill a vital role while the others fight on. You should also do a battlefield first-aid course. It will transform you from a parcel being delivered by a security detail into a potentially useful member of the team.

The other thing I'd like to touch on again is the question of carrying arms. I don't necessarily think that it's a great idea, it really depends on the individual, because if you haven't got the resolve to use a weapon, then you shouldn't carry one. Engineers and managers are happier firing away on slide rules and calculators, and that's the way it should be.

But you're in Iraq and you've been ambushed on the Fallujah bypass. One of your bodyguards is dead, the other wounded, and you and your Jordanian driver have been isolated from a second protection vehicle. At that moment, you might decide you'd rather have a go than be shot or measured for an orange boiler suit. That's when the basic weapons knowledge you can learn on a hostile-environment course might save your life. Do the course!

As I write, most journeys in Iraq undertaken by foreigners are between the Green Zone and the airport. Journalists now venture outside the security zone only if they're embedded with coalition troops or by strict agreement with the militias that will escort them into areas like Sadr City in Baghdad or around Basra in the south. That's the Shia militia, of course, as no deals at all are being struck with the really evil axis of former Saddam Ba'athists and Al Qaeda types who run the Sunni insurgency.

Businessmen and engineers travel outside the country, but that is generally in armed convoys the length of a Wild West wagon train, which are whacked the moment they are spotted, or else they travel British-style and go covert.

And that's where I come to my number one rule for surviving in Iraq. I've really taken it from the mantra of most Realtors, who reckon selling a house is about three things: Location! Location! Location! Surviving in Iraq is about three things, too: Low profile! Low profile! Low profile!

7. The City of the Dead

I T WAS AUGUST 2003 AND NAJAF WAS HOTTER THAN hell. I was in the city, which is located a hundred miles south of Baghdad on the west bank of the Euphrates, with a British TV crew and their regular Iraqi driver. I'll call him Hamdany. I loved Hamdany; he was a really warm, funny guy. He would often give me a bear hug and say, "You are my son." Sometimes his hand of friendship would be followed by the bonding words "When you are with me, you are Iraqi." He wasn't bullshitting. Like many Iraqis, he was a man of great heart and humanity, and when we drove past some scene of bloodletting and carnage, you could almost see him wince. He would shake his head, a deep sadness would fill his voice, and he'd say, "This is my new democracy? This is my new democracy?"

But that day, it was too hot even for Hamdany and the hugs and bonding sessions were put off until a cooler day. His new democracy would have to wait to be mourned, even though it had barely been born.

The TV crew was going to do a piece on the growing influence of the Shiite organization known as the Supreme Council for the Islamic Revolution in Iraq, centered on the Imam Ali Mosque, which holds the tomb of Ali. The top Shiite cleric, Mohammed Baqir al-Hakim, was based there with his Badr militia. The town was also home for the Medhi Army. It was a tense place and brimming with fear. As I said, it was hotter than hell, and I'm not just talking about the weather.

As we drove into the suburbs, we passed a vast plantation of tombs and graves, acres of burial sites, and Hamdany said something in Arabic.

"What's that?" I asked.

"It's named the City of the Dead. Every Shia wishes to rest here within sight of the tomb of Ali. They want to be near the martyr when they die. It is said it is the biggest cemetery in the world."

"The City of the Dead, eh? Nice one."

Then I saw it rising from the ground like an explosion of golden light, glittering and glinting as it transmitted a million reflections of the sun over the city. The Imam Ali Mosque. It was awesome and humbling, and it was real gold, too, thousands of solid tiles of it, but I remember thinking as I saw it that gold usually spells trouble.

We parked a good half mile from the mosque and set off on foot through the labyrinth of market streets with overhanging balconies closed to the day, their corrugated metal shutters all slammed down. Before we left, we'd had some intelligence on the PMC grapevine that there'd been trouble earlier in the day outside the mosque. A bloke had been beaten and carved up outside the gates. Apparently, he'd been taken for a Sunni spy, or maybe he'd even been one. We'll never know; it's history, and so was he.

But you could definitely smell trouble in the air. Everyone knew it was brewing even if they didn't know exactly why, and the sense of fear was palpable. I'd taken the decision to go on ahead unarmed. You have to weigh these things, and at that time the Badr and the Mehdi armies weren't considered insurgent; they were seen as militia policing their own communities for the general good, even if they were a bit on the volatile side.

I could have stashed the AK and just taken the Tariq pistol, one of those heavy Iraqi handguns that are a bit like coshes with bullets in them, but that might have been disrespectful. Why? Because we were being sort of hosted by the ayatollah and we were being allowed near the mosque after a couple of days of negotiations by the producer.

We kept walking. The cameraman had been well briefed, and I'd made him wear really bright, gaudy clothes so he looked like the locals' idea of a filmmaker. I even got him to wear a brightly colored hat, in line with the old maxim, If you can't fight, wear a daft hat. I grabbed his tripod and carried it in order to look like one of the crew.

As we neared the mosque, hundreds of eyes turned to watch us as we worked our way through the crowd. It was the time of day for Saturday prayers and the faces glaring at us were entirely male, which was intimidating in itself. Many of them were hostile, but a lot of the eyes in that sea of faces were genuinely surprised to see a group of Westerners in that place at that time and they seemed to register grudging respect that we had the balls to be there at all.

We got to the walls of the mosque and representatives of the ayatollah came out and handed us a written safe passage to be in the area of this most sacred place and a license to film. It allowed us to go into the outer courtyard of the mosque, in front of the magnificent gates to the inner sanctum and the tomb of Ali. Since it was prayer time, the place was thronged with worshippers.

It was a fraught time, the atmosphere uncertain, and we were receiving mixed messages and signals from the crowd. A large group followed us around, gawking and chattering as we filmed. There was some real hostility in the air, but word had buzzed around that the ayatollah himself had allowed us in, so those who were full of real hatred for Westerners bridled their feelings. Any questions and we just waved the magic piece of paper.

We finished filming in the courtyard and left, but the cameraman wanted to get some shots from above and wanted to go into a building overlooking the scene of the lines of men at prayer.

"We really need that shot to set the piece off," he told the correspondent, and they dispatched the moderator for the film, who was Hamdany's son, to ask a shopkeeper on the ground floor if we could go up.

I was thinking, For fuck sake, let's get out of this place. But I knew that cameramen don't see anything except through the lens. They're among the most disassociated and detached people on the planet. Nothing matters but getting the shot. Me? Well, it's different for me. I've got to worry about them, and nothing matters but not getting them shot.

The magic paper opened doors again and he went up two stories for his wonderful fucking shots of the Shia at prayer. Marvelous. I was really chuffed to be walking back to the car, swept along on a sea of men who'd just been wound up by their mullahs and whose eyes were alight with the fire of religion and patriotism. Of course we were infidels and, in their eyes, representatives of the forces of oppression. Oh well, only half a mile to walk in their company, I thought.

You've seen those pictures of Muslim men beating themselves with chains in an act of mass self-flagellation? Well, that was this lot mourning the death of Imam Ali at the festival of Ashurah. They were hard-core, and soon we were being jostled and cursed.

Some of them who spoke English said, "You shouldn't be here. Go home!" Others asked the question that, if answered incorrectly, would have invited a mob lynching: "Are you American?"

"Not American. English. British," we kept saying.

"Ah, we like British," said one of the crowd. Not that much, though.

I was getting really worried about the way things were going and I told Hamdany's lad to go ahead and warn his dad to turn the car around and get ready to roll. The last fifty yards were really tense and some anticoalition chanting had begun. I know some basic Arabic, but I got the message, because the names of Bush and Blair featured heavily. I don't like chanting; it numbs the mind of a crowd and gets people into that state of oneness that allows a thinking mass to become a mob.

I hurried the crew on, cursing the dickhead of a cameraman and his precious prayer footage under my breath. They were all loaded up and I had one foot on the ground, about to swing myself in and close the door, when four sharp cracks rang out one after another, kicking up dust and chippings of stone from the road around us. Only then did I notice that the crowd that had been following us hadn't come right up to the car. Had they known what was going down? I think so.

I slammed the door and spun the equation through my mind in a split second. Returning fire equals calling down the mob and getting the crew and me torn limb from limb! I told myself.

I kept my AK dormant and yelled, "Put your boot down, Hammy!"

"I can't! I can't!"

Shit! I looked at the road ahead and saw that it was filled by two looming 4 x 4's with running boards along the sides, heading straight toward us. Bearded men in sweeping black robes, bristling with weapons, hung off the sides.

Fuck! The Mehdi Army! I gripped my AK and began sweating like a pedophile in a toy shop. Too much booze the night before.

"Re—" I hadn't finished ordering Hamdany to reverse the car into the alleyway behind us when the two trucks full of fighters swept past us. What a relief. It wasn't us they were after. They were looking for the sniper who'd broken the word of the ayatollah. Whoever he was, he'd be split in two and barbecued before the day was over.

Hamdany didn't need telling; he was off down the road like a rocket as soon as it cleared. Then one of the crew asked, "Were those shots meant for us?"

"Nah," I replied, lying. "Just some stray rounds fired off by a hothead."

Hamdany and I looked at each other out of the corner of our eyes. We knew.

Those in the crowd had known, too. Like an agitated hive, they'd sensed something foul was brewing. And two days later, a massive car bomb exploded outside the gates to the tomb of Ali. It had been parked right below the balcony where our cameraman had been filming, and it dispatched the ayatollah and over one hundred worshippers to the City of the Dead. It was an outrage that pushed the Shias to take the offensive.

But we were safe for the moment. Hamdany drove off, muttering his usual doleful complaint, "Ah, so this is my new democracy?"

THREE WEEKS LATER, I was taking care of a different crew—Irish television this time—and we were in the ancient city of Nasiriyah. We were in the city center and the crew was filming an interview with an Iraqi who was making a living taking passport and ID-card photos with a homemade pinhole camera made from plywood. This was another example of how extraordinarily resourceful the Iraqi people are. The crew was filming what was going to be a positive, hopeful piece highlighting the ingenuity of the Iraqi people—a change from the usual reportage. Then all hell broke loose.

A huge blast about 150 meters down the street, opposite the police station, demonstrated the sinister side of the ingenuity and inventiveness of the Iraqi people. It was an IED detonated in a crowded shopping street near the precinct house.

It's hard to know which came first, the all-consuming sound of the blast or the piece of corrugated steel sent hurtling by the shock wave into the cat's cradle of power and telephone lines hanging over the street. Showers of sparks fell around us, followed by a confetti of shredded rubbish and a rolling cloud of dust. I managed to keep my feet, but the cameraman was bowled over onto the pavement and damaged his kit.

Focus, you've got to focus in those terrible, unreal, dream-time minutes that come with a bomb blast. The rest of the crew was fine. They'd been standing in the shelter of a building just around the corner from the pulsating wave generated by the bomb.

I saw a boy lying on the ground on the other side of the street, blood pumping out of a wound in his thigh. Right! Let's go! I thought. I was with him in a second, ripping the cover of a shell dressing—a U.S.-issue one, as the British dressings are rubbish, with the absorption qualities of a 1950s sanitary napkin.

The kid looked up at me, his big brown eyes vacant, as if some invisible tentacle of the blast had scooped the inside of his brain out. There was nothing to read in those eyes. No pleading, no shock. Nothing. Why subject a boy like this to the hellish lottery of a bomb blast? For a moment, I felt a savage anger, but I knew that the injury wouldn't kill him now, and I had the crew to sort out.

Scores of people rushing away from the site of the bomb blast were ballooning out into the small square we were in and they were in a terrible fury. I think the fact that I'd been seen treating that kid made a difference. They were looking for scapegoats and someone helping wasn't going to attract their anger. Not for a few minutes anyway.

A hail of gunfire followed as a battle broke out between insurgents and the coalition troops who were based in the police barracks, but there was no point in our being there without a working camera. The box camera, too, had been knocked over in the stampede.

It was my call. We were isolated from friendly troops, and I took a look at the crowd and then looked at the crew with the broken camera.

"Come on, we're off," I ordered, and ushered them toward the car about forty yards away.

I knew what had happened there. It was common knowledge that the locals got on really well with the coalition guys stationed in their town, and they especially liked the captain in charge of the detachment. I think they were Spanish. Apparently, the captain was a charismatic man with an instinctive political touch, a man they could do business with. Well, that was no good, was it? The terrorists weren't going to let such a cozy relationship flourish and take root, so they moved in to obliterate that relationship with a bomb.

I stood on the corner, looking down the bombed alley. Across the way, the photographer was trying to salvage the remains of his broken equipment, and I hope he got it back together again.

Looking down the street, I saw the body of a man sprawled in the gutter. He was wearing a distinctive red-and-green-striped shirt. I'd seen him only a few minutes earlier as he'd left the street photographer. He'd been clutching a new ID picture in his hand.

He'd looked pleased with the results, but he wouldn't be needing it now. I needed a drink.

I'D MOVED ON. It was still August 2003, but I was back with a British crew and down south again in Basra, where the summer heat was boiling people's brains. The fact of the matter was that a lot of Basrans were so badly head-cooked that mobs of them were on the rampage, venting their rage over the shortage of fuel. They needed fuel for generators to power the air-conditioning units they needed to unboil their brains. So, with the logic of brains rendered into haggis by heat, they attacked the only three petrol stations in town that were open, thereby increasing the scarcity of the very fuel they wanted to get their hands on.

To make things worse, fuel tankers were being hijacked by various clans or tribes, and so suddenly there wasn't any fuel at all in the petrol stations, causing those not in on the tanker heists to go crazy. There were even gangs trying to hunt down the garage owners and their families to extort fuel from them.

They'd created their very own catch-22 situation and they'd done it very violently. In the absence of any effective policing, it was the poor bloody British infantry who had to sort it all out. Their officers had insisted they not fire on the mob; instead, they'd issued them riot gear.

There they were—I think it was the Princess of Wales's Own Regiment—wearing heavy gear, swinging batons, and charging the crowds with plastic shields in a ninety-degree-Fahrenheit breeze that was blowing off that gigantic kiln called the Sahara Desert. It must have been like wrestling in a sauna. It's a testament to their training that they didn't flinch even when soldiers were collapsing from heat exhaustion and being dragged out of the line to be rehydrated.

At one point as I was accompanying the crew, we saw a thin line of infantry bashing people's heads to get them to back off from the petrol station. Then suddenly, a youth—he was no more than seventeen—appeared from nowhere clutching an AK that he looked far too comfortable with. A corporal on the flank of the infantry line pinged him immediately, broke ranks, ran to him, and grabbed the AK, twisting it out of the kid's grip. Then he butt-swiped him with it, dragged him twenty yards by the neck to a Land Rover, hurled the gun into the back, then slapped Plasti-Cuffs on the would-be gunman before you could blink.

It was a superb example of the brilliant work the British Army does, and that corporal was an unsung hero who certainly averted a complete catastrophe on the streets of Basra. We saw the same sort of raw courage and complete discipline in Basra in September 2005 when a Warrior armored personnel carrier was set alight during the rescue of two SAS men from the grips of the so-called police. Our troops stand their ground and do not overreact. As far as I'm concerned, the British Army is rock-solid.

My crew was busy filming, but I noticed that we were being surrounded by the mob, so I said to the correspondent, "I think we should go; we're getting isolated here. Have you got enough?"

He looked around, chatted to the cameraman, and said, "Yeah, we've got enough."

That's the way it usually went: a balance between their safety and their need to get great footage. I was the safety valve and it was always my job to draw their attention to the security implications of any situation they were in. I wasn't making judgments about what I would do if I were on my own and responsible for only my own skin. I had to think of the group and make sure they all survived.

As we were driving back to the hotel, a great bang on the roof, like thunder, heralded a stoning. Soon an erratic thumping and clattering filled the cab of the vehicle as we were rained on with rocks and bottles. On the road ahead of us, a UN 4 x 4 was being systematically smashed to pieces. We were lucky to get out of it and navigate a new route to the hotel without my having to fire a shot. Then the streets fell quiet as the thermometer rose to a point where rioting became a physical impossibility.

We were staying in the Hotel Mirbad in town. It's a family-owned business and all the boss is interested in is offering a safe haven to travelers, whoever they are, in exchange for their money. He had a simple view of the insurgency: He just thought it was bad for business. And he was always ready with a very robust response to any incursion into the peace and prosperity of his hotel compound.

It stayed quiet and the crew went to their rooms and got their heads down for an afternoon nap, but I just couldn't sleep. I may have been on the lash for a couple of months, but my instincts hadn't been completely shot away by booze and fatigue. I just knew something was going to happen.

Now, I can usually sleep through gun battles when the shit's going down a couple of streets away, but then when the position I'm in starts to become threatened, I'm up and standing, as though my brain is sounding its own bugle call. That night, however, even though it was really quiet, I lay awake on my bed, restless. I got up, thinking I'd just have a little look around.

Five minutes later, I was on the roof of the hotel, looking around the usual scrap heap of air-conditioning units and ducts. On the far side of the roof, there was movement. I froze for a moment; then I saw him. It was Bill, an old mate from the regiment, a real top-slice operator with a proven record, and he was doing exactly the same thing as I was.

I'd thought his call-sign group—there were four of them—was out on the ground with another media crew, but Bill had come back a day early for some admin reason or other. I knew Bill well and I'd worked with him in Northern Ireland and a couple of other strange places, as well.

"You get a bad feeling, too?" I asked.

"Yeah, John, I did."

"It's too quiet, isn't it?"

"Yes, mate, it's too fucking quiet out there by half."

"Have you found anything?"

"Yeah, I have. Take a look over here. There's a fire escape bridge between this place and the hotel next door. It's about ten-foot long, made of steel."

"Nice one. If they come at our place, I can get my people out across it," I said.

"There are a couple of call-sign groups with clients in there. They might want to come the other way if their place is hit," said Bill.

"Let's take a stroll across and find 'em."

There were two big gunned-up teams in the other hotel, with a couple of ex-Blades and a load of ex-Paras, and we quickly found them. A ten-minute chat had the deal worked out. We'd butt out to their position if anything hit the Mirbad, and vice versa. Bill and I were happy. We'd have eight seasoned ex-army lads and two bang-on Blades in our gang if the night erupted.

I got back in time for the routine six o'clock RV with the crew in the editing room, when they'd usually have a debrief on the day's work, discuss plans for the next day, and take on any orders from London. Then, quite often, the cameraman would go onto the roof and take some sunset footage looking out over the city. I'd be asked for any contributions before the meeting broke up.

"John?" Everyone looked across at me as the producer asked for my call on the day.

"Okay. It's like this. I don't want to worry any of you, but it's too quiet and it's been too quiet since this afternoon. It's time to talk about our escape route if the hotel is attacked. I've had a recce and talked to some security call-sign groups who are staying here and at the hotel directly behind this building.

"If anything or anyone hostile comes through the front gate of the hotel, do not go to the vehicles. I want you to go upstairs to the roof and I'll be with you. That guy Bill who's been around will be with us. Is that clear? Get onto the hotel roof, keep your heads down, and wait for instructions."

They all nodded. They'd had lots of briefings—and every briefing is serious in a place like Iraq—but I knew I'd conveyed my sense that something nasty was imminent.

We went down to the dining room for our evening meal, but we hadn't even finished the soup before it started. I'm serious. I jumped up and turned the corner into the hotel lobby, and there was an armed mob pouring through the gates. There was an old guy who seemed to be a permanent fixture as gatekeeper. Anytime you went through the gates, he seemed to be there. But he'd moved, and I watched him scuttle across the courtyard to the building as fast as he could. Not just any night watchman, this fellow; he was swinging his AK behind him every ten steps to fire a burst at the angry gunmen pouring into the courtyard.

Then all hell broke loose as waiters abandoned the half-full soup dishes and AKs appeared in their hands like rabbits conjured out of magicians' hats; then they began laying down fire on the gate-crashers.

At first, a lot of the incoming was pistol fire and the UN cars in the courtyard were riddled with small holes in seconds. Metal shutters appeared from nowhere and were placed over the front windows under fire. Can you believe men risking their lives to protect a fucking window?

Cooks and bottle washers in their whites charged out of the kitchen. Ladles and whisks had been abandoned for AKs, but wicked kitchen knives were held in reserve in the bands of their aprons. They deployed at various key points and started banging out an unvaried menu of lead. I know that top chefs call their cooking team the "kitchen brigade," but Gordon Ramsay has never had one like that lot. And they were all harder nuts than Gordon, too.

Our cameraman was gagging to get to work. "I've got to get some shots of this, John."

"Where's your gear?"

"In the room."

"Oh for fuck sake, get it on the way to the roof."

I had the crew waiting at the restaurant door. To the right were the lobby and the firing line. Left was the stairs. Rounds were tearing into the facade of the building and the odd one or two were whining into reception like lead wasps that were trying to register.

I was just waiting for the kitchen brigade to begin laying down enough fire on the perimeter wall to suppress the incoming rounds.

I judged it was time. "Okay, let's go! Up the fucking stairs! Sharpish! Don't stop till you see the stars."

I hustled the crew along and the cameraman diverted to grab his gear before joining us on the roof. The air up there was like warm milk and thick with cordite. Bill, who had no one to look after, was already there, of course, laid up behind a parapet in the far corner, picking his targets as he used his AK to effect. He grinned at me as if it were a big game, then turned back to his work. I wished I could do the same, but I had a crew to nanny.

A couple of waiters who were still wearing their aprons were alongside Bill, firing wildly down at the walls and corners below that hid the unwanted guests.

"We'll try for some shots now, John," said the correspondent.

"It's not safe. Just keep your fucking heads down!"

"It won't take a minute."

I looked at him, then looked at the cameraman. They wanted their shots. "For fuck sake! All right. Keep low."

I guided him away from Bill and the two waiters, who would be attracting return fire, and got him about twenty feet away, behind the hotel sign, which was about three feet higher than the parapet around the rooftop. I managed to steer him into a position where he could just get his camera over the parapet and get his shots. Looking down at the dark, unlit streets around the hotel, I could see shadows flitting from cover to cover like huge low-flying bats, flashes of gunfire giving their positions away. I could see that Bill's pinpoint aim was making it very dangerous for them. I noticed someone being dragged away wounded, and experience told me that the attackers were losing the initiative and being forced back from the hotel perimeter.

I never saw the footage the cameraman took, so I don't know how it looked, although I imagine a load of flashes, bangs, and cracks would be pretty crap. Hell, what do I know? When he'd finished, I steered him back to the others, then pushed them to the far side of the roof, away from the cutting edge where Bill and the waiters were at work.

"Just keep your heads down. Don't be heroes." I didn't want them catching ricochets and I reckoned they'd be unlikely to be hit by any incoming where they were positioned as long as they kept their heads down.

One of the waiters was a big burly bastard with a mustache. He looked like quite a hard case, a chubby Saddam type with a hard eye, and he was well into it. I could see he had a blood lust up. His face was glowing and his eyes, lit up now and then by gun flashes, were wild and excited. He was firing away quite happily when suddenly he had a stoppage in his rifle. You should have seen him. He went into a complete fit. He bashed the AK on the floor, whacked it here and there, desperately trying to get it to fire again. Then the furious waiter moved away from the edge, sat on his arse on the flat roof, and took it out on his weapon even more, cursing as he flailed it around.

Bill looked at me and I could see he was laughing like a drain at the absurdity of it all. He told me later that he thought it was hilarious that the waiter couldn't serve up a dish of hard metal jackets.

"Go on, Johnny, give the fucker a hand," he shouted across to me.

"All right, all right." I ran low and fast across the roof to the waiter and took the gun from him before he crippled it. I unloaded all the rounds, then looked in the breech and saw he had a hard extraction. The casing of a cartridge had split inside the mechanism and wouldn't eject, blocking the works completely. The thing was filthy, and I remember hoping that he kept the cutlery cleaner than his gun.

Rounds thumped into the masonry just above my head as I leaned back on the parapet, got my foot on the cocking handle, and jumped on it hard. The split case tinkled like a bell as it fell out onto the floor. The waiter reached for his gun, but I pushed his hand away and sprinted across to the air-conditioning unit, which had one of those old-fashioned oil cans with a long spout sitting on top of it. I grabbed the can and poured oil into the workings of the AK, then ran low back across the roof to hand it to the waiter.

He was beaming with delight to have his weapon, unseized and serviced mid-battle, and he was soon back at it with gusto, firing like fuck into the darkness.

Our producer had called the QRF, the quick-reaction force, at the start of the shoot-out, but they didn't arrive until forty minutes later, when they did a drive past and reported there was nothing to be seen. That's because it was all over and the gunmen had melted back into the night.

And that was the first and last time I've acted as gun bearer for a waiter during a battle on a hotel roof.

8. Convoy!

WHAT'S GOING ON IN RECEPTION, JOHN?"

"No idea. I'll have a look."

I was in the bar of the Baghdad Sheraton and the usual drone from the huddles of media types, businessmen, and hard-nosed security guys had been drowned by bedlam in the lobby. As I turned the corner from the bar into reception, I was confronted by a jabbering, animated party of forty or so Japanese people of all ages and sizes. Chubby little women mingled with inscrutable teenagers, all kitted out in designer gear. It took me a second to work it out. Unbelievably, they were tourists, and for a moment I could have fooled myself that I was in the entrance hall to the British Museum. Something was wrong, though. For one thing, there wasn't a single still or video camera in sight; for another, they were all milling excitedly around a pile of labeled suitcases and luggage being brought in by the porters and the baggage looked as though it had been ripped open and tipped out.

Two well-dressed but disheveled-looking young European men

who'd been with the Japanese party broke away from the chattering group and headed for the bar, obviously in search of a cold
beer. They seemed dismayed and looked anxiously around in
search of a drink. That's because the word *bar* was a bit of a liberal
description for the room. There was no bar and you couldn't buy
a drink; instead, you got your drink from two or three booze vendors who'd set up stall at the hotel entrance and did a roaring
trade. When you'd bought your booze, maybe a bottle of whiskey
or a six-pack of beer, you just went into this big room full of tables
and chairs, where there was a running buffet laid out on trestles at
the far end. It was the same buffet every night, so you'd have your
meal, then settle down for a drink.

I collared them. "Fancy a drink, you two?" I asked.

When they had their beers, we made our introductions. They
turned out to be two Danish archaeology students from a town
somewhere near Copenhagen and they were tourists, too. They'd
been traveling around the ancient sites of Babylon in a car they'd
hired in Jordan and they'd met up with the Japanese contingent at
the Hanging Gardens of Babylon. Hard to believe, isn't it?
Sightseeing in the middle of an insurgency.

They'd decided it would be a good idea to tag on behind the
Japanese's convoy of 4 x 4's, figuring that they'd be less likely to get
lost following someone who knew the bus routes. At one stage,
they'd lagged behind a bit, and when they caught up again, the
convoy had pulled over and the Japanese were all being held at
gunpoint on the roadside by a group of what I describe as ban-
dits/insurgents.

These men were relieving the tourists of enough camera gear
and top-of-the-line cell phones to open a T-Mobile branch in
Baghdad. The Danes wisely kept on driving. That was a good call,
because it turned out the Japanese had made such a racket that
the insurgents, struggling badly with the language barrier, had
just loaded them all back on the bus and sent them on their way.

They were so desperate to get rid of the babbling tourists, they even spared their driver to make sure the group would be driven away in double-quick time. Normally, they would have slotted him and dumped him in a ditch. On the other hand, two English-speaking Danes would have been a much better proposition as hostages, so it was just as well they hadn't stopped and that eventually they'd all gotten back to the hotel.

The Danes, whose names now escape me, joined me and a man named Tony for a couple of drinks and we got chatting. When they learned what I did for a living and the fact that I was taking a cameraman and a sound technician back to Amman in the morning for a crew change, they pleaded to be allowed to join us. They were nice young blokes and obviously scared shitless. It had dawned on them that coming to Iraq had been a big mistake. Why not take them, I thought.

"Okay, we leave at six on the dot. If you stop for any reason, you're on your own. I don't run a breakdown service."

"No, no. We won't be stopping for anything."

I believed them. They looked like they wanted to hang out with us and get really pissed, but they went to bed early. I don't think they wanted to miss the convoy.

Tony was a utilities engineer. He was involved with water or electricity—I'm not sure which—and he'd been around for a while and knew the correspondent I was working for, but I'd only met him that night. Tony was a really nice bloke. Quiet and self-assured, he obviously had some mettle, because not everyone has the balls to do business in Iraq. He'd completed his job—some sort of assessment for a tender—and was relieved to be going home in the morning, when he'd be picked up by a security team that his company had hired. There was nothing else to do but drink and enjoy each other's company in the more or less relaxing surroundings of the Sheraton.

The Baghdad Sheraton was expensive but grubby. Not surprising really, considering the hotel's situation. And to be fair, the staff tried hard and were always charming. The carpets were shabby, the furniture worn and threadbare, and the whole place needed a lick of paint, but I could live with all of that. It was the chained and padlocked emergency exits that worried me. I suppose the management thought they'd lock out any insurgents, but common sense should have told them terrorists would bomb the place rather than try to storm it. That's just what happened in October 2005, when a huge bomb was detonated nearby, killing several Iraqis.

Anyway, the chained doors gave me a bit of a headache because I had a TV crew to look after. The solution was a big pair of bolt cutters placed close to the door of the room we used as an office and editing suite. You see, we practiced escape drills in case of attack and I insisted we practice them often, so when the signal was given, we'd all head for the designated emergency exit, with me in the lead.

Normally, I'd have had my Kalashnikov stuck in front of me, but during the drills I had to sling it over my shoulder and make for the exit with my big "bugger off" bolt cutters as an alternative AK-47. We'd all run down the stairs, I'd simulate a bit of chain destruction, and then I'd unsling my AK to demonstrate I'd be ready for action if the time ever came when we might need to burst through the emergency exit into the open.

We never did do any bursting through the doors, which was a real pain in the arse, because I had to check the alleyway outside every day to make sure we'd have a clear run in case of a real emergency. It was just another madness in the catalog of insanity that I had to deal with.

Still, the Sheraton had been home on and off for months and it was better than kipping in a pioneer camp. That night in October 2003, we'd done a day's filming around Baghdad and the crew had finished their feed. That doesn't mean they'd had their supper; it's TV jargon for sending an edited piece back to the studio.

I'd developed my own routine for when the day's work had ended and I usually took a shower and got into the bar by six o'clock, ate, then went on the lash with the crew. I'd start on gin and tonics and move to Jack Daniel's by about eleven and I'd keep drinking as long as there was someone to drink with. I'd been on the piss like that for about seven or eight weeks. But every morning, I'd be up again and back on the road, bleary but unbowed.

Tony poured me another whiskey and we settled in for a long night. Then around midnight, two blokes arrived in the bar, obviously looking for someone. It turned out to be me. They had a quick word with a hotel employee, who nodded in my direction, and then they came up and introduced themselves. Even I was surprised at their identities.

The tourists in Iraq were mad enough, but these two were right out on the far edge of sanity. They were Israeli Jews who'd been wheeling and dealing in Iraq, trying to pin down some oil contracts. Fucking hell, being a Jew was dodgy enough in Al Qaeda's Iraq, but they were carrying their Israeli passports, as well. They might as well have brought their own set of orange boiler suits with them. And they looked Jewish, too. I'm not racist and I don't mean to be offensive, but that's the way it was: They just looked Jewish.

"Nice to meet you guys," I said, trying to avoid giving them a "dead men walking" look.

"You, too," said the bigger of the two with a friendly beam. "We've been told you're a bodyguard. They say you're the best."

"That's absolutely right," I said. "How can I help you?" No time for false modesty, and there's nothing like a compliment when you're half drunk, but I can see now that he was playing me with a line straight from a cowboy movie.

"Well, we've been here for two weeks and we've done about all we can businesswise, so we've decided to leave in the morning. The security situation is getting worse."

"Great, good luck with the journey."

"Yeah, thanks, but we think we should get some security for the trip out."

"You mean you've been driving around for two weeks without any?"

"Sure, protection is very expensive. We thought we'd be fine if we just kept a low profile."

"Well, you've been lucky. It seems to have worked for you. So far."

"So far, yes, but we thought we should get some protection for the journey out. They say the road's very dangerous."

I nodded agreement. He asked, "How much will it cost to hire you for the day?"

"Well, how's six hundred pounds a day sound to you?"

"Six hundred pounds you say, not dollars? It's too much."

"Really. So tell me, friend, how much is your insurance policy worth?"

"What do you mean? You're joking." He smiled.

"No joke. I'm deadly serious. I bet your wife will collect a packet if you're killed out here."

"Maybe she will."

"So maybe it's worth paying six hundred pounds to make sure some other bloke doesn't share it with her."

He wasn't smiling now and I was already regretting my words. There'd been no need for that. Oh fuck it! I thought. I relented, ashamed by my dig at his marriage.

"Listen, guys, I'm leaving at six in the morning. Be there on the dot and you can follow us. If you stop on the way, tough. We don't stop until we get to the border."

"We don't have to pay?"

"No, you don't have to fucking pay, but remember, if you stop, you're on your own."

"We won't stop."

I believed him. They drank some of my whiskey; then they headed for bed.

That left me, Tony, and a few other diehards there drinking, including my boss—the correspondent—and the two crew who were shipping out with me in the morning.

The lights dimmed—not for the cabaret, but because the power had failed again. We could hear the drone of the generator as it kicked in somewhere down in the basement. Pissed, we watched a couple of nocturnal flies as they wove in and out of the blades of a fan that barely turned for lack of power.

Tony broke the silence. "John, what's the chance of me going back to Amman with you guys in the morning?"

"Why'd you want to do that, mate? You've got a complete team to nurse you back down the Highway."

"I know, I know, but I don't really get on with those guys. I suppose they know what they're doing, but I just haven't gelled with them over the past three weeks."

"I know them. They're a good team, mate, believe me."

"I'm sure you're right, but I'd just feel happier with you. I just have more confidence in your ability."

I knew he wasn't feeding me a line like the Israeli guy and I appreciated what he'd said, because basically he was willing to trust his life in my hands, but I tried to put him off.

"Remember what I said to that Israeli guy?"

"About what?"

"About the insurance."

He raised an eyebrow and I quickly explained. "Nothing to do with your wife, old son. No, what I mean is, if you travel with me and it all goes pear-shaped, you probably won't have any insurance at all, because you should be with the team assigned to you."

"Fuck it. I don't care. Will you take me? I'll pay you, of course."

"Ask the boss over there. If he okays it, I'll be fine with it. Forget the money."

A couple of minutes later, the correspondent gave me the thumbs-up across the room and Tony rejoined me. We had another drink.

So there I was. Big-time hero. Everybody's safety net. I was drunk, and in about four hours' time I was intending to ride the most dangerous road in the world. Like some wagon-train master, I was taking the fate of a completely random group of people into my hands.

I'd been getting more and more stressed as months riding as lone shotgun on scores of protection runs took their toll. I was making huge amounts of money flying solo because there were no company middlemen taking their cut. I was getting the premium rate and it was virtually all profit. But that profit came at a price, and I was paying it in stress and I was paying in spades.

Eventually, I'd started drinking with the media crews. I suppose I was trying to bury the stress. The drinking had gotten completely out of hand, until I found myself in a cycle of fatigue and stress, followed by late-night drinking, which compounded the fatigue, and that, in turn, increased the stress.

There'd been some close shaves since I'd returned to Iraq after that first six weeks with Bungo immediately after the Gulf War ended. But it had gotten to the point where I had become the most dangerous man to be with on the most dangerous road in the world, because I should have been sober and pulled together. I should have been doing the job SAS-style, not media-style, and I knew in my bones that it had to stop before it all went terribly wrong.

Sure, it was during this period that I'd sorted out the guys in the black BMW, and I knew I hadn't lost my skills, but I also knew that I was blurring my hard edge with the life that I was living. The drinking was just part of it; it was also the stress of riding shotgun alone with the media crews and the responsibility of keeping them alive that was wearing me down.

The worst thing was that I was beginning to dwell on the past. I was thinking a lot about the mates I'd lost in battle.

And yet there I was in the bar of the Sheraton, drunk, and agreeing to take people on the terrifying roller coaster back to Jordan. I was like some John Wayne figure walking tall, straight to the saloon. Perhaps I was fooling myself that I really was the Duke. I was certainly acting like a cowboy.

In the morning, it would be wagons roll, but I'd be lucky if heads didn't roll. I was going to be taking the wackiest convoy you could dream of down the road past Fallujah and Ramadi. A two-man camera crew, a brace of Danish archaeology students, a couple of Israeli wheeler-dealers, and a British engineer who, on the strength of a night on the booze, preferred to be with an ex-SAS man rather than with four perfectly capable ex-soldiers.

Not only that. Five of them weren't paying me a bean, and here I was, deluding myself into thinking they were the ones who were mad. I knew it had to stop, but I was drunk and I thought, Fuck it, one last time, and let's hope it isn't the last time.

How the hell had I managed to end up in a state like that?

I SUPPOSE I COULD TURN to the old cliché and say I blame the press. After all, it was the media I had been working with and it was the media's big drinking habits that I'd fallen into step with. I mean, I always enjoyed a drink, but those people go for total immersion on a regular basis. Hand on heart, though, I honestly don't blame my dealings with the media for my fall off the more or less straight and narrow.

There are a couple of things I should get straight. First, my boozing all took place over a relatively short period of time, a three-month period at the most, out of the eighteen months that I worked in Iraq in total. Also, a lot of people would think that the amount I was drinking was nothing much compared to the quantities a really hard drinker will consume, and I never drank at all during the hours of daylight. Set against that, and what made it a potentially acute problem, was the fact that I was operating with a hangover nearly every day in the most lethal and hostile military environment on the planet. That was extremely foolhardy and dangerous. I'm not proud of it.

While all that was going on, I began to dwell on the past, particularly on the friends that I'd lost in combat operations. Steve Prior, a comrade who'd died bravely in the Battle of Goose Green, was on my mind and I kept hearing the words he spoke to a frightened eighteen-year-old paratrooper in his section as we sailed to the Falklands: "Don't worry, if it comes to it, I'll die so you can live." I remembered how Steve had indeed died saving life instead of taking it as time and time again he dragged wounded soldiers into cover. I replayed those moments at Goose Green over and over in my mind. There were friends who'd died in SAS operations, too, and they kept coming back to haunt me. They call it "survival guilt" and that's what it is. I felt as guilty as fuck.

There was another fallen comrade whose face kept coming to mind in those days and he was one of the most ballsy guys I've ever known, an old SAS mate, Nish Bruce. He was a crazy fuck and one of the finest and most courageous free-fall parachutists in the world. Nish was pivotal in the development of the high-altitude, low-opening tactic, known as HALO, used by Special Forces to insert troops in secrecy.

Nish had parachuted into the South Atlantic with an SAS patrol and swam ashore to be one of the first British troops on the Falkland Islands a couple of weeks ahead of the fleet carrying the main task force to retake the islands. He was tall and hawkish-looking, with a vicious sense of humor. He was very popular and I'm proud to say that we were best mates.

But years of stress had left him flawed by depression. Nish himself believed his psychological problems stemmed from the effects of the decompression-chamber training he did for his planned attempt on the world's highest free-fall jump in 1993. I'm not sure, but I know that, like many other regiment guys, he was stretched to the limits by nonstop operational cycles, which ultimately take their toll.

I visited Nish many times when he was a patient at a psychiatric unit. I'd sit for hours with him, just talking shit; then I'd return the next day and talk the same shit again, because the lithium drugs gave him a memory like a goldfish.

In 1998, Nish wrote a painfully honest book about his military career and his descent into depression and, with no little irony, he called it *Freefall.* Then in January 2002, while flying over Oxford, England, with his girlfriend, Gail, his mental problems got the better of Nish. He simply opened the door of the light aircraft he was in and made his last free fall, this time without a parachute. True to Nish's huge personality, he'd even ensured that his death would be as spectacular as it would be tragic and so, in turn, it inevitably attracted a spectacular amount of publicity.

The warmth of his friendship stays with me to this day, but then, in what were relatively tough days for me in Iraq, it was his illness that I found I focused on. I began to wonder if I was beginning to experience the same demons that had tormented Nish. They were not comfortable thoughts.

Strangely, though, it's while I've been writing this book that I've thought most deeply about those events and what propelled me on a dark carousel of Jack Daniel's and stress, and now I've come to realize when it began and what triggered my months of recklessness. It was the events at a dust-choked hole called Al Majar al-Kabir.

I T WAS THERE in Al Majar al-Kabir, a place of treachery and execution, that six lightly armed British military policemen were summarily butchered by a mob after the Iraqi police officers they were supposed to be working with abandoned them to their fate.

God knows how terrifying the last minutes were for those men. My heart truly goes out to their families. You see, for three days I thought my son, Kurt, had died in that shithole community thirty kilometers south of Al Amarah.

At the time, I was just getting started as a freelance operator in Iraq, but I was still hanging out with Bungo. Kurt was serving in the Parachute Regiment. The Paras had been assigned to the Al Amarah area, about 130 kilometers south of Baghdad. It's a strategic place, quite close to the Iranian border and on the highest navigable reach of the Tigris River for small commercial boats. The area is on the northern edge of the Shia area, but it's just close enough to Baghdad to have had a large Ba'ath party spy network. It was also the place where Ali Hassan al-Majid, the infamous henchman of Saddam, known as "Chemical Ali," was raised. He was the man who gassed the Kurds. Since the area is also close to the border with Iran, it was alive with Iranian agents. In other words, the whole region was full of stroppy insurgents who hated everything and everyone, including their own shadows. Nice place.

I should tell you a bit about Kurt. He's a cheeky, hard bastard who was born with Army stamped on his forehead. From his earliest days, he was a tearaway. I can tell you I was really proud when he joined the Parachute Regiment after passing the tough P Company selection process for the Airborne. When I saw him wearing his red beret, I had a touch of moisture in my eyes, but of course with the rivalry of an old stag, I told him it was harder in my day.

When he got to Iraq, Kurt and his unit were not "crows." Far from it. They were the heroes of an entire country, and I'm not talking about the UK, where these days far too many people don't realize just how much they owe our armed forces. No, they were and are the true heroes of the people of Sierra Leone, whom they rescued from a horrifying civil war and years of rampant hand-chopping anarchy at the whim of gangs like the infamous West Side Boys.

Things came to a head when the West Side gang seized eleven British soldiers from the Royal Irish Regiment and held them hostage with some locals in the hamlet of Magbeni against demands for guns, ammo, and drugs and the release of their leader, a psycho called General Papa, from jail.

A negotiator did a bit of seriously dangerous coming and going into their camp and came out with accounts of cannibalism and serious communal instability brought about by fierce drug taking and drinking.

Five of the hostages were released, but the man doing the talking, a sadistic clown who went under the nom de guerre of Colonel Cambodia, was getting more and more crazy, and it was decided to go in and get the remaining hostages out.

SAS guys had been moving around the swamps of the Rokel creek, where the hamlet was located, and they'd been observing the goings-on in the village and seen mock executions of the Irish lads. Nothing for it but to go in, as it looked like the Irish were going to get bits chopped off them. So at first light on September

10, 2000, a hundred or so guys from 1 Para went in hard under the cover of Chinook helicopters, deliberately using the downdraft from their rotors to knock the flimsy roofs off the huts and cause maximum confusion among the hostage takers.

The SAS were there, too, of course, and the only casualty on our side in Operation Barras, as it was called, was a tremendous character from the regiment, Brad Tinnion, who tragically failed to "beat the clock." He died from gunshot wounds after showing incredible courage during the difficult operation of loading the hostages onto a helicopter to get them out.

About fifty or so West Side Boys were wasted, including Colonel Cambodia, their chief negotiator. The rest were taken prisoner, including their leader, Foday Kallay, as the whole of the country first breathed a sigh of relief, then burst into spontaneous celebration at their final release from the daily and indiscriminate terror that had stalked the land. As I said, the Paras still carry the status of demigods among the people of Sierra Leone.

I heard that Kurt had acquitted himself well in that textbook Special Forces attack and it goes without saying, then, that Kurt could already handle himself when he arrived in Al Amarah, the armpit of Iraq.

Anyway, it was Sunday evening about 9:00 P.M. when I heard that six Paras had been killed in an attack near the city and that several others had been wounded. I can't clearly remember how I heard, but I think it was a phone call from another PMC. I don't think I've ever experienced the feelings I had over those next two or three days as a mixture of anxiety and anger consumed me. I started making frantic calls to anyone I thought could shed more light on the situation, but it was no good. There was a news black-out.

Twenty-four hours dragged by and still I had no news about Kurt and I was worried sick. It was only then that I began to real-ize how my family and loved ones must have been feeling over the years I'd been going to trouble spots when serving with the regiment and again since my SAS days while wandering all over the globe doing PMC work. I'd just cheerfully said my good-byes and not once really and truly considered the worry and anguish they would be going through. Never once had I really considered what it's like to sit at home fretting about the safety of a loved one and being totally unable to communicate with that person or even get a briefing on where and how he is from his superiors.

So it came back to me in spades as I was unable to find out whether my boy was hurt or not. Now I was the one who was fretting and feeling impotent over the fate of my son; I was the one who was incommunicado and I was the one who was left behind to worry. I learned then that the phrase "No man is an island" is among the truest ever written. No Special Forces soldier is an island, either. I knew something else, too. I knew that those first figures of dead and injured Paras that we'd heard meant that there was a high probability that Kurt was a casualty. I had to find out.

We were in Baghdad and Bungo suggested that we should wing over to the British embassy compound within the Green Zone. He'd remembered that he had a mate there, an officer who'd done some time in Northern Ireland with a surveillance unit. He was now in command of the Para detachment guarding the embassy and there was a chance he'd know something.

We slipped into his command hootch and Bungo made the introductions. "John's got a bit of a problem. His lad's down the road in Al Amarah with 1 Para and John's obviously worried about him since the shit hit the fan. He's called Kurt Geddes."

The officer was sympathetic and said, "I honestly don't know any names, but I can tell you that there are no dead Paras. The six dead soldiers are all MPs. They were bottled up in the local police station and killed.

"The Paras were in a firefight about the same time, maybe a couple of hours later, with insurgents about five klicks away and they had seven wounded, but they slotted about eighty of the other side. That's why there's been some confusion about just who got whacked, because the MPs were being done over at around the same time. None of that came from me."

An almost overwhelming sense of relief overtook me as I learned from this conversation that at least Kurt was alive (even if there was still a possibility that he'd been wounded in the firefight). I looked at the officer and thanked him with a couple of words that never could have conveyed just how grateful I was for his intelligence on the incident.

Bungo summed it up, the relief evident in his voice: "Thank fuck for that, John. Someone would have died tonight if that kid had been killed."

I just looked at him. Bungo was right. If Kurt had been killed, I would have tooled up and gone looking for serious trouble. I'd have gone to Al Amarah, but I wouldn't have gone in all guns blazing. I'd have slipped in there and used all my old skills to get revenge. It would have been tricky, but I'd have gotten some intelligence on known suspects in the area and then slid in and made myself an observation post from which to watch and wait for a few days. When I'd identified some of those low-life insurgents, I'd have moved in on them quietly and taken some of them out in the night. I'd have used my knife and I might even have taken their heads off to bring some terror down on them before slipping away again. In the end, there was no need to do it. My lad was alive and my rage had gone.

IT WAS ANOTHER TWO days before I learned that Kurt hadn't been wounded, either, and about a week later I saw him. He was in a canteen in Saddam's palace, where he and his mates were on guard duty at the embassy compound.

I saw him across the room as he was shoveling food into his ugly face and I just strode over and gave him a big hug in front of all his mates. If he was embarrassed at the demonstration of his father's relief in front of his mates, he didn't show it. None of them seemed to want to take advantage of the situation, which would have been the normal thing among Paras. Anyway, I didn't give a fuck. I was just pleased to see my lad in one piece.

Kurt didn't talk about the fighting and I didn't press him about it. I know how he felt; it wasn't the time to glory in combat. We just were both thankful he'd come out of the other end in one piece.

Later, through official sources, I was to find out about the Paras' action at Al Amarah on June 24, 2003. Two truckloads of 1 Para were ambushed by a strong contingent of insurgents and called in the QRF, which arrived in a Chinook, but just as they were putting down, the helo came under fire, too, and seven guys were wounded. Scimitar light tanks escorted a second QRF by road into the town and Kurt was in that detachment. They quickly deployed and dealt out a lot of death with their withering and accurate fire. I heard that once again Kurt had acquitted himself in the finest tradition of the Airborne, fighting an effective battle and slotting a few of the enemy.

Much later, he told me just one thing about that battle.

"It was the strangest thing, Dad," he said. "We were heavily engaged with the enemy, but all the dogs in the town were going mad. They were running around between us, snarling and snapping. We had to shoot them all."

It's only in hindsight that I've been able to reflect on what was truly going on in my mind at the time. Now I know that no man is an island, not even an SAS man. At the time, I was just buffeted by a series of disconnected and conflicting emotions that set me off along a strange personal highway. It was a morbid path, but when I was on it, I played the role of the tough, competent soldier to perfection, although it was only luck that I carried it through.

My son was alive, but that still left six military policemen dead, murdered by treachery in a scruffy room in a sunbaked, flat-roofed police barracks. They'd been there by appointment on a training mission and I firmly believe they were set up by insurgents in police uniforms.

Later, it was said the locals were furious about search missions involving their homes and the mob took the law into its own hands and killed the MPs in a spontaneous action not connected to the attack on the Paras. Crap. That was a carefully coordinated double whammy that had the stench of Iranian agents all over it. And it had given me a terrible jolt.

THE ROAD TO AMMAN stretched ahead as our wacky convoy left Baghdad and the rising sun behind us.

We watched the Japanese tourist group load up into a coach and leave with a military escort; then we spun along at a hurtling pace, and the two rental cars containing the Danes and the Israelis stayed so close to our tail that they looked as though they were attached to us by a tow bar.

The road is basically a motorway and for much of its length in the city it's higher than the housing that flanks it. As you leave Baghdad, the road arrows through an industrial area with many oil-processing and -cracking plants belching steam and smoke and the occasional flame where venting waste gases are burned off. It's a busy, bustling arterial route, one that all too often sees real arteries opened up.

I preferred to travel early because I figured that most of the insurgents would be tucked up in their bed pits or busy with their morning prayers and that by the time they'd gotten their shit together and decided to wander out onto the shooting gallery, I'd have left Fallujah and Ramadi well behind me.

Generally, traveling early worked, but when you'd been on the booze into the twilight hours, the strategy had some obvious disadvantages. For one thing your tongue felt like the bottom of Saddam's sandal and for another you had to perform monumental feats of concentration just to keep your eyes open.

Tony, the engineer, who was riding with us, was in the back, stuffed between the two crew members, and was first to speak after the tension of the Ramadi Ring Road bypass.

"John?" he asked quietly.

"Yeah."

"How the fuck do you do it?"

I paused, conscious of the burning fatigue behind my eyes, and said, "Don't know, mate. Suppose it must be practice."

"Anyway, thanks for the ride," he said as he closed his eyes and did what I was desperate to do: sleep.

There's a really dangerous choke point at Ramadi where a Yankee JDAM bomb hit an elevated section of the highway, so traffic had to come down off the fast dual carriageway and crawl around a dusty contraflow before being guided back onto the motorway. It was a favorite hangout of insurgent sharks, who used to bask there while they eyeballed the passing traffic, looking for likely targets to prey on. I always kept a sharp eye out for them, but that day it was fine and we were back on the fast road with no problem.

I wound my window down after Ramadi, adjusted my AK-47 on my lap, put my shades on, and let the warm desert air pour over my face as I scanned the road and my side-view mirror for unwanted interruptions.

It wasn't long before I noticed that the last car, the one with the

Israeli guys in it, had started lagging behind a bit. Their fucking problem, I thought. I'd warned them I wouldn't be stopping and that was that. Now and then, they'd put a spurt on and catch up, but they kept fading away. I tried not to take any notice. Their problem, their fucking problem, I kept telling myself.

We'd just passed one of the Iraqi versions of a motel and restaurant—I don't know what they call them—which are dotted along the length of the highway, when I saw them in my side-view mirror. There they were. More bandits/insurgents. They were driving a scruffy white BMW 7 Series, just pulling out of the dusty car park at the back of the café, throwing spurts of gravel into the air as they accelerated toward us.

Here we fucking go, I thought. I've read this script before.

I knew for sure that whoever was in that BMW was up to no good. The way they'd rushed out onto the road and that surging and intent way the car was being driven told me they were scumbags on a mission and I knew in my gut that they were out to hunt down the Israeli guys, who were well behind us now. Sure enough, they latched onto the two Israelis and pulled alongside them. A gun barrel poked out of the window of the Beemer and I watched as the Israeli guys pulled to the side of the road, the BMW close behind them.

No! No! No! I said to myself. I'm not getting involved. I told them, no pay, no play.

Fuck it, though. I knew in my heart that I couldn't leave it at that. I wouldn't leave it at that. They'd be headline news on CNN in the morning and it would be my fault. But then I told myself, No, if they get slotted, it will be their own fucking fault for being in Iraq in the first place.

The arguments for and against stopping, for and against breaking my own self-imposed rules tussled inside my head. Then, tails, they won.

"Oh fuck it!" I said out loud.

The driver had seen, too, and so had the rest of the traffic, but the herd didn't bat a collective eyelid as it kept moving along the highway. They were used to this sort of stuff, the people of Ramadi. Anyway, most of them were complicit in the terrorist activity because most of them approved of the actions of their young warriors.

The driver was looking at me questioningly and I nodded at him to pull off the road. The Danes, still attached to our Range Rover by the invisible tow bar, came straight off after us. I was going to break all my own SOPs and take back my own dire warning to the hangers-on who'd been following me. I unsealed the car and trotted back to the Danes.

"Out of the car and into the ditch," I ordered them. I didn't have to ask twice. They'd seen what was happening down the road and they were crapping themselves.

I could see the Israelis standing at the side of the road with three insurgents shaking them down, but the really rough stuff hadn't begun. I knew that would begin the moment the insurgents found their passports and saw they were residents of Tel Aviv. The two of them would be on the road to al-Zarqawi and it wouldn't be a pleasant ride. They'd be tortured every step of the way because of their religion and birthright.

This is no way to be fucking doing this, I thought as I clipped down the bipod on the front of my RPK, dropped to the ground, and took up a firing position by the rear wheel on the side next to the ditch. I glanced at the two Danes and saw they were cowering down, waiting for the worst to happen. I looked across the slight curve in the road at the unfolding drama down the road.

The only good thing was that we'd been just far enough ahead for the insurgents not to have noticed us, and they still hadn't pinged us, because we were a fair old way up the road. They were too intent on their prize to be looking about, and one of them was actually lifting his AK into the air and whooping in triumph.

They were about four hundred meters away, I reckoned, and

the heat caused the air to shimmer and swirl up from the road and reflect off the tarmac at the site of the ambush. I'm a trained sniper, but this wouldn't have been an easy shot even with optics and a sharp mind. I was going to do it with open sights and a hangover. Have a look at four hundred meters sometime. Pace it out in a park. It doesn't sound very far, but it is quite literally a long shot with a rifle. Especially with a hangover.

Oh well, fuck it. It's now or never, I told myself.

Crack!

Shit! I thought. I couldn't believe it. The shot was short and I managed to hit only the wanker doing the war cry in the ankle. He was wounded, though. At first, he hopped around, doing a strange dance that wouldn't have been out of place with the rifle waving and the ululating he was already doing. Then he fell to the ground, screaming.

One of his mates, who'd been searching the Israelis, spun around as he heard the crack and witnessed the thump, then started firing in all directions. He had no idea where the shot had come from. Good, that gave me time—a precious fraction of a second as I put fifty meters on my sight to lift the shot and gently squeezed the trigger.

Crack!

It whacked the gunman in the shoulder, maybe the chest. I couldn't be certain. He crumpled onto the ground like a sack of fertilizer, still pulling on the trigger. Rounds burst all over the place, kicking up around the two cars and narrowly missing the Jewish blokes. The third of the tough guys proved to be a real hero, as he jumped into the white Beemer and sped off, leaving one wounded comrade and one dying comrade on the side of the road like dogs that had been run over.

The two Israeli guys were also back in their car before you could blink and were screaming up the road toward us as we surged up the Highway without waiting to see what was left behind us. They didn't drop back again and were tailgating at 160 klicks all the way to the border.

I never learned why they'd dropped back in the first place. I reckon they just got complacent and had been chatting away like Israelis do. I don't particularly like Israelis. I know the score on the West Bank and I don't like seeing unarmed children shot in cold blood just because they've hurled a few rocks at the troops. I have mixed feelings about their policies and I think a lot of the trouble in the Middle East, including Iraq, can be laid at their doorstep. Why, I ask myself, does a nation born out of the ghettos of Europe then put the Palestinians in ghettos, too?

Nothing was said about the incident back on the road. I wasn't in the mood for chatting. When we got across the border and then into the suburbs of Amman, the two rental cars kept following. They tailed us all the way to the Sheraton Hotel and pulled up right behind us. I got out and walked back to talk to the four of them as they climbed out of their cars. The Israelis started pouring out effusive thanks, but I just put my hand up to stop them.

"Just shut it. I don't want to fucking know!"

I didn't, either, but I wondered why they were still with us, so I asked them, "Are you lot staying here?"

They looked nonplussed; then they sheepishly shook their heads. Of course they weren't. I realized straightaway what was going on. They were like little chicks following the mother hen and they'd been so terrified on the Highway that they were too frightened to let go. They hadn't realized yet that their dependency on me was over.

"Well, I suggest you get those fucking cars back to the rental offices before you scratch the paintwork," I said.

One of the Danes looked close to tears from the stress of the drive and I had no doubt he'd spent the entire journey wondering what would have happened if they'd had a flat tire. The Israeli guys were apparently going to head off to the border and see if they could wangle their way across the Allenby Bridge and back into Israel. Not recommended, but nothing much they'd done so far on this trip had been.

Me, I just wanted to have a coffee, take a shower, and get some sleep, but what I didn't know was that someone had spotted me through the big plate-glass window of the hotel.

A HUGE BROAD BACK confronted me as I walked up to the reception in the Sheraton. I'd have recognized that back anywhere and I moved up and put my arm around his waist.

"Johnny! How are you, boy? I saw you coming in earlier," a big Welsh voice boomed as Mike Curtis turned around to look at me.

Then as he saw me, his voice lowered a couple of decibels and he said, "Fuck me, you look rough, boy. What have you been doin' to yourself? You look as though you've seen a ghost."

I told him I'd nearly seen my own; then I sat down and related the whole story over a glass of mineral water and a jug of strong coffee. It took some telling, too, and he sat there, his eyes full of concern, occasionally laughing at the more ludicrous turns to my tale.

"So, Johnny," he said at last, "to sum up, you've been rocking up and down the Highway and around the arse end of Iraq minding media crews and you've been doing it all on your fucking own-some?"

I nodded. "Yup. That's about it."

It was his turn now and Mike waded into me and gave me one of the biggest bollockings I've ever had in my entire life.

"Who the fuck do you think you are, John? Zorro? No, that's not it, is it? You're the Scarlet fucking Pimpernel, aren't you? Come on, man, tell me. I'm fucking fascinated."

He squeezed his finger and thumb close together as he went on. "You're a living legend, mate, but you're that close to becoming a dead fucking laughingstock. It's got to fucking stop, John. This Lone Ranger act has got to fucking stop or you'll be dead within a month."

I was too knackered to argue. Anyway, I had no arguments to make. He was absolutely right and I knew it. But I needed someone like Mike to tell me. I needed a Blade who'd worked with me; I needed a man who'd fought side by side with me and had my absolute respect and loyalty. Only someone like Mike could read me my fortune and tell me exactly how it was. Anyone else who'd tried would have gotten a slap.

"When you going back in?" he asked.

"Tomorrow, six o'clock. It's a crew exchange."

"On your own?"

"Yeah."

"No, you're fucking not. You're going at eight o'clock because I've got five gunned-up wagons going then and you can join them. All right?"

"Great. I think I'll get my head down now."

"Good idea. And John . . ."

"What, Mike?"

"Remember, bread always lands on the buttered side."

"What the hell does that mean?"

"Fucked if I know, boy."

He roared with laughter and I knew that I was among friends again.

THE TRIP BACK into Iraq was a total relief. No hangover, sharp as a razor, and twelve mates to fight with if the shit hit the fan. I still had eyes in the back of my head; I was still keyed up and ready to rock. But what a difference a day makes, I thought as we bowled along the Fallujah bypass. I kept my eyes peeled for the spot where I'd shot up the two bandits/in-surgents, but there was no sign that anything at all had happened except for a dark brown patch of sun-dried blood on the side of the road. No white BMW in the parking lot at the greasy spoon café, though.

That twenty-four hours marked a sea change for me during my time in Iraq. From then on, I worked only in teams and never alone. I sometimes worked with Bungo, sometimes with Mike's guys, but never alone. I was still a gun for hire, but I wasn't for hire on solo jobs anymore.

I slotted back into a proper routine, as well. Instead of shower-ing and going on the lash with the clients, you'd find me running up flights of stairs in the Palestine or whichever hotel I happened to be staying in. If my memory's correct, there were eighteen flights of stairs in the Palestine and I'd grind up and down them with a pack on my back, passing other guys who were also in training. Any locals I happened to pass on the high-rise concrete treadmill looked at me as though I'd lost my marbles. What they didn't know is that I'd really just found them again.

I also had a long stint, lasting months, back in Basra. The city was relatively quiet again after the fuel riots and the Shia majority were content to police themselves and more or less lay off the British Army, which was on their patch. That was to change a year or so after I left, what with the Iranian agitation and a series of at-tacks on our lads, culminating in the taking of two SAS men by the local police in August 2005.

Basra was good for me because there was no drinking down there. The reason? Well, there'd been three or four attempts to set up liquor stalls in the town, but the ayatollahs had them dealt with summarily by whacking them with RPGs and the street vendors and their booze supply were obliterated. License refused! Happy fucking days.

So it was that I reestablished some of the old stabilizing routines into a life that, in any event, was, by its very nature, pretty abnormal. I had a couple of runs home, too, which were a real blessing, and the power of family is one thing I no longer took for granted.

But there was one more thing that needed to happen to restore my pride and self-esteem completely, and predictably it happened on the Highway. The Highway had become my own personal hell on earth in Iraq. I saw it as fate, the way that the Highway and my life as a mercenary had become intertwined. But first there was other business to take care of.

9. Baghdad Babes

A GROUP OF FOUR PEOPLE WERE ENJOYing a quick lunch in the bustling canteen of a coalition base north of Baghdad. Two of them were dressed quite formally in safari-style tropical kit they'd picked up in a smart New York department store especially for the trip. They were bankers in Iraq, on a mission to gauge investment needs and to audit the schemes that money had already been spent on. They were big cheeses in the business world and a precious cargo for the team guarding them. You never wanted to lose any of the customers, but especially not clients like these.

The other two at the table were dressed in the usual PMC garb—kit vest, body armor, cargo pants with pockets everywhere, and assault carbines, MP5s resting on the table, close at hand, even in this relatively safe haven. They were all picking away at their food. It was a hot day and even in the air-conditioned environment of the canteen, they had little appetite.

WHOOMPH!

Without warning, a mortar round exploded just outside the

canteen, cutting out the lights. Soldiers dived for cover under tables as two more mortar rounds thumped into the ground outside, the blast smashing crockery as the kitchen wallahs screamed with terror.

But the two bankers were already on the move as their close protection dragged them in the opposite direction of the incoming rounds and out through the flap of an exit on the other side of the big temporary building.

"In the car! Quickly!" one of them said.

The two bankers obeyed the voice immediately and without question, even though the PMC giving the orders was a tall, stunning blonde who looked like she could have been a fashion model in another life. And the other guard was a babe, too.

Within seconds, they'd ferried their VIP charges across the compound on a military airfield and out of the firing line. Cool as ice, tough as whipcord, and crack shots, the two of them were from the elite handful of close-protection women working on the Highway. They'd earned themselves the name "Baghdad Babes," and not needing to be politically correct because they were so unique, they'd taken no offense at the name and used the title with pride.

There are hundreds of women involved in security work in Iraq and many of them are British. A lot of them come back after a stint in the most frightening country in the world and boast of their working on the front line. They're right to be proud of the fact that they are working in Iraq at all, but 99.9 percent of them are not the real thing. Their jobs are mostly confined to bag searching inside Baghdad International Airport. Most of them fly into the BIA, stay in the on-site accommodation, with its bars, clubs, and cinema, do their shifts, then fly home again without ever driving through the gates. They stay on the entry level and never progress into the combat zone.

But a very few women are the real deal. There are six of them from Britain, and there are also a handful from Eastern Europe. I met one from Italy and one from France. I don't know of any from the United States, though. You could probably number such women on the fingers of three hands. In these days of feminism, women are claiming the right to equality in the armed forces, too, and this is all viewed as though it's some bold new departure in the history of warfare. But there's nothing new under the sun about women being involved in warfare; they have been at the sharp end of conflict for thousands of years.

In Britain, we have one of the great women of war in our history, the tempestuous Boudica, who came so close to kicking the Romans out of Britain. In fact, Celtic women traditionally fought alongside their menfolk.

In classical mythology, the Amazons were characterized as the thing men should fear most—women who could fight as well or even better than they could. There is some archaeological evidence to suggest that the legend of the Amazons may have come from the people of Georgia, on the Russian steppes, in ancient times. Many of the warrior graves there contain the skeletons of women and their weapons.

Our own Alfred the Great had a daughter who went by the wonderful Saxon moniker of Aethelflaed. When dad wasn't around, the flaxen-haired princess tied up her braids, unsheathed her sword, and led the Saxon shield wall against the Viking invaders. There was Joan of Arc, of course, who routed the English from Orléans and paid for the trouble she caused the British by being burned at the stake for wearing men's clothing and for witchcraft.

In World War I, the French had Moroccan women mercenaries fighting in the trenches, and in World War II some of the most skilled and feared snipers fighting in the rubble of Stalingrad and Leningrad were formidable females.

And in many of the African civil wars of the past thirty years or so, women have been partnered with the ever-present AK-47 to fight alongside men. In 2005, Liberian women were fighting as mercenaries in the Ivory Coast.

The countess of Pembroke; Dame Nicolaa de la Haye; "Black Agnes," the countess of Dunbar—all women warriors down through the ages.

But of all of these women, the one who really sets my imagination alight is another princess with a wonderful name. She's Sichelgaita, an eleventh-century princess of Lombardy, who married a Norman mercenary against her father's will, then joined the family business. Described as long-limbed, strong, and striking in looks, she fought alongside her husband, riding to battle with him and vowing to live or die as he did. She took no shit, this Sichelgaita, and personally executed deserters. Some woman!

I'm really dodging the issue a bit, because it's only fair that I give my personal view of women on the front line. Well, it is a difficult one, because all the women's rights in the world can't make them a match for men on the battlefield (with, of course, notable exceptions now and down through the ages).

Women will certainly never be able to perform to the standards required by the SAS, Delta Force, or other Special Forces units around the world. I'm not some unreconstructed male who's in the business of dissing women because of some chauvinistic attitudes. I'm just coldly and rationally looking at the military facts.

Of course, there is one leveling factor in modern warfare, and that is the development of modern weapons. A woman who can shoot straight with an AK or some of the lightweight composite plastic rifles on the market is on the face of it as good as a man.

One great example of sexual equality at the end of a barrel is the Danish woman soldier deployed as a gunner in a Leopard tank in the Balkans, who took out two Serbian Bofors guns that had been playing havoc in the Drina Valley. She was the best shot in her unit and she did it with just two rounds, one for each gun. Hats off to her. She did a fantastic job. But there's more to war than sitting a thousand meters away from your enemy and taking potshots at him.

Personally, I just take each person as he or she comes. Some women are brilliant in certain very dangerous roles and they have my absolute respect, but they've got to earn it, just as a bloke does. You meet men who look the part and talk the part, but I just run my gimlet eye over them and wait to see how they pan out. One thing's for sure: I don't rely on anyone, man or woman, until I've seen how that person performs.

But back to Iraq. One of the two women in the coalition canteen really stands out as a bit of a Sichelgaita figure. Tall, long-limbed, and striking in looks, Paula was the first female PMC in Iraq. She's the original Baghdad Babe and she's a woman I respect and admire in the male-dominated world of close-protection work.

Paula's been a mate for years and I used to do close-protection work with her when Mike Curtis and I were looking after certain Middle Eastern royal families in London. She'd had a fascinating and dangerous career in covert units of Scotland Yard in London and became a very good pistol shot. When she left the force, she went into security work, and then in 2003 she found herself in Iraq.

It was her first time in a war zone and, true to type, she performed brilliantly. I'll let her tell you the story of the Baghdad Babes in her own words. It's a fascinating insight into a very exclusive world.

I'll never forget the day I got a call from a guy from another company. I can't name the company for various reasons, but he was a bloke I'd worked for before. But I didn't expect the question he asked, I didn't expect it at all.

"Paula," he said, "I'd like you to go to Iraq and get involved in some close-protection work out there. We need a woman out there to get involved with client protection. What d'ya think? You up for it?"

"Let me think about it," I said, and I got off the phone feeling quite stunned at the request.

This would be my first foray into a war zone, so I spent the next couple of hours working out all the options in my mind—the options being the number of ways I could get killed—and as I worked them back from being blown to bits by a car bomber in Baghdad to getting run over by a cab outside Terminal 5 at Heathrow, I realized I was going to do it.

Anyway, ever since I was a little girl, I've had this funny idea fixed in my head that I was going to live until I was eighty-seven, so I just thought, Yeah, I'm not going to die for a long time yet, so I'll take the job.

I rang the guy back and said I'd do it, but I persuaded him to let another girl go with me. I'll call her June, and she was someone with a great deal of experience, too.

We flew out to Baghdad a couple of days later and you'd have paid for tickets to see the faces of the guys from the team waiting for us at the airport. The boss back in London had just put our initials on the manifest and hadn't told them we were women. We weren't just any women, either, because, without boasting, I can truthfully say June and I both turn heads. We're both real lookers.

The guys from the team stood there, mouths gaping, when we checked through passport control. One or two of them had real sneers on their faces and I could see they were thinking, Why have we been lumbered with these two silly tarts?

It didn't phase me or June; we're both used to being looked upon as silly tarts in a man's world. I've found though that the higher up the PMC food chain you go, the more tolerant and accepting the men are. The SAS guys are at the top of the chain and people like you and Mike Curtis and Bungo just watch and wait to make their judgment on an individual. You can't ask for more than that.

Anyway, we began with some range work with our new weapons. We were both familiar and competent with pistols, but we'd not fired rifles before, so we had a crash course with MP5s, and once again we attracted a lot of looks as we stood up and did our stuff. After that, we spent a lot of time on the ranges and a lot of time practicing escape driving routines, U-turns, J-turns, all that sort of stuff, on the big parade ground in front of Saddam's giant crossed swords of victory.

I can remember looking at the famous crossed swords and thinking, God, a couple of weeks ago I was playing Scrabble on a boat cruising down a river in Norfolk. What the hell am I doing here?

I used to get cheesed off with the driver training, because in the police you're always involved in chases on the streets, so you don't need to practice. The army guys are right, though. They just say practice keeps your blade sharp, and they're bang-on.

After the rifle training, we started work almost immediately. We'd be in a team of four and we'd work long hours on close protection of very high-level officials. You're guessing they were bankers and economists. You could be right, but I'm not going to comment.

Our chosen method of movement was low profile. We'd have good, fast vehicles, but they were soft-skinned and we'd bash the bodywork around a bit just so the car would blend with the Baghdad background.

As you can imagine, there aren't many six-foot-tall blond women in Baghdad, so I would often wear a burkah when I traveled and keep my face reasonably well covered, but not so much that I couldn't see what was going on.

I'd be sitting there in the car, a big blond bird, smothered in a burkah, with an MP5 across my lap. I suppose it was a hell of a strange sight, but it worked, because it gave the impression that this was a local group traveling through Baghdad.

First impressions are everything in Iraq. That instant impression that we were locals gave us the split second we needed while any potential enemy was doing a double take. By the time they'd decided we weren't all that we seemed at first glance, we'd have vanished.

It was a good scheme for operating and it largely kept us out of trouble. As I said, our clients were very important people and they really loved the female close-security operators. They weren't phased by us at all; in fact, they were impressed that we were in the country at all. And I can honestly say that to a man they behaved like perfect gentlemen. There was no bottom pinching or anything like that, but then, you might not want to chance groping a girl with an assault rifle in her hands.

June and I were so popular that in the end the company had six girls working rotations out in Iraq. Two were ex-police and four ex-army. All the girls were British, and I don't know of any female teams except ours. There were no American women, to my knowledge, and I know of only one Italian girl who worked out in Iraq as a full-blown personal bodyguard.

We were a small and elite number of women who put ourselves at risk, and the risks were considerable. I had no illusions about what would happen if we were taken by the insurgents. There's no doubt that we would have been subjected to gross physical and sexual torture if we'd been taken alive, and I would be lying if I didn't admit that this was one of the most terrifying thoughts on our minds.

We all knew what would happen, because two Scandinavian aide workers had been kidnapped and killed by the insurgents. The two women had had enough of Iraq and wanted to go home, so they went to a café around the corner from their base to get a cab to the airport. Well, you can imagine the rest. They'd been warned, but they'd gone ahead and done it.

The "cabbie" turned out to be an insurgent and they were driven off and horrifically tortured to death. I didn't want that to happen to me, so I knew that I would do anything rather than be captured.

But if I thought I was going to be taken alive, I vowed to keep one bullet in the magazine and use it on myself. I know that sounds melodramatic, but was it really so melodramatic to consider that sort of extreme case in modern Iraq? I don't think so.

We all talked about it and the other girls felt the same. I have doubts whether I would have done it in the end if I had been captured, because my survival instinct is so strong, but I wanted to feel that I had the option.

Eventually, we became known among the men as the Baghdad Babes—not to be confused with a porn movie called Babes of Baghdad, which, needless to say, wouldn't be our line of work. We didn't find the name offensive; in fact, the reverse is true. To be quite honest, none of us are feminists in that mouthing-off sense. We all felt quite confident enough in ourselves and what we could do not to have to shout it from the rooftops. So we took the name in the spirit it was meant, and now the name has become a badge of pride for those of us who were involved. We even posed for a Web site publicity picture, but our faces were never revealed.

Scary times? There were a lot of scary things happening in Iraq while I was out there. It was nothing to have bullets flying all around you and you honestly never knew whether some of them were meant for you or not.

I lived through a few mortar attacks and a couple of near misses from RPGs, but none of us ever had a contact in the sense of a full-on shoot-out. It was our job to avoid those situations, so I think from that point of view, our low-profile tactics and our burkahs worked.

One of the most sinister things that happened was on a bridge over the Tigris River. There was an armed group out on the street and one of them was taking photographs. He took a photograph of me through the car window and I really didn't like that. The thought that I was on some insurgent's file made me feel very uncomfortable. I felt almost violated, and I remember wanting to get out of the car and do something about it. We had a client with us, though, and he had to come first. That's the way it was.

We used to cause a real stir around the place with the locals and you could tell the sight of a blond-haired Western woman carrying a machine gun used to get the local Iraqi guys going. Knowing that, we used it to our advantage, because we knew for sure that some of the local police, militia, and private security guards were working as dickers—that's the jargon for a spy or spotter—for the insurgents.

Sometimes when it was needed, we'd just wander out to a checkpoint or a hotel entrance and chat up the guards until one of our call-sign group vehicles had whipped through the gates and gotten off on their way. That way, the dicker didn't have time to make his call to the bad guys and a chance for them to make a hit was lost.

Unashamed use of sexuality. Yeah, maybe, but women members of the Resistance would act out almost exactly the same role to distract Nazi guards in occupied France during World War II. If it works, it works.

Sometimes we'd go into the banking district in Baghdad with our clients. It was a strange area, busy but extremely tense, as of course it would be a great hit for the insurgents. It was surrounded with concrete barriers to keep the car bombs out and there was generally a high level of security. But just looking around made you aware that the place was heaving with insurgency dickers.

We'd go in low profile as usual and park in the basement garage of the building; then we'd head for the boardroom of a particular bank or institution, which was generally on the upper floors of high-rise buildings. It used to give me a really strange feeling to be so high up, and you'd feel really exposed and wonder how you were going to get your client out in case of a bomb.

Those visits were always a bit surreal, because from the moment I got through the door and whipped my burkah off, I'd be followed by a crowd of women, who were no less fascinated by the sight of a tall blond woman with a machine gun than the Iraqi menfolk were. They'd literally be pulling at your clothes and chattering around you, which made it difficult to keep an eye on the client.

Once, I took an American principal to the banking district. He was a really nice bloke, tall, distinguished-looking, iron gray hair, perfectly turned out, with a lean, fit-looking figure.

"I think it would be nice to take the stairs, don't you?" he said.

No, I bloody didn't, but he was the boss. He set off with a long stride, eating up the stairs two at a time, with me trotting after him. Unbelievable. It took me only a couple of minutes to work out there was no air-conditioning in the stairwell. I was wheezing as I tried to keep up with the sly old goat. I had all my kit and my weapon, and by the time we'd gotten to the twenty-seventh floor, I was dribbling and nearly fainting from the effort.

I quickly recovered and gave him a sick smile when he said, "That was invigorating, wasn't it?"

There was a lot of comradeship in Iraq and I found that most of the men were prepared to give you a chance. Of course, you got more than a fair share of the "little woman" stuff, but I really don't think it mattered. I'd been a female in a man's world for a long time and I'd learned to cope with the crap. I'd usually just ignore it, and, as I said earlier, the people who really counted didn't come at the situation in a negative way.

I think the worst individual was a South African guy, who I actually thought was a good bloke at first, but then he really had a go, saying a lot of shit stuff about shooting blacks in the townships and how women were shit and should stay in the kitchen. He went on and on, blah, blah, blah.

I know what it was all about. Some guys sort of put out to you and then when they realize that sex is not on the agenda and you're just there as a professional, they round on you and attack you for being unprofessional because, of all things, you're a woman.

I just told him, "Look, mate, you think you're tough, but when I was a nineteen-year-old, I was patrolling the streets of Brixton in London with a truncheon as my only weapon. You'd have been afraid to go out on those streets without your big gun, so don't give me any more crap."

I really should have done what I usually do and just let it roll over me, but I just got fed up with him. Some of those South Africans just make it their business to get on your wrong side. They're a really cussed lot.

There are definitely a lot more women involved in security work these days, but in Iraq they're mostly employed as searchers and airport processors. A lot of girls get into the business through martial-arts skills, which take them on to nightclub door work, that sort of thing. Then they want to get into the real world of close protection, which they fail to do, and they end up in the Baghdad airport searching bags.

Close protection, now that's another world, and the best people in that particular world come with an army or police background. You get women who've served with specialist British Army units like 14 Intelligence who are absolutely expert at surveillance work, and that goes for women with a background in specialist police work, too.

I came up through the Scotland Yard mill and I was on the streets when I was quite young. I saw all the worst riots in London when I was in my twenties. You learn certain things in those situations. It's that awareness of what's happening all around you. It's being one step ahead. Even if it's just the ability to read the signs that tell you there's a choke point in the traffic ahead and that you'd better take a turn and go a different way. It's the ability to look a man in the eye as you sit in your car and know with your every fiber that he's weighing up his chances of taking a shot through the car window, but your look tells him he'd better try on another day.

Like I said, none of the girls had a full-on shoot-out with insurgents, but some heroic stuff was done. There are things I simply can't talk about because they would give away operating procedures that are still being used to convey people in safety. But the girls did some heroic work and displayed courage on a daily basis. We thwarted suicide bombers and we kept our clients out of harm's way. And there was an X factor, too, because the clients really took confidence and courage from the fact that they had women minding them.

That day in the canteen, for instance. All hell broke loose and there was confusion and chaos all around us as the rounds kept coming. Later on, the clients told us that they'd really taken a huge boost from the fact that they were with two women who remained cool, calm, and collected through those terrifying few minutes. I think that was a great testament.

Was there any romance under the desert skies? People always ask. Afraid there wasn't for me. I'm single, but out of the thousands of alpha males on the loose in Iraq, I never saw one I fancied. It hardly seems fair, does it, but I was out there to do a job for good money. I wasn't looking for love. As for the other girls, well, none of them had a fling, at least not while I was there.

I think the serious thing is that there's this huge army of mercenaries in Iraq and among them are a handful of women who are prepared to match the men for courage and devotion to the job.

I'm proud of that and I hope with all my heart that in some small way I've helped the Iraqi people on their journey to reconstruction and shown two fingers to the insurgents, who'd like to take them back to the Bronze Age.

THERE YOU HAVE IT, the story in Paula's words. I'd really like to underscore one thing: The fact that the Baghdad Babes have not been involved in any firefights—or contacts, as we call them—really stands as a testimony to the skilled way they move around the warscape in Iraq without attracting attention to themselves. I hope that they never have to fire a shot in anger and that their low-profile, covert style of operating keeps them out of trouble for the duration.

I did hear a story that an East European woman was involved in a shoot-out northwest of Baghdad. Apparently, her vehicle was hit by an IED and she staggered away from the wreckage and fell to the ground a few yards farther on and kept screaming. But she'd only been pretending to be badly wounded, and when a couple of insurgents ran in to make the capture, she malletted them with her rifle.

That's the story, but I simply don't know if it's true or not.

I do know that having seen the Baghdad Babes on the ranges, I am convinced that they are more than capable of providing that hallmark military skill, sustained, accurate fire. One thing is for certain and that is there is a place for women in the PMC lineup.

IT WAS NOVEMBER 4, 2005. Four Iraqis, one of them a woman, were tearing down the Iraqi Highway on their way to Jordan. They were going with the determined intention of creating their own miniature hell on earth. The four rented an apartment in west Amman. A few days later, they took three taxis to three separate hotels.

Three of the Iraqis then blew themselves up; the woman's device failed to detonate. The explosions ripped through the hotels, causing massive devastation and loss of life. They had carried out the attacks in the belief that the Kingdom of Jordan had defiled the purity of Islam. Whose Islam had been defiled? you might ask. And that's a bloody good question. It's one the Jordanian security services came closer to answering when the failed female suicide bomber was captured and detained.

Her name was Sajida Mubarak Atrous al-Rishawi, and while she was being grilled, the streets of Amman were filled with crowds baying for her blood and the blood of her close friend Musab al-Zarqawi, the head of Al Qaeda in Iraq. It was not the effect those Al Qaeda psychos had intended.

One thing's for sure: The thirty-five-year-old woman came from the nest of Al Qaeda vipers at the heart of the insurgency, so the Jordanians kept her arrest secret at first, hoping to get a location for al-Zarqawi and with it the possibility of capturing the Sheik of the Beheaders.

Just how close Sajida was to the leadership is demonstrated by the fact that she was the sister of the former right-hand man of al-Zarqawi, Mubarak Atrous al-Rishawi, who had been killed by coalition Special Forces in Fallujah.

The other three suicide bombers who attacked the Grand Hyatt, Radisson SAS, and Days Inn hotels, killed fifty-seven innocent people, as well as al-Rishawi's husband, Ali Hussein Ali al-Shamari, who was an Al Qaeda lieutenant in Iraq's Al Anbar province.

The Jordanian security services were playing their hand close to their vest and not giving out too many details, but I heard on the grapevine that this black widow of a woman had deliberately chosen to target the Radisson, where three hundred people were attending a Jordanian-Palestinian wedding feast in one of the hotel's ballrooms.

It appears that this excuse for a woman wanted to turn another woman's happiest day into a nightmare. Her belt of powerful RDX explosive was packed with ball bearings, like those of her comrades, to cause the maximum amount of personal injury to the guests.

Al-Rishawi walked into the wedding reception with her husband, but when he noticed she was having trouble detonating her bomb and was tugging at the primer cord with no result, he pushed her out of the ballroom, then blew himself up.

I have no doubt she was given a real going-over by the Jordanian interrogators, and personally I have no sympathy for her whatsoever. I also have no doubt that she gave them a lot of information, which meant that al-Zarqawi would have lost safe houses and key operators. All of that would have limited his options and brought him one step nearer to his eventual death.

As for al-Rishawi, I believe they still have the death penalty in Jordan and no doubt she'll join her husband in hell one day. She was the first of the "black widows," as they are known, and she was followed by the strangest, and perhaps most sinister of them, a white Belgian woman named Muriel Degauque.

Muriel was a thirty-eight-year-old from Charleroi, Belgium, who converted to Islam after marrying a Moroccan immigrant who also happened to be a radical Muslim. Muriel Degauque's mother, Liliane, reckoned that after her conversion and marriage in 2000, the former Roman Catholic became more "Muslim than a Muslim."

Liliane had tried without success to contact her daughter for three weeks before Muriel carried out a suicide attack in Baghdad on November 9, when she tried but failed to take out a patrol of U.S. troops.

The radicalization of the quiet, unassuming Belgian woman took place quickly and she moved from wearing a simple veil to donning the full head-to-toe chador. Then after a thorough indoctrination, she moved through Syria into Iraq, where she became the first female European bomber in Iraq. Those in the Syrian government would, of course, deny any knowledge of her traveling through their country, but they bear a heavy responsibility for a lot of Al Qaeda's activities in Iraq.

The chilling thing, of course, is that she could have come from any country in Europe, including Britain, where new terrorism legislation introduced in 2005 seems to have had little impact on radical imams. They were still preaching violence and hatred and praising suicide bomb "martyrs" with little interruption even as Muriel Degauque was blowing herself up.

In December 2005, there was a blood-chilling double act in Baghdad when two black widows blew themselves up in the police academy, killing twenty-seven students and wounding thirty-two more. One woman blew herself up in a classroom full of students during roll call, the other in the busy mess room, where young officers were eating a meal. The two women were believed to be students at the academy, planted by Al Qaeda, of course, and that's why they weren't subjected to a search.

Simply put, they got their feet under the table, then waited to blow it up. They took five other female police officers, Muslim sisters, with them. It was a dreadful act, and it's the type of terrorism that is the hardest to combat.

10. The Power
of Love

YOU'D THINK THAT CUPID'S ARROWS WOULD be torn to shreds by the assault rounds and car bombs in Iraq. Even if it weren't a war zone, you'd imagine that being surrounded by the prohibitions of an Islamic culture would dampen the ardor of the thousands of Westerners in the country all on its own.

Don't believe it for a moment. Love finds a way even in Iraq and there are countless affairs, romances, and even scores of marriages between locals and the coalition troops and PMCs. In practice, that means male U.S. soldiers marry Iraqi women, female U.S. soldiers marry PMCs they've met in the theater of operations, and PMCs marry Iraqi women. What I've personally never heard of is an Iraqi man being involved in this complex triangle of love.

Why? Because these romances depend on one thing to survive, and that's a marital home and a life outside Iraq. Those are things that Iraqi men aren't generally able to supply. And of course when

I talk about the marriage surviving, I don't mean there's a shortage of marriage counselors in Iraq. No, what I mean is that the happy couple would be slotted and dumped in the Tigris before the groom could carry the bride across the threshold.

When I was in Iraq, the center of this marriage bazaar was the relatively safe Green Zone, where the Coalition Provisional Authority operated, because literally hundreds of local women worked inside the zone in secretarial, clerical, and catering jobs. Naturally, they met the men from the military and the mercenary army as they went about their daily work and relationships began to flower. There's a lively social scene inside the zone, with discos and bars, and it's easy enough for them to chat one another up in the day, then plan an RV to meet again in the evening.

It's like the fifty-third state inside the zone, and when I was in there, I always felt as if I were inside an alien craft with some sort of force field surrounding it. Outside was bedlam and anarchy, where nothing and no one was safe. Inside is where the alien invaders and the Iraqis were able to interface and evolve their own unique culture. It was as if they were grafted onto the city outside.

I'm sure all sorts of relationships flourished inside the zone from the purely platonic to the totally lustful to those of true love. But I reckon a lot of the Iraqi girls, and there are some real lookers among them, set out to get a Yank by hook or by crook so that they could move out of the hell of Baghdad and across the world to the States, where they hoped to find relative safety and a good life in the greatest consumer society on the planet.

And that's exactly what they did, because as soon as they got married, there was no going back home. They were on a marriage conveyor belt that plucked them from one culture, then took them halfway around the world to drop them in another.

The women would keep their arrangements totally secret, sometimes not even telling their own parents. Then on the big day, they'd bring their luggage into the zone with them and have it ready to go when the civil ceremony had been performed. All the vetting and visa arrangements had to be done by the U.S. Immigration people, who had their own bureau in the zone, too.

The couples would make their marriage vows in the Presidential Palace, which is at the heart of the Green Zone, tucked into a great bend in the river. The marriage ceremonies were held in one of the garishly painted state rooms with high stucco ceilings inside Saddam's very own version of Versailles. When they'd finally tied the knot, there was only one way to go, and that was down the road to the airport in a protected convoy and straight onto a flight out of Iraq.

While I was around Baghdad, there were so many marriages taking place that they had special wedding days up at the palace. I knew three or four Yank PMCs who took the plunge and married Iraqi brides from Baghdad. Those Iraqi girls were certainly keen to get married and jet away to their new life in the States.

There's apparently been a big falloff in the number of mixed-religion marriages between Shias and Sunnis, but I reckon the new marriage market between Westerners and Iraqis in the Green Zone ghetto is making up some of the shortfall.

IT WAS A QUIET EVENING in the bar of a Baghdad hotel in July 2003 and I was relaxing over a drink with the British correspondent I was guarding. He'd invited a couple of members of one of the international news stations to join us and we were chatting about the usual stuff. Where was the latest hot spot in the insurgency? Who'd had a contact? How many people had been killed in the latest bombing?

One of those present was a woman journalist. I'll call her Jasmine. She was in her late thirties, dark and quite attractive. I was to discover that she was on the lookout and hungry for love. It was only about twenty minutes after we'd been introduced that she deftly turned the subject away from the endless talk of the "situation" and onto my personal life.

"Yeah, I've got a steady girlfriend. We've been together for years. We're really happy," I said.

"I'm happy too," she said. "My husband and I are close, but we don't keep each other on a lead. You know what I mean. I think the expression is 'We have an open marriage.'"

"Really?" I said.

"Yes, we're very understanding of each other's needs. He knows I have certain needs and of course when I'm in a place like this, he knows that there's a certain de-stressing factor involved and he knows that sex is great relaxation."

By now, her foot was going up my trouser leg and I'd gotten the message loud and clear.

"Obviously, it has to be no strings attached, but that's fine, isn't it?"

Now, if I had agreed, it would have seemed like I was accepting her advances, and on the other hand, if I'd said it wasn't fine, then I might have sounded a bit rude, so I settled for the diplomatic course.

"Suppose so," I offered.

She smiled seductively then and gave me a look at the fob of her room key. "There's my room number. Shall I see you later?"

I know that refusal can cause offense, but I found some of the man-hungry media women more scary than the insurgents. Most of them were fantastic at their jobs and kept everything on a professional level, but some of them were real prick mangles who knew what they wanted and set out to get it. And with all the alpha males of the PMC community around them with testosterone levels that must have been near the top end of the safety guidelines, they were like kids in a sweet shop.

Still, she had to be told, so I said, "Don't think so. I've got an early start tomorrow and I love my girlfriend."

It sounded rather limp, but that's how I felt. A few of my mates, especially the ones that weren't too seriously attached, got well into the female correspondents, though. They're formidable women. You can imagine that the networks don't choose them for their bad looks and they're not exactly shy. Those girls know what they want and were determined to get it.

They're not the only women out there, either. There are a lot of businesswomen out in Iraq, as well—high-powered executives representing some top companies and corporations. Most of them stay inside the relative safety of the Green Zone, where they conduct their business with executives of oil companies or Iraqi utilities, who come into the zone to meet them.

Once again, they're mixing with the whole range of people involved in the Iraq project, so where there's attraction, there's opportunity inside the self-contained Green Zone. You get liaisons between women execs and senior officers, interpreters, and, inevitably, with the PMCs who are assigned to protect them.

It's a natural thing. Put yourself in the woman's situation. You're in a strange and dangerous country. Along comes the hunk assigned to protect you on your occasional forays outside the Green Zone. He's an alpha male and he's got his own wants and desires, too. That feeling of vulnerability and not a little fear then throws you into his arms.

It happens a lot. One of my mates, Mac, had a passionate affair with a corporate executive from the States. He was divorced, she was single, and she wanted to ship him back home to New York, shower him with cash and presents, and love him for the rest of his life. Perfect. Well, apparently not.

"She's a cracking looker, mate," I told him. "You could do a lot worse for yourself."

"I know, Johnny, but I just can't do it."

"It's not because she's an American, is it?" I asked. "They're great when you get into their way of thinking."

"No, it's not that."

"What is it, then?" I was really curious now.

"The trouble is that she just wants me to hang around while she's working. She's told me I can have all the toys I like—fast cars, a superbike. She's even said she'll get me flying lessons. It's all there for me, Johnny. Skiing in Aspen every season. California. Flights home to see the kids whenever."

"Fucking hell, Mac, move over, son. I'll have her," I told him, joking.

"You wouldn't, mate."

"So what's wrong with her?" I was exasperated now.

"She's told me I can have it all but that I'll have to give up the Highway. No more jobs."

"You're kidding?"

"No."

"Tell her to fuck off, Mac. You've got to keep your balls."

"That's what I've been trying to tell you," he replied.

ONE OF THE MOST unusual sets of relationships that I saw spring up in Baghdad was between three of the lads and three Iraqi sisters. They were beautiful girls, members of the small Christian community in Baghdad, and they had been working for a company that the lads had been ferrying clients around for.

One thing led to another and they would sneak into the hotel for nights of passion with the lads, but it had to be kept very secret, not because the hotel might not like it but because they'd get malleted if word got out.

If I had to go and find one of the boys, there'd always be a pause until he was certain it was me; then the door would open and I'd be allowed in just as the girl was coming out of the closet. The reason was that these women were absolutely paranoid about being spotted by one of the cleaners or by room service, in case they were recognized.

When you think about it, these women were running huge risks, but I'm sure it was all a big exotic game for them, and the lads seemed to enjoy it, too. But there is danger out there in Iraq for illicit lovers. It's a very real and present danger, which can end in terrible tragedy, and for one famous British soldier it did.

BRIAN TILLEY WAS RELAXING after supper in the lounge of a comfortable villa-style house in the smart Baghdad suburb of Al Dawrah on a warm evening. His bags were packed and he was ready for an early night because he was catching a flight back to the UK the following morning. He'd already missed a flight two days earlier and he didn't want to lose the next one out.

Brian was a forty-seven-year-old veteran of the Royal Marines' elite Special Boat Service, the Brit equivalent of the U.S. Navy SEALs, and a man with a fantastic military record. As a Special Forces soldier, he was a man who attracted immense respect and he was extremely popular with his comrades in the SBS—"boaties," as we call them.

Life was sweet for Brian at the time. He was making a good living as a PMC and he'd sorted out his routine to make life work for him. Not for him the anonymous walls of a hotel room and the same old couscous buffet in a tatty restaurant every mealtime. No, Brian had done better for himself and with all the resourcefulness that had made him a hard-core SBS operator, he had set himself up in the villa with all the comforts of home. He had good home cooking, comfortable informal surroundings, and a good social life, which included enjoying the passions of a beautiful Iraqi woman.

But a knock at the door that evening in May 2004 heralded a tragedy that was still unfolding eight months later with all the twists of a nightmare crime thriller. There were five other people in the house with Brian that evening, a group that included his lover, her sister, a woman friend of the sister, an Iraqi man who worked with Brian, and a pretty teenage high school girl, the daughter of Brian's mistress.

The Iraqi guy opened the door to see who was calling, only to be confronted by four police officers, who calmly asked to be let in on official business. Brian must have heard the conversation at the door, but there was no commotion, so he stayed relaxed and at ease. The police uniforms must have pacified any fears the occupants of the house may have had. Mistake. Big mistake.

The IP officers came into the lounge, and what happened afterward is largely a matter of conjecture. They probably jumped Brian Tilley without warning before he could arm himself and put up a fight, because I cannot imagine he didn't have a weapon somewhere near at hand. One of the cops shot him in the foot, presumably to disable him, as they would have discovered it was going to take more than four IP police faggots to hold down a man like Brian. Then they dragged him into another room as the screaming women watched.

We can only imagine what was being shouted and screamed among all those involved. Maybe Brian was told that he was infidel filth and he should keep his hands off Iraqi women. Maybe he was told to beg for mercy and refused. We simply don't know because Brian Tilley was then executed with a shot in the back that smashed his vital organs and killed him instantly.

The so-called cops then went on in cold blood to summarily execute the three women and the man in the house. The fifteen-year-old girl, who'd come out of her bedroom, rubbing the sleep out of her eyes, disturbed by the noise, was shot in the neck and

The Power of Love

left for dead. But she survived to give investigators the vital evidence they needed to establish that the perpetrators were police officers. She told the investigators it was cops who'd slaughtered those in the house, and not only that; she was able to identify them clearly.

After the Iraqi forces arrested the cops, the PMC community was awash with rumors: He'd been jumped leaving the house and they'd tortured and mutilated his body before shooting him; the cops were part of an insurgent hit squad out to get any PMCs who strayed into the community; and so on.

Well, it doesn't appear that he was tortured and mutilated and it doesn't seem to me that he was the victim of insurgents. The best theory I've heard is that the cops were paid by the woman's family to warn Brian off, but when they got into the cage with the tiger, they found themselves completely out of their depth and had to shoot him before he tore their throats out. That done, the witnesses to the murder had to die, too. I believe that in the Muslim world, these cowardly murders would be called "honor killings." What honor is there in killing women and girls? I wonder.

Brian's home in the UK was in Dorset, not far from the SBS base at Poole, where he'd served with such distinction, and the local coroner ordered a police investigation, headed by Detective Superintendent Phil James. Nearly two years later, in the winter of 2005, the superintendent was no nearer to closing the file to his or the coroner's satisfaction, and that was through no fault of his own. What he'd come up against was the Iraqi factor, which amounted to a complete reluctance on the part of the authorities in Baghdad to move things along, and that could have been for a variety of reasons.

Perhaps it was because the Baghdad authorities had a lot on their plate. More likely, they had a cultural sympathy for the men who had killed an outsider, a non-Muslim, who'd brought shame and dishonor on an Iraqi family. On the other hand, it could have been that tribal loyalties, which are complex and intertwined in Iraq, together with a few well-placed bribes, were keeping the officers immune from justice. Because that's what they were, insulated from justice, and, believe it or not, in December 2005 the bastards were back on the beat.

The girl, the only witness in the case, provides another twist to the story. Apparently, it was only through a chance encounter in the Baghdad hospital where she was being treated that the girl spotted the killers. How much of a chance that actually was, I don't know. Maybe they were planning to finish off the job but she spotted them first and told the authorities. Anyway, it was immediately recognized that she was in mortal danger, and it was even suggested that she could be given asylum in Britain in return for giving evidence at the inquest in Dorset.

But Dorset coroners don't hand down Baghdad jail sentences, and suddenly the girl vanished from the protective custody that she was being held in. Without her, there could be no trial, but on the other hand, turning up to give evidence might have exposed her to a death sentence. So there's a dilemma: What's more important, justice for the people who were murdered or life for the teenager? Personally, I don't think there's a choice. That girl's life is paramount; after all, you can't bring the rest back from the grave.

Someone thought it was her life that counted most and she vanished from protective custody. Detective Superintendent Phil James thought it was pretty certain that she'd been spirited away by friends of Brian. That suggests one thing to me: It's those Baghdad cops with blood on their hands who'd better be watching their backs now. If anything goes for cops in Iraq, then I think anything might go for friends of Brian Tilley, who have the skills to move in and out of the shadows at will.

There are lessons to be learned from this tragedy, and unfortunately, that means I'm going to have to speak frankly about the actions of a dead man who was held in high esteem when he lived. But first I think we should look at Brian Tilley's record a little more closely, because he was some man.

Born in Derby, he'd served for twenty-two years in the Royal Marines and fought in the Falklands, Northern Ireland, and the Gulf War. In 1997, he was awarded the Queen's Gallantry Medal for outstanding courage.

But it wasn't just his military career that marked Brian as a special bloke, even by Special Forces standards. He was also a qualified paramedic, a diver, and a talented mountaineer who'd been on expeditions to three of the world's four highest mountains. On two expeditions, he was the man who saved the day when he used his medicals skills to save people's lives.

When he left the Marines, he set up his own security company, which was called Peak, and in 2002, when a plot to kidnap David and Victoria Beckham was exposed, it was Brian Tilley who was called in to beef up security. He became friendly with the Beckhams, who were apparently delighted with the way he improved their close protection after retraining their civilian security staff. Quite a CV, isn't it?

But it's plain to me that Brian Tilley succumbed to Special Forces invulnerability syndrome. If we're honest, all of us in the world of Special Forces will put up our hands and admit there have been times and situations when we chose to believe that we were Superman. I know, because I've done it myself.

For 99.9 percent of us, the outcome is fine, for we either realize in time that we're wearing our underpants outside our trousers or luck carries us safely through whatever the situation may be. But some don't realize their vulnerability or their luck doesn't hold and they pay the price.

I don't know what verdict the coroner will arrive at regarding

Brian's death, but in my judgment he all but killed himself when he broke every rule in the book by going native. He became complacent and too comfortable in his cozy berth at his girlfriend's villa. He didn't believe anyone could get the drop on him and he exposed himself as surely as if he'd gone onto a mountain glacier without an ice ax.

I don't want to upset his family or any of his old comrades in the SBS, but I'm sure that, hand on heart, they must know that he should never have been in that villa on a routine basis in the first place. If he took his liaison seriously, he should have chosen to carry on the romance in a more secure environment. Even Jordan would have been infinitely safer than the suburbs of Baghdad. But Brian had a lovely girlfriend back home in Poole and he surely never meant his Iraqi liaison to last. It's a crying shame. A man like that had a lot left to offer.

THIRTY DAYS HATH SEPTEMBER, and so on and so forth. And February has twenty-eight days, and twenty-nine in a leap year. Well, it was leap day in February 2004 and I was back in my old stamping ground, staying at the Mirbad Hotel in Basra.

The night of that attack on the hotel when we'd taken cover on the roof seemed a lifetime away and the old chap who owned the place was in great spirits. He was pleased to see me and patted me on the back as he kept repeating, "Welcome, Mr. Johnny, welcome!" And the waiter who was a Saddam look-alike gave me a conspiratorial wink, as if he'd been initiated into the brotherhood of men who know how to free up an AK-47 jammed by a split case, as I had done that night on the roof.

It was nice to be there on familiar ground and it had the feel of a bit of a homecoming. Even the insurgents put out the welcome mat at dusk as they started a firefight under cover of the fading light.

I was with a team of guys and they immediately started deploying, together with guys from other call-sign groups. The odd shot in the dark was cracking into the outer wall of the Mirbad, but I noticed the old night watchman, installed in his hut at the gate again, didn't seem inclined to move. So rather than rush around like a headless chicken, I asked the owner what was going down.

"Oh, not to be worrying, Mr. Johnny," he said gravely. "Tonight they are busy killing one another."

I knew he was right, so I just settled down in the corner of the car park to watch the eerie phosphorescent muzzle flashes on buildings a hundred meters or so away from us. There was some tribal or clan dispute to be settled and they were too busy sorting out matters of honor to be bothered with us.

Just as the battle reached fever pitch, my satellite phone began jumping around in my vest pocket, but the sound of the rifle fire, joined by the steady tattoo of a machine gun, made it impossible to hear it ringing. I pulled it out of my vest pocket and pressed the receive button.

"John?" It was my long-term girlfriend, Emma.

"Hi, darling," I bellowed into the phone.

"What's all that noise? It's a terrible line," she said.

Terrible line? The only lines were the occasional luminous streaks of tracer rounds.

"Hang on, doll," I shouted as I ran away from the shooting and crouched down on my knee behind a vehicle.

"That any better?"

"Yeah, much. What's going on?"

"Nothing much, babe, just a bit of a firefight across the road."

"Oh God, are you okay?"

"Yeah, I'm fine. Safe as houses."

Emma had been with me for eight years and had learned to accept that when I said I was all right, then I was all right, so the conversation moved on.

"You know it's a leap year, don't you, John?"

Well, I did, but I hadn't really spent my waking hours characterizing 2004 as a leap year.

"Yeah, what about it?"

"Well, it's leap day today, isn't it?"

Once again, I supposed it was, but still I hadn't twigged, and I might even have been getting a little bit impatient at being quizzed about my knowledge of the calendar in the middle of a gun battle.

"Really, I suppose it is," I replied.

"Well, you know that a girl can take the initiative on leap day. . . ."

Booph!

An RPG round hit the side of an apartment block about 150 meters away and drowned Emma's voice out.

"What was that, babe?" I asked.

She was shouting now. "John, will you marry me?"

For a second, I was stunned as I realized where the whole conversation had been leading, but I wasn't stunned for long. Emma is a beautiful, caring woman who just tunes in to the way I am. There was only one answer.

"Course I will, darling."

A crescendo of firing drowned out the conversation again, but she'd heard me accept, and three months later, on my next trip home, we were married. Mike Curtis was my best man. Who else?

So I know from personal experience that the power of love works even in war-shredded Iraq, and I'll never forget the day I went down on one knee to take cover for a proposal.

11. Outtakes

IT WAS JULY 2003 AND THE PEOPLE OF BAGH-dad navigated their way around the pools of sewage leaking out of cracked pipes in the streets. Down one of those streets, a slightly built young man with a thousand-yard stare clutched the steering wheel of a car as he drove it straight toward the concrete Jersey blocks barring the way to the Baghdad Hotel.

A first glance would not have revealed that this was a suicide bomber on his chosen route to paradise, but a second look would have revealed something very strange about the young man's face. He had a bulldog clip from the end of a set of jump leads, with wires dangling from it, clenched between his teeth.

The armed Iraqi guard at the hotel checkpoint probably didn't have time to see the bulldog clip, but he certainly must have known what was about to happen as the car ignored his signals to stop and kept coming.

Later on, eyewitnesses told how the guard had pumped several rounds through the windshield of the truck. The bullets thumped one by one into the driver and he died instantly from the wounds, the bull-dog clip falling from his mouth. The metal plates snapped together in a vicious bite, completing an electrical circuit to the bomb loaded in the car, which would kill six people and savage scores of others.

We felt the quake created by the blast vibrating under our feet only a second after we heard the massive blast reverberating around the Palestine Hotel. No time to fuck about, we were out of the door and heading for the scene of the huge suicide bombing at the Baghdad Hotel.

I was with an Irish TV crew and we were first on the scene of desolation. The carnage caused by a suicide bombing is difficult to describe. I'm sure you've seen the pictures on the news channels of smoke, debris, and mortar dust filling the air. But seeing it on TV is one thing; being there, right in the thick of it—that's something else.

People were rushing around without any rational thought; others were staggering, with gaping holes in their clothing and their bodies. The horrible epicenter of it all was a smoking hole, piled with rubble that used to be a building full of living, breathing people. But it had become a place of screams as those trapped in the center of it wailed in agony. Some of them were wailing their lives away.

As we got closer, we were surrounded by pieces of the suicide bomber mingled with pieces of his victims. Scraps of flesh were everywhere, pieces of anatomy thrown here and there in a haphazard rearrangement of bodies—a leg here, someone else's foot there.

And the smell—it wasn't the mouth-filling stench of decomposition. Too soon for that. No, this was different. The air was full of fresh smells like a slaughterhouse on a busy day. There was the hot steam of eviscerated guts, but everywhere, too, was the metallic scent of blood. It wasn't just the scent, either; you could taste the iron tang of it in the air all around, where the blast had sprayed it like an aerosol.

A small crowd was gathering now, but the military and the police hadn't even arrived at the scene. I guessed they were standing back, counting to twenty, while they waited to see if there was a second bomb meant for them.

The cameraman had taken the scene in and decided what he needed to do to get the best shots of the carnage. He was struggling to get a clear shot over people's shoulders of what was happening and he was being bumped around and jostled. For him, it was a nightmare in the midst of a nightmare.

"John! John! I need some height."

I looked around and homed in on the construction site about seventy meters away, opposite the hotel. There were some workmen standing in front of it, obviously in shock, and I asked if any of them spoke English. One of them nodded and I said, "Irish television. Can we go up?" He nodded again and we legged it up the open staircase to the second floor. There was a big open square that had been created for a window to be fitted on the corner of the building. The cameraman decided this was the spot to film from, but he wanted to be back away from the edge for the best shot. I think he wanted the concrete hole to frame the pictures.

I didn't like it. Back in the shadows, with a piece of kit over his shoulder, he'd look as if he were aiming a rifle or mounting an RPG.

"Come on, move forward to the window," I told him.

He didn't like it. Let's be fair: He didn't like me and he resented taking instructions from me. Why? Well, he was from Southern Ireland, he was a staunch Republican, he knew I was ex-SAS, and he'd put two and two together and decided that I must have been involved in anti-IRA operations. Maybe I had been. But that was none of his business. I was out there to protect him, end of story. I didn't give a fuck what he thought. He wasn't going to get shot up on my watch if I could help it, whether he was an IRA sympathizer or not.

"Get across to the fucking window," I snarled.

He knew I meant it, and he moved, grumbling all the way. He stood about five feet back from the open window frame, facing the hotel. I was standing at a window frame just behind him, on the opposite corner to the hotel, looking back up the street. Just as he moved, a convoy of U.S. Army Humvees came down the road. They had .50-caliber guns mounted on the back, which were being swiveled around in threatening arcs.

I leaned out and showed myself, holding both hands in the air, and waving as I shouted, "Irish film crew!"

Those guys with the big "fuck off" .50-caliber guns don't look at you with their eyes; they look at you with their guns. Where their eyes go, the barrels follow. A couple such barrels were now trained on me as the army guys sized me up. And their eyes were large, dark, and reflective, like sinister dragonflies' eyes, behind their army-issue Coyote shades.

Then one of them shouted, "Okay, man, we got you. You're fine."

I was relieved and I know with a fair degree of certainty that if the cameraman had stayed out of the light in the back of that construction site and then been spotted as a shadowy figure seemingly carrying a piece on his shoulder, those guys on the Humvees would not have hesitated. They would have ripped him apart with lead, and he knew it, too.

"Enough," I asked.

"Enough," he said grudgingly, and we went back to the street outside the blitzed hotel, where the correspondent and the interpreter were waiting for us. By now, the driver had joined us. It was my old friend Hamdany. You have to understand that these drivers are not hired cabbies; they come complete with a set of vehicles and they are proud businessmen who are well paid for a high-risk job. I admire them and their families, and I had great affection for Hamdany in particular.

The correspondent filmed his piece for the camera and we decided it was time to go. There are invariably three phases to these atrocities among survivors and those who come to witness events. The first is the trauma phase, brought on by the obvious shock of what has been perpetrated. The second I'll call the postoperative phase, to use the military term, when the necessities of aiding and saving the injured and trapped are under way. The third is anger.

In such situations, it's a real wave of fury that seems to be thrashing around, looking for somewhere to vent itself, and inevitably the media are often the target for that volcanic frustration. It's quite understandable in a way, even if it's not very fair. It's just a variation of the old adage about shooting the messenger, but at a time like this, there's a real danger the messenger will be shot before he's even delivered the message. No surprise then that I always aimed to get my crews out of those situations before phase three kicked off, and usually I did.

But the phases can overlap, and that day in Baghdad the anger began to spill out while the rescue operations were still under way. A huge crowd of locals was pressing up against the line the military had thrown up around the site. Most of those in the crowd were people who feared relatives were dead or injured in the awful tangle of concrete and metal. Many of them were hysterical with grief or fear for the lives of their loved ones and they were becoming hostile.

We exited the building and the cameraman spotted a concrete bus shelter. I knew what was coming: "John, I need that shot." Oh shit, I thought, this is borderline phase three and he wants to set up on top of a bus shelter for one last shot. Go on, mate, I thought, but make it fucking quick. Five minutes felt like five hours; then he was finished and we were moving. He was a wild-arsed Irishman and I had to admire him.

I had the tripod over my shoulder and a pistol in my belt, but I didn't have any body armor on. Normally, I would have been wearing it, but we'd left in such a hurry, I'd forgotten it. We pushed the correspondent and the cameraman against the street wall and Hamdany put his big arm around me as we formed a scrum to walk back to the vehicle against the human tide coming to the scene. The interpreter kept telling people we were from Irish TV, and that deflected most of them. A few cursed us; some spat. Eventually, we got to the car and the crew were shoved inside. Someone aimed a blow at me from the crowd. Hamdany deflected it. My hand was on my pistol.

"What a time to forget my body armor," I said as Hamdany pushed the attacker to one side and replied, "You are my friend. Today I am your body armor."

I'll never forget those words, and now and then I wonder how he and his family are getting on.

T HAT STORY of the Baghdad Hotel and the Irish cameraman I was minding contrasts starkly with the tragedy of Mazen Dana, a Reuters news agency cameraman, who was killed by machine-gun fire from a U.S. Bradley fighting vehicle in August 2003.

His death led me into a heated debate with an ABC staff correspondent over the "trigger-happy" military and the "shit rules of engagement" of the U.S. Army.

Dana was belly-shot while filming near the notorious Abu Ghraib prison in Baghdad the day after a mortar attack there had malleted six Iraqi civilians. The accounts of his death differ in detail and emphasis, depending on whom you hear the story from. Journos tend to play up the fact that twenty minutes or so before he was shot he'd been allowed to film at the prison gates by the military.

So what? Dana and his soundman then moved a third of a mile away to film a wide-angled shot of the prison from a river bridge.

He might as well have been a world away from his original filming position. Everyone agrees that Dana had called it a day and the crew members had packed their kit into the car and driven off toward the Reuters office.

Dana then spotted the armoured column coming directly toward him and stopped to film it with the prison in the background. He jumped out of the vehicle and set up his camera with a built in microphone as his soundman lighted a fag. Within ten seconds, he was clutching his belly and bleeding to death.

You see, what he'd done was jump out of a car, which, by the way, had no press marking on it, drop to one knee, and mount his camera, which was swathed in a dark blue padded canvas cover, onto his shoulder. That is an action that precisely mimics the way an insurgent would mount an antitank weapon or RPG onto his shoulder before firing.

Add another element, the fact that Mazen Dana (as you can probably tell from his name) was of Middle Eastern origin. I think he was a Palestinian, and you can easily see why he was mistaken for an insurgent.

International journalist groups, on the other hand, claim that from fifty meters the camera would have been clearly visible. I don't agree. When I took up media-protection work in Iraq, the illusion of the camera as a potential weapon was one of the most contentious issues. Could a highly trained U.S. soldier really mistake a camera for a weapon? I decided to find out for myself by conducting a little experiment.

I got a cameraman to kneel behind a low wall with his kit on his shoulder while I paced out fifty yards, a hundred yards, two hundred yards. Each time, I spun around as if in a combat situation, and I am convinced that I could not have differentiated quickly enough between a camera and, say, a 66-mm LAW, a Stinger, or even a MILAN antitank weapon if my life had depended on it.

I would ask that, instead of pointing fingers media people put themselves in the skin of the nineteen- or twenty-year-old marine on a coaxial machine gun that day at Abu Ghraib. He saw what he took to be a local man hurriedly dismounting from an unmarked car and raising what might have been a weapon onto his shoulder. At that point, his training would have been screaming at him, TANK ACTION! He had only seconds. His pals were depending on him for their lives. He fired. An innocent man died. War is shit.

Every media person I met poured real venom on the U.S. forces for Dana's death and blamed the Yank rules of engagement for his shooting. That's bollocks. Why do they seem to believe the media can go to these places with some force shield around them? Why are they so foolish as to believe a soldier would hesitate and put his own life and his buddies lives at risk? Surely they can't seriously believe a young soldier would look down his barrel and say to himself, Ah, there's a media cameraman. I'll shoot him and pretend I thought he had an RPG.

As I said, that's bollocks. It was Mazen Dana's own rules of engagement that were at fault, and I am convinced that if he'd had a PMC with him, he would never have been allowed to engage in that almost suicidal posture.

I briefed all the camera crews under my protection to look like what they were and not dress in a paramilitary style, unlike some dickheads, who would wear cargo pants tucked into their boots, that sort of thing. One of my guys used to wear a big floppy hat to mark himself out as a definite civilian. I taught them all to infiltrate slowly into their filming positions and to be deliberate in the way they set up a tripod and camera. They learned to be aware of what was going on around them and not just what they saw through the lens. They learned to look at the troops and make eye-to-eye contact and to wave at any troops they thought hadn't spotted them. In short, they were trained to do anything that would make them stand out as film crew.

During my career, I've taken countless risks that other people might think crazy, but as a soldier you know that at some point you are going to have to put your life on the line to tip the balance in a battle. Taking a stupid risk for a bit of footage of a Bradley vehicle trundling past a prison was foolish, and I'm sorry that he had to pay for it with his life. His colleagues should learn from it, not whine and blame.

'D WORKED WITH MEMBERS of the media a couple of times in the 1990s, long before my experiences with them in Iraq. This was back when Mike Curtis and I were out of the regiment and up for adventures. The first time was when a mate from the *Daily Express* in London called us, asking if we could give him a hand.

There was a celebrated case at the time of two British nurses held in a Saudi Arabian jail for eighteen months for allegedly killing their flat mate, another UK nurse, Yvonne Gilford. One of them, Deborah Parry, had been sentenced to public execution and the other, Lucille McLauchlan, to five hundred lashes and imprisonment.

The women, who were now known as the "Saudi Nurses," had been pardoned by the king and released by the authorities out there and were jetting into London Gatwick the following day. There was bound to be a bun fight at the airport, he said, and they needed some professional help. He introduced us to John Coles, the *Express* reporter in charge of the job, and off we went.

Well, there *was* a bun fight and the nurse in our charge, Debbie Parry, was photographed immediately as we left the terminal and fought our way into a waiting Range Rover. We were tailed to London, but we slipped into a private car park, got a friend's wife to dress up in Debbie's clothing and leave in the Range Rover, with the press pack pursuing her.

Meanwhile, we wanted to put Debbie into the trunk of a Golf

GTI to smuggle her out of the underground garage, but she was too nervous to get into it.

"Don't worry, lovely. I'll get in there with you," said Mike.

The sight of the two of them curled up there in the trunk, the burly ex-SAS man and the tiny nurse, was unforgettable. First the princess, now the nurse—Mike just seemed to be cuddling up in the line of duty all the time.

Anyway, we gave the rest of the pack the slip, got our nurse to a nice country hotel in Wiltshire, where reporters from the *Daily Express* were able to interview and photograph her at their leisure. For what it's worth, I thought Debbie had been well and truly set up by the Saudis just so they could write the murder off as solved and not have to bring a Saudi citizen to trial.

J OBS LIKE THAT WERE an introduction to the madness of the media and the frantic, crazy existence its members live. I love some of the characters I've met through the media, but in a war zone they can drive you nuts.

The problem is that many of them, particularly photographers and cameramen, think they are bomb- and bulletproof. They have a curious way of looking at the world through a lens. As far as I can make out, they believe they are utterly detached from the events going on around them and so they take bloody stupid risks that a professional soldier would never expose himself to. They are voyeurs and have a complete belief in their immortality, which makes them hard to look after.

Businessmen just want to get to the job or project they're contracted to do quickly and safely. Journalists are the same, except with them the job is the war and they want to see it. They want to get to the action; consequently, looking after them is a very tricky balancing act. It's particularly difficult when the bosses of a media station dictate a hard-and-fast "no guns" policy.

The big media corporations have a very businesslike attitude about guns, and those in their employ travel in well-coordinated columns with enough firepower to fight off a large insurgent ambush. Sometimes, when it suited my purposes and usually when I was in a hurry, I would tag onto the end of a big media convoy bound for the site of a bombing or a shooting.

At the other end of the spectrum, the BBC now have their own in-house hostile-environment security team. It's made up of some top operators, led by an ex–Special Forces officer. They have a "no weapons" policy because the BBC sticks to the notion that a journalists must remain neutral if he or she is to report a situation fairly.

I don't know if those BBC protection guys could suddenly conjure a gun out of a hat like a magician's rabbit if they needed to, but I do know that I would not like to be responsible for a media team in the Iraqi situation without a gun in my hand.

I remember as a kid looking at replays of those old newsreel style films taken during World War II, with famous correspondents like Wynford Vaughan-Thomas and Richard Dimbleby, who hit the D-day beaches with the troops. Everyone seems to think embedded correspondents are something new on the scene. But those blokes weren't just embedded; they were entrusted to bring the news from the front without subjecting the troops to politically correct analysis of every action they took. War is not some sanitized, bloodless exercise. It's a fierce bloodletting, where kill or be killed is the norm.

Today, the nature of war has changed dramatically with the emergence of Islamic fighters who not only don't heed the rules of the Geneva Convention but actually despise those rules and the world order that created them. It is their often-stated and avowed aim to topple that world order and create a new Islamic one, which they call a "global caliphate."

Article 79 of Protocol I of the Geneva Convention says, "Journalists engaged in dangerous professional missions in areas of armed conflict shall be considered as civilians" and "shall be protected as such. . . ." They've got a nice ring to them, those words, but they don't mean jackshit in downtown Fallujah. The only protection a journalist has in modern Iraq is his wit and a man like me watching his back with a gun.

In 2005, one American print journalist based in Baghdad, *New York Times* staffer Dexter Filkins, brought the whole debate into the open when he ostentatiously carried a pistol on his assignments.

There was a lot of soul-searching and hand-wringing in media circles along "Should we or shouldn't we?" lines. The right to defend oneself was not considered an option for a journalist. The argument was that one's very membership in the profession was one's defense. An armed press is a vulnerable press, which has become combatant, rather than just observing hostilities, they argued. How could an armed reporter claim that he was not a spy or a military agent?

Well, that's what radical Islamists are going to call any captured reporter, whatever his status, and the fate of American reporter Daniel Pearl is a case in point. He was kidnapped by a fundamentalist gang in Pakistan and beheaded in 2002. His killers are all part of the same loosely affiliated worldwide network of Caliphists who want global Islam, and they immediately claimed Pearl was a spy.

Well-made arguments about his journalistic impartiality didn't count for a thing among his captors. Their world is a different world with different values and they recognize nothing of ours as being of any value or honor. That's just the way it is.

I've never met Dexter Filkins, but I know he must be a realist who worked out the odds for himself. He made a rational appraisal of the men out there in Iraq just waiting for people like him to fall into their hands. He weighed up the risks and thought that shooting it out would be a better option than being beheaded after a period of terrifying and humiliating captivity. In my opinion, he's bang-on and absolutely correct. I take my hat off to him, with one proviso, which is that I hope he's been on the range and that he knows how to shoot straight and how to handle his weapon safely while in the company of his friends and allies.

There's another tragedy that opens up all the arguments about being armed and the way the media operates in a war zone. It involves one of the most respected British TV correspondents to die on the front line in recent years.

TERRY LLOYD WAS ITV'S longest-serving correspondent when he died in Iraq in March 2003. He was a veteran of several conflicts; a man of proven courage, Lloyd was loved for his cheerful outlook on life and admired for his unyielding professionalism.

The circumstances of his death and the deaths of two of his crew, cameraman Fred Nerac and translator Hussein Othman, are complicated, but essentially they were in a two-car convoy in 4 x 4's. Nerac and Othman were in one vehicle, while Lloyd and Belgian cameraman Daniel Demoustier were in the other, with Demoustier, the only survivor, at the wheel. Both cars were clearly marked with TV symbols.

They were near Al-Zubayr and they were being pursued by Iraqi troops. Demoustier thought the Iraqis might have been trying to give themselves up to the journalists. Subsequent events show the reverse was probably true.

In any event, they took incoming rounds, possibly from U.S. troops ahead of them, as well as from the Iraqis behind them. They were quite clearly in a cross fire. An ITV investigation later concluded the Iraqis had been trying to capture the media crew, then used their presence as a shield to fire at the Americans when they ran into them.

Their car went into a ditch and burst into flames. When he looked across the cabin of the 4 x 4, Demoustier saw that Lloyd's seat was empty and the passenger door was wide open. The cameraman was hurt, but he managed to escape and was picked up by another media crew, who sped off with him on board, at which point he saw Nerac and Othman being taken out of their vehicle alive and well by Iraqi soldiers. He never saw Lloyd again.

Later, U.S. troops said they had fired on vehicles marked "TV," which were among Iraqi troops, fearing suicide bombers may have been using vehicles disguised as those of a media crew.

Six months later, an Iraqi civilian emerged to say that he had been driving some of his country's soldiers to the hospital in a civilian minibus and had picked up Terry Lloyd, who was wounded in the shoulder and was pretending to be a Russian journalist, possibly to protect himself. Lloyd, he said, was actually killed when a U.S. helicopter gunship strafed the bus. He took Lloyd's body on to the hospital in Baghdad. Eventually, a post-mortem in the UK showed Terry Lloyd had two wounds, either of which could have been fatal. One was from an Iraqi round, the other from a U.S. bullet.

It seems Nerac and Othman may have been handed over to Saddam's version of the SS, a sinister group called the Fedayeen, and were shot out of hand. The Fedayeen went on to become the core of the Ba'athist insurgency in the months and years to follow.

I found myself in a ruck of an argument with an ITV correspondent just a few months after Terry's death. It went along roughly the same lines as my argument over the death of Mazen Dana. The scars of loss and mourning for their hero Terry were still fresh for ITV staffers and one of them, another well-known face on the television, was trying to give me a beasting over his death.

"You military," he said, "you're all the fucking same. Trigger-happy fuckers. Terry should never have died. He should never have been shot. His car was clearly marked with 'TV' all over it. Then he was finished off in a civilian bus. It's obscene."

Well, he was right: War is obscene. By then, he'd had a couple of drinks, and although I wasn't particularly looking for an argument, I couldn't let what he'd said go unchallenged.

I told him then and I say it again now: Terry Lloyd and his crew should never have been in the position they found themselves in during a full-on battle. Not only that. They should never have been in the field without a PMC team to advise and protect them. The truth is that they made themselves hostages to fortune by making up their own rules of engagement on the hoof.

I never met him, but if he could speak to us, I believe that Terry Lloyd would probably acknowledge that he pushed his luck and then it ran out. I don't care how experienced a correspondent is in front-line coverage; he is not a soldier and he cannot fully understand why events take the turns they do or what is propelling the course of fortune on a battlefield. It's tough enough for a battle-hardened soldier to do that, and only the best of them can really see much at all through the fog of war.

I'm not saying that if I had been there, they'd all have lived. But I am saying that if I'd been with them, I doubt whether they'd have gotten caught in that lethal cross fire in the first place.

The fury of ITV staff and executives is futile. Do they think that an Apache helicopter pilot can't see men in military uniform clambering into a seemingly civilian vehicle? Do they think it's impossible for a helo pilot who's looking through enhanced sights to see military uniforms through the side windows of a bus?

I've not had the benefit of speaking to the Iraqi who picked Terry Lloyd up, but I think he's a very lucky man, because it's been my experience that when an attack helicopter turns its attention on a target, it's almost inevitably curtains. Just a single burst from a .20-caliber machine gun will rip a vehicle into a blazing wreck and shred everything inside it.

What I'm trying to say is that Terry Lloyd was moving independently across the battlefield; they call it "busking it" in the media. You cannot send a brave cavalier dashing around the place and expect him to be immortal. You cannot expect dreadful things not to happen. What you can do is pay him proper respect, mourn him, and learn from his death.

It seems that in the fog of war, both sides fired at him in a civilian vehicle, but bleating about which of two bullets killed him and which side was more responsible for his death is a fruitless exercise. I believe his superiors would do better to reflect upon whether they should have allowed him to go where he did in the first place without military experts at his shoulder.

It's impossible to say what might have happened if these men had had some top operators guarding them, but I have a strong feeling that the pursuing Iraqis would not have been chasing a 4 x 4 that was capable of returning accurate fire.

I'm sure that privately the company learned the lesson of Terry Lloyd's death. They decreed that ITV crews from then on never traveled without top military operators watching their backs. If that alone was his legacy, I know for a fact that some of the ITV colleagues who followed Terry had their lives preserved by the actions of their PMC call-sign groups.

A Note of Advice to Wanna-be War Reporters

I think at this point there's some basic advice I'd offer to any journalist going to a place like Iraq for the first time. I'd counsel that person to think very hard about whether going is really the right thing to do at all.

We've all got different personalities and some people will never settle into any sort of comfortable existence within a war zone. If you're not absolutely certain, then my advice is not to go.

There is no shame whatsoever in saying that you don't want to put your life on the line and turning down a war-zone assignment. However, it would be a shame if when you got there, you were in such a state of fear that you became a burden and a danger to your colleagues. Better not to go.

Chris Ayres, a journalist who reports for the *Times* of London, wrote a hilarious account of his unwilling days as an embedded war correspondent paralyzed with fear in Iraq in 2003. *War Reporting for Cowards* describes the dilemma perfectly, and it's worth a read.

When you've made the decision to accept a war-zone assignment, there are a number of things you should then address. The first decision you should make is to go on a good course that will give you at least a certain amount of acclimatization to military jargon and the world of the PMC. More important, you will be subjected to simulated attacks during such a course, and this will introduce you to the shocking flash-bang world of a terrorist ambush in a controlled environment. A simulated attack is never like the real thing, but it is an introduction that could save your life, and the instructor will run you through the options you would have were you to be in an ambush. You'll also be taught how to survive if you're separated from your team during an encounter and given some basic advice on how to keep your wits about you if you're captured. You should also be taught how to use a GPS navigation system and basic radio communications and signals protocols.

Situation awareness is very important in a hostile environment like Iraq. You'd be taught how to recognize that different situations present their own particular threats, such as the approaching flash point of an angry crowd or the aggressive, hostile driving that distinguishes the insurgent pursuing you. Allied to that would be the ability to recognize an IED (an improvised explosive device). That's very important knowledge if you want to avoid having your arse blown over your head.

Off-road driving and a few escape driving techniques are also useful skills to have in your locker, and it's well worth learning some of the tricks of the trade.

A vital part of any course should be trauma medicine. If you are attacked when you get to Iraq, you may not have the skills to fight back, but you can have the skills to staunch and dress a bleeding wound. That way, you may save a life and you won't feel like you've been a burden during combat. This type of training ensures you will be a useful member of the team above and beyond your own media skills.

I now run training courses for PMCs and I also give courses tailored for businessmen and journalists through my company, Ronin Concepts. We do a lot of work in the UK but also travel to Eastern Europe, where we're allowed to do live-fire training with AKs and machine guns.

Naturally, I think my course is the best available. But truthfully, there are others out there offering the same comprehensive war-zone training, and a couple of them are run by excellent men with a background similar to mine.

It's vital that you attend a course if you're serious about surviving a war-zone assignment. There is no substitute for a properly developed course run by professionals and certified by the official watchdog in Britain, the Security Industry Authority.

The next thing you should do is to check your insurance situation and make sure that your company has you adequately covered for combat situations. That's particularly important for freelances who may be sent to cover for a big company.

Check your blood group and have it and any other important relevant medical information recorded on a dog tag and keep the tag around your neck. If you're going to a country where HIV is prevalent, you can get an AIDS pack with needles, lines, et cetera, which can be used if you are wounded. In this way, you can avoid using possibly contaminated local hospital gear.

Most media people do their background briefing in detail and will have boned up on a country's politics, geography, and culture before they get to the airport, but remember to think about surrounding countries. Get entry visas for as many of the neighboring countries of the one you're assigned to as you can. They could prove lifesavers if you have to pull off a hurried exit strategy, and you never know when a situation might spill over and you'll find the story has moved across a border.

The best journalists I know have their entire kit, including clothing and laptop, in one bag, which they can take on board a plane as hand luggage. Cameramen will sometimes book an extra seat on a flight so their kit doesn't go in the hold. When these men and women arrive at an assignment, they're not watching luggage go around a carousel for an hour. They hit the ground running. So an important rule is always to travel light.

These days, a satellite telephone is a must, but in Iraq it can be used to help you get good intelligence and information from U.S. troops. No subterfuge here—you just operate on the principle that soldiers serving in a foreign country are very likely to be homesick and a free call home to a family member in the States is going to make you a helpful friend.

A more primitive intelligence-gathering tool is a six-pack of beer. Remember, the U.S. Army runs dry; in other words, they don't let their boys drink until they're officially on leave. I found that a few cans of beer or a phone call home could be traded for vital information and the supplies and ammo I needed. It worked like a charm every time.

AUGUST 19, 2003: a terrible scene of carnage and a turning point in the escalating insurgency in Iraq. The UN building in Baghdad lay obliterated in front of us when I arrived at the scene with a UK television crew.

When I look back at that moment, I realize it wasn't just a turning point in the war but also a moment of revelation for people who had not understood that the Al Qaeda psychopaths responsible for this outrage were operating in the dark forests beyond the walls of civilization. If they could hit the personnel of the organization of world governance and peace, they could hit anyone.

And hit them they did with a flatbed truck packed with explosives. The truck was parked right opposite the window of the UN special representative for Iraq, Sérgio Vieira de Mello, when the detonation occurred. The special representative died along with twenty-one other UN workers and scores were injured as their headquarters building, the old Canal Hotel, was obliterated.

The place was in utter chaos, with UN officials staggering around injured or blast-shocked. A lot of local people had found work there as interpreters, secretaries, cleaners, you name it, and crowds of relatives rushed to be there once word got out.

This was a difficult situation to gauge, because in such circumstances there's always the danger of a second device. My inclination was to sit in a cozy spot half a mile away, sipping a cup of tea and waiting to see if there was going to be a second explosion. Life's not like that, though, and the crew needed to film what was in front of them for a piece, so we just had to get on with it. More and more people were arriving at the scene and I can remember there was a great deal of emotional charge in the crowd, more so than usual. I think the ordinary Iraqi people looking on felt a great chunk of hope slipping away with the destruction of the UN headquarters. They'd always seen the UN as an acceptable middle way between the United States and the madmen.

A strange atmosphere develops in other ways at these scenes of annihilation, and as the emergency services set about the long slog of digging casualties out of the wreckage, the media crews settled in to wait for developments. They were hoping for shots of survivors coming out of the rubble, back from the brink of death. Meanwhile, life went on and fruit and drink vendors began to turn up at the scene, selling their wares to the assembled members of the media waiting behind a tape cordon. People began chatting just to pass the time away and I spent time making contacts with PMCs guarding other call-sign groups.

Bizarre as it may seem, a sort of barbecue atmosphere developed. It was surreal. There in front of us was a human and international catastrophe unfolding and we were shooting the breeze about old times, other jobs, and people we knew in common.

The media guys tell me it's something that happens to them all the time. They end up at bombings and sieges and there's nothing to do but kill time. So what do they do? Do they stand there observing a continual silence out of respect for those who have suffered or those who are suffering, or do they chat? They chat.

It wasn't long before the street kids started turning up. There are hundreds of them in Baghdad. Some have been orphaned by Saddam or by one of his wars or by coalition bombing. Others have families, but they've been pushed out of the home because they simply can't be looked after. We saw a lot of them, because they'd hang around the hotels, too, scrounging food and generally grifting and working the street to survive. They would move from one opportunity to another and were always on the lookout for a dollar or a can of Coke. When they rocked up at the UN bombing, we knew their faces and we just fed them. They didn't beg. They were there, we had food, and we shared it with them. It was as simple as that.

Most of them I saw around were addicts who got high on glue. You would see their noses streaming and their eyes ringed red against the brown faces, now turned a putrid green color from the glue. There was a real Dickens feel to the plight of these children. I always thought of them as the Middle Eastern version of Oliver Twist.

One of them was a kid who had a strange name, which we sort of translated into David. I liked him. There was something about him, and on every trip to Baghdad I'd slip him twenty bucks, but I made him agree to give up the glue.

"I will do it, Mr. John," he told me. "I do not like it anyway."

"Okay," I said. "It's good you don't like it, because it will kill you."

"Ah," he said gravely, "but what will kill you, Mr. John?"

A good question, I thought. But it was one I couldn't answer. He'd go off with his money and then the next time I saw him he would show me some clothes or maybe a pair of trainers that he'd bought with the money.

"I have a family, but they do not like me," David told me once. "If I go home, they send me away. They have no money to feed me."

I didn't know what to say to him about his family. How could I comment on the fact they'd pushed their son out onto the street. I simply didn't know what they had to cope with.

David saw I was uncomfortable with the subject and beamed a big smile as he told me, "Don't worry, Mr. John. One day I will have four or five big four-by-four trucks from the General Motor Company and I will hire them to the film crews. I will be very rich and I will have my own family."

David was there that day at the UN building with the rest of the feral street kids and I wondered then what would become of him and his buddies. I hoped he would make something of himself. Maybe, just maybe, he would get his fleet of 4 x 4's. But where would the media crews be then? Perhaps still in Iraq, or maybe they'd have moved on to Pakistan or Indonesia. Who knew where this madness in the world was going to take them. I just hoped that someday David would be ferrying passengers through peaceful streets.

I thought those Baghdad street kids were the story the press never wrote about, the story the TV crews never filmed. The story was right under their noses, but they never saw it. Yet in many ways, it was one of the most important stories in Iraq, where children have suffered so much.

12. Respect

NOVEMBER 5, 2003. IT WAS 3:30 ON A blazing hot desert afternoon on the road from Kuwait to Basra—a far cry from the cold mists and early darkness of fall in Britain. Two ex-Blades were driving a pair of brand-new GMC four-wheel-drive vehicles back to their forward operating base after dropping a couple of clients off in Kuwait City. An hour later, there would be four Iraqi insurgents lying dead on the roadside.

The four bandits/insurgents in a beat-up old Mercedes decided it was their lucky day when they spotted the two smart 4 x 4's moving in a convoy through the unrelenting landscape of shattered rocks. They decided to split the pair of them up and then hammer the man in the second 4 x 4. Bad decision.

The Blade in the first 4 x 4 was a Welsh bloke named Darren, a great guy and a really hard case. On his own, he would have been more than a match for those four and another four like them. But the guy in the 4 x 4 the insurgents were targeting was something else. That vehicle was being driven by a living legend of the SAS, a man whose exploits are feted throughout the world community of Special Forces. He's a Fijian known as "Tak" and he was about to become their nemesis. Picture a muscular, broad-shouldered Polynesian warrior who's polite, soft-spoken, and invariably gentle with his family and friends. But when his fighting blood is roused, Tak is the most terrible of enemies.

Tak told me about the contact himself. It's one of the most spectacular accounts of close-quarter combat I've heard of by a PMC in Iraq and I really can't do better than let him narrate it in his own words.

> *You know what it's like, John. I was a bit uncomfortable with the company's operating procedures and I was thinking of quitting and looking for someone else to work for.*
>
> *I didn't like the business of driving alone in Iraq. You need someone with you because you can't shoot if you need to with your hands on the steering wheel. I thought it was a bad risk. I didn't like the soft-skin 4 x 4's, either, and we had crap weapons and no body armor had been supplied.*
>
> *Anyway, we'd dropped the clients off in Kuwait and we were going back into Iraq for another assignment. At the time, we were spending a couple of days resting in Kuwait; then we'd go back in and hold the ground for five or six days.*
>
> *We went up the Mutla Pass, where the old border post is situated, and then we drove off down Highway Tampa into Iraq. I thought we'd vary the journey, so I called Darren on the radio and suggested we take the old route that runs parallel to Tampa. Basically, we were leaving the motorway to drive on a trunk road. Darren took the lead. It was about 3:30 in the afternoon and we were near the town of Safwan.*
>
> *There's a lot of nothing out there, but we'd gotten well on the way and we had about half an hour of the trip left to do. We were*

*near the oil fields that stretch out towards Kuwait from Basra
and I could see the installations on the horizon.*

*Then we came to a part of the road that does a big S bend
around an old burned-out Gulf War T-42 battle tank. The road
doubles around the tank, then over a bridge above the Highway.
At that point, there's a steep dirt track that serves as an unofficial
slip road between the trunk route and the Highway.*

*A car came up the bank on the track and joined our road
ahead of us. Darren went past them and then they pulled in and
stopped to watch me go past. I tried to look into the car to see if
there were any weapons in evidence, but I couldn't see anything.*

*Then they started off again and went past me before slowing
right down. I came up behind them and then as I went to overtake them, they suddenly veered out in front of me and forced me
to throttle back and fall in behind them again. I thought, well, I'll
just give them the benefit of the doubt, and I tried to overtake
them again.*

*This time, there wasn't any doubt about it, because they didn't
bother with the swerving nonsense; they just fired a burst from
an AK in front of me and I realized I was on the menu. I dropped
back behind them again and I could see AK's popping up everywhere inside their vehicle. Not good.*

*One option would have been to ram them. As you know, John,
we're taught certain ramming techniques in the regiment that
are best not described, for safety reasons. I could have rammed
them and that would have spun them. That would have been
great if Darren had been sitting next to me, ready to shoot them
up as soon as I'd done it. Basically, that would have been game
over, because Darren would have blown them away as they spun,
but he wasn't with me, so I decided that ramming them wasn't
an option.*

Instead, I just whipped the wheel over and drove off into the desert and drove across the rocks and sand about fifteen meters parallel with them. That didn't last long, though, because there were lots of rocks, and though it looked a bit clearer farther over, I reckon my wheels would have gone down into the sand.

I was really concentrating on the driving and cursing the company for their crap one-per-vehicle policy, when suddenly I saw a ridge of rocks ahead of me that I couldn't drive over. I wasn't going anywhere.

I stopped, and when I looked up, I thought, Shit. There standing in front of me were three of the bastards from the car. They'd obviously shot ahead at speed on the tarmac road while I was concentrating on not smashing my vehicle up on the desert. Then they must have just ran across when they saw where I was going and that I'd have no choice but to stop.

I forgot to say that they weren't just standing there nonchalantly. They were firing their weapons from the hip, too. There were AK rounds going everywhere, but none of them was actually hitting me. I'd pulled up on an angle, so most of the rounds were going in on the passenger side.

I had an MP5, a pistol, and an AK on the floor behind my seat. The MP5 is fine for close-quarter work, as it's shorter than a AK, so I just fired a burst through the windshield at them. Then I put it back on my lap.

I don't think they'd realized at first that I'd fired at them, they were so busy doing their own thing, and they were making so much noise that they probably never heard my burst. Maybe they thought it was their rounds that were hitting my windshield. They just kept coming toward me, firing from the hip.

I don't know why, but then it just came to me. I dropped the gun onto my lap and put my hands up as if I was surrendering. They stopped shooting. They were right in front of my hood by then. They must have thought I'd given up, and for an instant they stopped firing. It was all I needed. Just that fraction of a sec-

ond. A hesitation. It was just a blink of time and they probably did blink, too, but by the time they had, the MP5 was back in my hands again.

I fired through the screen and this time two of them dropped. I can remember how they looked. Really surprised. Like, What the hell's happening? This is all going wrong.

They were wearing long gowns, local-style. I think one of them had a shemag wrapped around his head. They just fell down when they were hit. But the third one was standing to one side of my car at an awkward angle and he was still firing. He looked desperate because he'd seen his mates slotted and he knew what had to happen.

I was out of the car as quickly as I could, around the front of the vehicle, and straight at him. I could see the fear in his eyes because he'd seen his mates slotted and he wasn't feeling such a tough guy anymore. But I knew there was no fear in mine. His eyes told the story. He was desperate and he knew that it was him or me. We both knew that.

As I came around the front of the car, I hit him with a shot from the MP5, but he was still standing with his AK and he was firing. I think he was so scared, he was shooting wildly and not hitting me. I kept going and I think he must have hesitated, or maybe he just froze. I was on him before he knew it and then I smashed him with my weapon. I don't know why. I think I'd run out of ammo and I didn't have time to put another magazine in.

I knew I had to get that AK off him and I think it was while I was clubbing him that a round went off from his weapon and hit me in the thigh. At that stage, he'd been so badly clubbed that I don't think he even knew he was shooting. He was in bad shape by that time, so I wrestled the gun off him and finished him with his own AK. Then I walked back to meet Darren, who'd just slotted the driver of the car and was coming to help me.

He drove me to the military hospital in Basra and I was even-

tually flown back to the UK. Luckily, it was just a flesh wound, or I'd have been in big trouble. Those assault rounds from an AK will track right through your body if they hit bone. It's a terrible effect: The presence of harder bone will deflect the round, and instead of going straight through you, it will travel in the most extraordinary way through your body. You could be shot in the leg and the bullet could end up in your lung.

I was lucky and it's fine now. I've been wounded a couple of times before and I've been quite lucky really.

When he'd given me his account, Tak smiled and said, "They got me in the head as well, John."

"What d'ya mean?" I asked.

"Well, quite a few rounds smacked into my bag, which was on the passenger seat beside me and one of them hit right in my passport photograph. I had to go down to the passport office to get a new one, and when I told the girl at the counter what had happened, she asked me, 'Is that what saved you, then?' I just told her, 'I don't think so. I really don't think so.' "

THAT'S TAK'S STORY, but there's more. He's the sort of bloke who should have his history tattooed on his forehead as a warning. That way, those local scumbags would have given him a wide berth and might have lived to fight another day.

Tak was one of the team that stormed the Iranian embassy when those images of the SAS at work went around the world and made the regiment internationally famous. The operation was courageous, cool, superefficient, and very public. But the embassy was not Tak's finest hour, because Tak is also one of the heroes of the Battle of Mirbat. That's the Battle of Mirbat in Oman, not to be confused with the skirmish at the Mirbad Hotel in Basra.

It happened in 1972 and it is one of the most gallant stands ever made by the British Army. It was at dawn on the nineteenth of July that a nine-strong SAS detachment, under the command of Capt. Mike Kealy, fought off four hundred Adoo rebels who'd come down from the hills to attack the port of Mirbat in Dhofar province. The Adoo were tribesmen who'd been indoctrinated into communism and wanted to overthrow the Omani royal family.

The SAS patrol bunkered up in a house near the strategic Wali Fort on a hill above the town with two machine guns and a mortar and fought off wave after wave of Adoo. Tak's fellow Fijian, Sgt. Talaiasi Labalaba, ran five hundred meters to a gun pit at the fort, where he manned an old World War II twenty-five-pound artillery piece to bring it into play against the enemy.

Scores of rebel fighters threw themselves at the fort as both SAS machine guns fired until their barrels were literally white-hot. In the gun pit, Labalaba kept firing shells at zero trajectory straight into the oncoming rebels until he was wounded, at which point Tak went to his aid, running a gauntlet of tracer bullets and mortar shells to dive and roll into the gun pit.

He found Labalaba firing the big gun alone and Tak helped him man the weapon for the rest of the engagement. Tak was hit, but he kept firing the big gun as the rebels reached the edge of the gun pit, and then Labalaba was hit in the neck and killed.

A few more of the boys arrived to help in the gun pit. They were about to be overrun, when twenty-two members of G Squadron appeared on the horizon and stormed in by helo. The rebels were then driven back with the help of air support. The battle had lasted six hours and around eighty-seven Adoo rebels were dead.

When it ended Tak, severely wounded in the back, walked calmly to the helicopter to be lifted out, when most men would have collapsed. His friend lay dead in the gun pit behind him, and no one in the regiment doubts that both Fijians should have been awarded the VC.

Don't forget the Alamo. Davy Crockett got totaled there. But when Mirbat ended, Tak and most of the boys were still standing, and they'd been fighting against the same sort of odds—about forty to one.

One more thing you should know about Tak. When he killed those four insurgents on bonfire night 2003, he was fifty-eight years old. In December 2005, at the age of sixty, he enrolled in my course because new regulations meant he had to have a diploma to be employed as a PMC. Imagine trying to teach a man like him about tactical awareness and close-quarter combat!

And after that contact on the Highway Tampa, some of the guys joked that Tak was still young enough to go out clubbing. What a phenomenal man.

THERE ARE SOME other guys whose work in Iraq I respect. Among them are three young guys whose exploits have earned them the scary epithet "the Horsemen of the Apocalypse." They got the name because of the sheer number of contacts they've survived and the large number of insurgents they've killed in these encounters. I'll call them Andy, Mel, and Cules.

I feel particularly triumphant when I mention the Horsemen, because I actually trained them during my first course in August 2004, then waved them off to Iraq. Mel and Cules were both 1 Para soldiers and served in Sierra Leone with my son, Kurt. Andy was from the SAS Signal Squadron, and when he left the army, he did a variety of barmy jobs, including a spell as a professional bare-knuckle cage fighter in England's West Country. He's a hard case.

They'd only been out there a couple of weeks before they were in a scrape, and that set the tone for these lads, who were involved in shoot-outs and bombings with a regularity that was anything but monotonous.

They tot up contacts with insurgents like other people tot up speeding points on their driving licenses, and to date I think they've been blown up four times (or should I say, there have been four attempts to blow them up) and they've been in over a dozen firefights. They've had four or five vehicles totaled and still emerged from the scrap-heap challenge alive, well, and triumphant. Some people think they're indestructible, and I really hope they are.

It was the Horsemen who got into that sad shoot-out with the lone insurgent that I mentioned earlier in the book who ran from one rocky position to another before he got totalled by an Apache helo. They've had some really wild flash-bang fights, too, and one of them was a police matter.

I T WAS OCTOBER 2004 and the Horsemen were on a routine journey north of Baghdad—that is, if there is such a thing as a routine journey in that corner of the planet. Riding in three armored GMC 4 x 4's, with a gun vehicle in the rear, they were on their way to collect a couple of clients.

An unusually hot wind was blowing off the desert that day and it had left everyone feeling tetchy and short-tempered. That's how they felt when they arrived at a police road check on the outskirts of a one-mule town, but they were going to get a lot more tetchy in the hour that followed.

They pulled up at the VCP (vehicle checkpoint) and went into the usual routine of showing their passes to the cops. There's always a lot of eyeballing and close observation in these situations. To be honest, you find yourself looking into the eyes of everyone you meet in a place like Iraq. You look for the slightest sign of hatred or unease that might tell you that something is going down. It becomes a way of life, that business of looking deep into the eyes, searching for the sign that says friend or foe.

The Horsemen said later that they'd smelled a rat at that road-block, but they'd driven on anyway, because that's what you do: You keep going forward. When they got into the town—which I can't name, for a couple of reasons—they thought it looked a bit deserted, to say the least, and they got that Clint Eastwood tumbleweed feeling. They then saw a group of police officers scuttle into their barracks on the main street as soon as their convoy came into view, which only heightened their suspicions about this shithole.

"See those fuckers," Andy called over the radio.

"Yup," came the reply from Cules.

"Heads up," said Andy, and they all knew what was coming.

Whak! Whak! Whak!

Heavy machine-gun rounds started thumping into the ground to their right and soon these were joined by the chipping, flinty kicks of lighter rounds. A few smacked into the vehicles and the lads immediately pinged the source of the shooting and returned fire.

Mel and Cules unsealed their vehicle and sprinted into a building as the Minimi in the gun vehicle roared a chain-saw reply at the ambush. They were looking for a vantage point to pour shit into their attackers, but then they ran up against fire from the back of the building.

Back onto the street. Pandemonium. A full-scale battle ensued, with the guys smacking rounds into any bastard with a gun who dared give away his position. Six or seven of the insurgents were dead or wounded, but there were others still firing away, and the lads hadn't been able to take out the enemy machine gun, although they had it well suppressed. Time to fuck off and leave the Minimi to say their final farewells.

"Oh fuck my old boots!" Cules was watching the literally depressing sight of the back wheel of the gun vehicle deflating while rounds kept chipping and cracking all around them. It was shredded.

"Bollocks!" Mel had spotted it, too.

"Cover me!" shouted Cules. "I'll sort the fucking thing out!"

"What you gonna do?"

"Change the fucking thing, of course."

Mel shrugged and kept up his fusillade of well-placed shots as he joined the others in keeping the enemy fire suppressed. That's the name of the game: Win the firefight, outshoot the bastards. Don't give them the time to aim. You don't need the time to aim. They do.

Cules had the jack and the spare wheel deployed from the back of the vehicle in record time and was winding the wheel nuts off in a blur. Forget those guys in the Formula One pit stops. Sure, they're really quick, but I won't rate them until I know how fast they can do it under fire. The Horsemen estimate their record stands at about six minutes under continuous fire and that was just two men, remember. Perhaps there's a challenge here some-where, but somehow I can't see the Ferrari team taking it up.

Cules slammed the fresh wheel on, screwed nuts in a way that suggested his life actually did depend on it, then dropped the jack under the vehicle and chucked it into the back of the gun wagon before hurling the flat tire in alongside it.

"Get that fucking thing out," yelled Gus, the man on the Minimi, as the tire slammed into this weapon and threw his gun off target, sending rounds tearing down the main street just past Cule's shoulder. Cules grabbed the wheel back, and this time he tossed it up onto the big metal rack on top of the vehicle, where it slid around on the roof as they roared out of town and carried on toward the base.

By now, the incoming was thinning out as the sheer weight of fire from the call-sign group vehicles bore down on the ambush, but to drive on through the town would have been a bad move.

Then as they flashed past the police station, a red mist descended over Andy's eyes and he called out on the system, "Wait one. Contact right." The convoy skidded to a halt and Andy raked the front of the police station with about two hundred rounds. Windows popped, masonry flew out in lumps, and the front door was splintered as the rounds smacked into the facade. "That'll teach those arseholes to set us up," he snarled.

TIKRIT IS SADDAM'S HOMETOWN. It's where his clan live, it's the heart of his old power base, and it's full of Ba'ath party pigs who fed at the trough of his regime while the rest of the people suffered. It's not a place where you'd want to buy a time-share.

The Horsemen were driving through town one day and found themselves bowling along the long, straight piece of dual carriageway on the eastern side of the city. They'd been shuttling clients around the area for most of the day in armored 4 x 4's and, as you can imagine, they were on a high state of alert.

As they rattled down the carriageway at a considerable speed, Cules noticed an old white Japanese sedan standing stationary at a strange angle, about the width of a car out from the pavement. Its position gave it a view straight down the road for at least half a mile, and the lads immediately pinged it as suspicious. Not only that but one of them, sharp as fuck, had noticed it earlier in the day.

"Same car as this morning," he sang out on the radio.

No doubt, then, that this was a dicker's car, and the way it was lined up suggested there was more to come—a lot more.

Then they saw another dark sedan parked by the side of the road on a long, empty stretch, with nothing next to it but a length of two-meter-high concrete wall. Why would someone park there? What are they doing? Visiting a section of wall? Don't think so. These thoughts went through Mel's mind in a rapid-fire calculation and then a couple of voices came to the same inevitable conclusion, delivered over the radio at the same time.

"Kamikaze!"

Simultaneously, the rear gunner spotted a gunman on a high-rise building to his left and began firing burst after burst. A split second later, their front windshield was crazed by the massive orange flash of an explosion as the car bomb to their right was detonated and the dark sedan erupted.

Cules was at the wheel and won the battle to keep the car on the road, then drove it right out of the killing ground of the ambush the insurgents had laid on for them. Incoming fire poured at them, but even though they'd just driven straight through a bomb blast, the guys had the presence of mind to ping the firing positions of the enemy.

"Right! Right! Right!" Andy screamed, and concentrated bursts of fire poured from the vehicle that the insurgents had hoped would be a mangled wreck full of shattered bodies. Wrong. The Horsemen rode on, and they reckon four insurgents were killed or wounded in their return of fire. This contact was all the more remarkable because the whole thing was filmed by one of those dashboard cameras that traffic cops use.

Two of the Horsemen are still riding the Highway, but Cules decided to call it a day. I asked him why when I next saw him.

"It's not that I'm scared or anything, John," he said. "I really can't put my finger on it, but I think it's just that I've had enough of being blown up all the time."

Fair point. The Horsemen have my respect and my admiration, but there are those who didn't make it, and I salute them, too.

IT WAS MAY 2005 and a convoy in western Iraq was hit by the Al Qaeda group called the Army of Ansar al-Sunna. It was an effective ambush and one of the guys was cut off from the rest and outnumbered. He was surrounded and held at gunpoint as the convoy limped away, leaving him to his fate, as the clients' lives were given priority.

These so-called men must have thought they were in for some hostage fun. But this was no ordinary man they'd captured. This was Akihiko Saito, a modern samurai who'd served in Japan's First Airborne Brigade before enlisting in the French Foreign Legion. The bristling AK-47s of the Fedayeen didn't subdue Saito, and he chose death rather than the indignity of prolonged torture followed by a beheading.

Although he was badly wounded, he pulled a concealed automatic weapon out of his vest and used it on his captors, wounding two of them. He had only so much gas in his tank, and with his wounds, they were able to nail him with a burst of fire. He took many more rounds, but still he refused to die.

Instead, the terrorists dragged him off, beating him without mercy as they fled the scene before the approaching U.S. quick reaction force team arrived. Akihiko died later of his wounds and his body was eventually recovered by U.S. troops.

Later, the Ansar al-Sunna released a video of his broken body. The video, filmed at the time, was accompanied by a commentary replete with Islamic propaganda. These were just babbling words from empty vessels compared to the indefatigable courage of Akihiko Saito.

I'd met him briefly sometime before his death. He was a polite, reserved man whose manner befitted his culture, but even then I thought he had the haunted look of a ronin, a samurai without a lord—the original Japanese mercenary. Respect.

13. Changing Times

THE YEAR IS 2015 AND THE MIGHTY UNITED States is still the world's dominant force, thanks to the development of new hydrogen fuels and gene technology. The war against terror continues unabated and the U.S. president feels compelled to act against a fundamentalist state harboring terrorists somewhere in the Middle East.

More shock and awe as the U.S. Air Force strikes with pinpoint accuracy at several terrorist bases. Ground troops are inserted under the umbrella of air strikes to hit at specific targets and to hold a key town on the country's border. It's not a Special Forces raid, but a much larger endeavor, a medium-size invasion.

The general image of the troops is similar to what we saw during the Iraq war. There are a few differences, though. The helmet design has been changed to incorporate a micro night-vision and target-designation kit as standard. And more of the soldiers' bodies are now encased in a new suit of lightweight molded ceramic body armor, so that they look like twenty-first-century plastic knights.

But there's another much more fundamental difference outside the realms of technology, because this U.S. force is not made up of good old boys from the States. It's a unit of highly paid PMCs whose allegiance is not to the president or to the Stars and Stripes, but to a binding contract with the Pentagon. Some specialists have negotiated lucrative individual contracts, but most of the soldiers are hired out by companies from around the world— Brits, Germans, French, Italians, Aussies and Kiwis, probably quite a few South Africans, Ghurkas, and Fijians: a global rental army.

They will have a few things in common: complete fighting skills, great experience in war zones, and excellent English so that they would fit in seamlessly to the command structure of the client state. And loyalty? Of course loyalty. Loyalty to their comrades and loyalty to their ideals of soldierly behavior. Loyalty to the contract. People might prefer patriotism as a motive for military service and some of history's greatest heroes have been patriots. But for every one of them, there have been hundreds of willing conscripts who, with the best will in the world, will always be better clerks than commandos. They call them "cannon fodder."

No room for fodder in the mercenary army, though. Just fighters. You can imagine, too, how they might be organized in the American style, along the lines of major-league football teams. The British contingent would probably be called the Bulldogs, with a suitably Churchillian emblem; you might have the Everest Gurkhas and the Kangaroos, too. These legions might even get ad deals, industry sponsorship, and product-placement contracts. They'd probably get win bonuses, too.

Far-fetched? Not at all, and some of the best minds in the

Pentagon see the PMC option as a model for the front-line American forces of tomorrow. They think the U.S. Army of the future will be like the Spanish army of the fourteenth and fifteenth centuries, which was a mercenary army filled with the best fighters recruited from all over Europe and paid for by Aztec gold and Incan silver brought back to Spain in treasure galleons from South America. From my conversations with U.S. Army officers and with leaders of the PMC companies, it's an option that is firmly in the Pentagon's future thinking.

Who knows? By then, advances in DNA science will see suitable recruits with the right profile given gene therapy that will build muscle and courage, too, so that SAS or Delta Force selections become a dawdle. I doubt that somehow, but I do believe the battlefield will be dominated by drones in the air and the increasing presence of robots and remote-controlled fighting machines. And like the fighting men alongside the machines in the U.S. new-model army, it's probable that they'll be on hire from PMC companies. But to understand completely what may come in the future, we should first look at the past.

S OME HISTORIANS BELIEVE that the profession of mercenary soldier is the second-oldest in the world. Certainly there have been stories and accounts of mercenary soldiers fighting for pay since Egyptian times, right through the Greek and Roman eras. They were even employed in ancient Mesopotamia, the country now called Iraq.

Britain has had its fair share of mercenaries in its history, too, and during medieval times knights with a weapon for hire were literally free lances.

The emperors of Byzantium based in Constantinople used to hire mercenaries as their personal bodyguards, and a Viking chief,

Harald Hardrada, was one of them. After taking part in eighteen battles, Hardrada became head of the Imperial Guard. He next fetched up in Yorkshire, where King Harold of England defeated his Viking army at the Battle of Stamford Bridge in 1066. A few weeks later, Harold was shot in the eye after marching his army from Yorkshire down to the Battle of Hastings. No wonder the English lost to William of Normandy and his knights; they must have been exhausted!

Many of the legendary longbow archers who wreaked such havoc on the French at Agincourt for King Henry V were actually paid-to-fight Welshmen. Those blokes were more likely to have cried "For enough silver to buy a new flock of sheep" than "For England, Harry, and Saint George."

At around the same time, the city-states of Italy were employing mercenaries, called *condottieri* to fight their battles for them, and it was the particular excesses of rape and robbery perpetrated by these men that began to give the trade a bad name.

Look at modern Switzerland, home of neutrality, the cuckoo clock, expensive chocolate, and secret bank accounts. Hard to imagine, but in the sixteenth century it was a ragged-arsed, landlocked rural society that barely managed to survive from one Alpine winter to the next. The hard life made them into hard men who became more than handy with eighteen-foot-long pikes, which proved to be a deadly riposte to cavalry charges. Naturally, those pikemen were in demand, and so the solution to Switzerland's dire economic straits was to hire out their soldiers to surrounding countries as mercenaries. To this day, we can see Swiss citizens who are still formally hired out to the Vatican as mercenaries and who swear an oath to protect the pope. They call them the Swiss Guard and they're a familiar sight on TV reports of papal ceremonies.

So it went down through the ages. In the fourteenth century, hard-bitten mercenaries formed "free companies" to fight in the Hundred Years' War between France and England, sometimes on both sides. The most famous of them was the White Company, commanded by Sir John Hawkwood, whose exploits became a byword in courageous fighting. Another was formed by a Welshman, Owain of the Red Hand, who presumably got his name because his hand had been steeped in blood. Red Hand fought for the French against the English before he was assassinated by a Scot named John Lamb. A Scotsman hired to kill a Welshman by the English. Mercenary warfare was a dirty game in those days, make no mistake.

In the sixteenth century, bands of colorful and highly skilled mercenaries, known as Landsknechts, dominated fighting forces throughout Europe. The Spanish employed them during the Eighty Years' War, which they fought to keep possession of the Low Countries, the nations we now call the Netherlands and Belgium. These were the best of the soldiers from various European countries. They were British, German, French, Scandinavian, Tyrolean, and Italian, and the only qualifications they needed were skill with arms and undaunted courage.

But it was during this period of history that the concept of nationhood was becoming more defined as the power in various countries shifted from the sovereign and his God-given rights to the people in general and the rich in particular. Eventually, revolutions in France and Italy in the eighteenth century, together with the amalgamation of a lot of princedoms to form the huge state of Germany in the nineteenth, accelerated this process. The Industrial Revolution, which gave rise to a new class of powerful business interests, sealed it as war became a means of protecting trade, an engine of the economy, and the endgame of failed diplomacy.

There were still some mercenary adventures. The East India

Company conquered India for the English Crown by using an army of hired guns who wore the company's uniform. Then Britain's colonies in North America rebelled and King George, short of manpower, paid for a thirty thousand–strong Hessian army from his native land to fight George Washington's own Continental Army. The mercenaries lost, and ironically it is now the U.S. Army, founded by Washington himself, that is hiring a similar number of PMC fighters in Iraq because they're the ones short of manpower now.

But in the nineteenth century, the tide turned decisively against mercenary armies. At the end of the eighteenth century, the French came up with a new idea for creating a modern army: conscription, or *la levée en masse.* In Britain, conscription was referred to as the call-up, or National Service. In the United States, it is called the draft.

Allegiance to the flag and nation became the order of the day and patriotism the motive for fighting. Now governments could call their citizens to arms, on pain of imprisonment if they didn't show up. Generals could have all the soldiers they wanted, and guess what? The cost was mere peanuts.

Imagine the course of World War I, the so-called Great War, if those mule-headed, ignorant generals had been obliged to rely on mercenaries to fight it. I'm pretty sure that the idea of trench warfare would never have gotten off the ground. Months bogged down in a hole, staring at your enemy across no-man's-land, then a catastrophic burst of action, with countless thousands dying in each battle. Fine, as long as the generals had a stream of conscripts to waste on their nonsense, but not if the government had to pay for it. They'd have soon dreamed up something a bit more efficient.

Of course, to keep the conscripts coming, they had to play up the jingoistic elements of war and paint those prepared to fight for money as real villains. Words such as *rape* and *pillage* were attached to the term *mercenary*, but throughout the ages mercenary soldiers tended to behave no worse, and generally a lot better, than official state troops. In fact, it's been huge national armies that have perpetrated the worst outrages on civilians. You don't have to look any further than the chillingly efficient army of Nazi Germany during World War II. They butchered millions of civilians and no one had to pay them any overtime to do it.

IT WAS DURING the breakup of European colonies following the end of World War II and the onset of the Cold War that the mercenary soldier attracted fresh disdain. The world was awash with ideologies, most of them left of center, and the idea of a soldier who fought for money was firmly linked to concepts of fascism and colonialism.

Africa then became the stamping ground of a new breed of mercenaries, and their client base was relatively straightforward. It tended to be the newly independent African leaders or their opposition in exile. Wars and conflagrations paid for by blood diamonds ebbed and flowed across the continent and mercenaries were often employed to train the opposing armies and sometimes to lead them in battle.

Mercenaries from many European countries flocked to fight for the Biafrans during the Nigerian Civil War, which lasted for three years, ending in a mess in 1970. British soldier Mike Hoare was heavily involved in the Congo crisis of the 1960s and in a failed coup on the holiday islands of the Seychelles in 1981.

Then the former Portuguese colony of Angola became the favorite destination of mercenaries in the 1970s. There they were fighting for the FNLA against the MPLA in the long-running civil war. The LA in the names of both factions stood for Liberation of

Angola; one faction was the National Front and the other the Popular Movement. Who gave a fuck?

When they were captured, the white mercenaries in Angola got short shrift. Nine were jailed for a long time and four, three Brits and an American, were executed. Among those topped on the gallows in a high-profile case was Costas Georgiou, the self-styled "Colonel Callan," who had served in the British Army. A charismatic French figure, Bob Denard, was also involved in numerous plots in Africa, the last of which was a failed coup in the Comoros in 1995.

This was the era of the "dogs of war" and the "wild geese," made famous in movies, and it continued in later years with the interventions by well-organized PMC forces in Sierra Leone in the 1990s. Then in March 2004, the latest African adventure ended with the arrest of a former SAS officer, Simon Mann, in Zimbabwe. Apparently Mann was hell-bent on a coup in Equatorial Guinea. Famously, Sir Mark Thatcher, Lady Thatcher's son, was implicated in that plot.

Meanwhile, the Soviet system collapsed in Russia as the Warsaw Pact folded like the house of cards it had always, in reality, been. Millions of troops were redundant around the world and the best of them looked for work that involved their professional skills.

In Russia, a lot of them became involved in organized crime, and many Muslims who'd been trained in the Soviet era made their expertise available to the growing Islamic revolution. In South America, former intelligence agents and some Special Forces soldiers allied themselves with drug cartels and narcoterrorists in a bid to make a fortune. In Britain and South Africa, both homes of well-trained and highly experienced Special Forces, companies were sprouting up and vying for position while looking for the main chance. They were in the United States, too, and the first major PMC contracts handed out by the Pentagon were to support and supply firms in their ill-fated incursion into Somalia and the Horn of Africa.

But the big opportunity opened up in May 2003 when the forerunner of the CPA in Iraq, a body known as the Office of Reconstruction and Humanitarian Assistance, gave the British company Global Risk Strategies a contract to protect their staff and assess the potential risks they would face.

It was like turning on a tap. The floodgates were open as PMCs became official in the war zone, and the number of PMCs began to rise exponentially in line with the intensifying of the insurgency, until it leveled off at around forty thousand and stayed there. Practically all the protection work in the country was then hived off to the private sector, with the CPA itself and also the British Foreign Office hiring guns to protect their diplomats. That worked down from the tip of the pyramid, so that everything and everyone moving across the landscape that wasn't a coalition combat force had a PMC guard.

It's natural that with the growth of such a huge force there came concerns, and those concerns centered on the chain of command and the accountability of PMCs. True enough, most PMCs in Iraq operated in a vacuum, where U.S. citizens in particular, who made up most of their number, could not be touched by American law and were more or less given carte blanche by the CPA. Some U.S. lawyers have even gone so far as to describe PMCs working in Iraq as falling into the same legal no-man's-land as the unlawful combatants being held at Guantánamo Bay.

Certainly some of the interrogators at Abu Ghraib prison involved in those notorious humiliation tortures were never prosecuted, while their serving army counterparts faced courts-martial. Very galling for the troops. These are issues that need clarifying by U.S. legislators and international bodies.

But as democratic processes began to be implemented and a fledgling Iraqi government started to take shape, then a greater degree of regulation was established, and by August 2005, it was the Iraqi administration that was licensing PMCs and the weapons they carried. The rules of engagement still entitled

PMCs to fire at Iraqi civilian vehicles they believed posed a threat on the Highway, the practice I described earlier in the book as common among the big American companies.

Ironically, though, it was video of this practice carried out by personnel of a British company, Aegis, that surfaced on a Web site. They were working on U.S. contracts in accordance with U.S. rules of engagement, but personally I thought film of vehicles, with no weapons visible inside them, being shot up was a dreadful advertisement. As I watched, I couldn't help thinking, What if that was my country and it was my insurance claims going up in smoke? I found myself wondering who the driver of the shot-up vehicle might be. Perhaps it was an ordinary bloke rushing to the hospital with a sick child. Whoever the person was, I don't reckon that shooting him up on a whim was sensible or fair, and I'm certain that Lt. Col. Tim Spicer, who runs the company, would agree with me. He's a decent and honorable man and has been a strong voice in advocating the cause of PMCs. As it turned out, he acted promptly, sacking all those involved.

I hear that he's since presided over a root and branch cleaning out of the bad elements in his corporation. I should hope so, too. Pity the bosses of Blackwater don't put their hands up, admit the way they've been operating is worse than a disgrace, and sort out the fucking mess they've caused. Much more about them later.

Some companies use a special round called the Hatton, which is basically wax and lead powder. When a Hatton round is fired at a car radiator grille, it gives it a hell of a smack and lets the driver know that a nervous man with a gun doesn't want him coming any closer. A better option, I think.

Another layer of irony in that story is the fact that it was Aegis that won a multimillion-dollar contract from the CPA to collate and monitor information on the number and types of PMCs who were working in Iraq as the mercenary gold rush ran away with itself.

But glitches and complaints aside, the plain fact is that PMCs are here to stay, and this was recognized even before the Iraq War by the

British government, which published a parliamentary consultation document, known in the UK as a "Green Paper," on the issues.

Of course, it wasn't just the moral issues that led to this move by the Foreign Office. Even before the Iraq situation, the companies were making shedfulls of dollars, and the British tradition links registration inexorably with taxation. In other words the government wanted to get a handle on every UK citizen involved in PMC work, then take them for as much money as they could.

So by 2005, it was ruled that anyone in the UK who wants to work as a PMC has to attend a course properly approved by the Security Industry Authority, which suddenly found itself thrown from regulating nightclub doormen to dealing with really hardcore military types—a whole new ball game.

But all the criticism and academic suspicion of the PMC industry don't address the problems. It's up to governments, not companies, to provide an acceptable set of national and international regulations as a proper template for any industry, including the mercenary industry.

What's certain is that the reality of PMC power that we've seen in Iraq is the one that is now accepted as the way forward by the military and political establishment of the world's leading power, the United States. It's not going to go away.

But there's more to it than that and to examine some of the strongest arguments for a well regulated and ethically motivated international pool of PMCs we have to go back to Africa and back into the heart of darkness.

IN 2005, at a refugee camp near Bunia in the Congo, two senior UN officials were inspecting the camp, looking for evidence that soldiers in the peacekeeping force had been sexually abusing the women, girls, and boys, whom they'd been charged to protect.

As they walked near the perimeter fence, the investigators heard a child sobbing. They continued toward the sound and soon the reason for the young girl's distress became evident. Lurched over her body and engaged in a filthy act of forced sex was a UN soldier. No doubt about it. He was in uniform and his UN blue beret lay on the ground beside his victim.

I'm sure the investigators were shocked to find such a graphic illustration of the allegations, literally under their noses, but I doubt that they were surprised. The allegations of pedophile activities and systematic rape by UN troops in the Congo are legion.

I know the Congo well. Remember the incident during the pay strike at the diamond mine? It's a country that has been ravaged by civil war on and off for the past forty years. War there is like the weather. Some years, it's better than others.

For six years, civil war had not been the only problem plaguing the Congo. The area had also become a focus for the ambitions and rivalries of neighboring countries. Militias from Zimbabwe, Rwanda, Angola, Namibia, and Uganda were all fighting like cats for a share of the Congo's enormous and barely tapped mineral wealth. Diamonds are the obvious magnet drawing outside support, but there's also coltan. It's a rare mineral that few have heard about, but everyone who uses a computer or a mobile phone will have a chip of coltan inside their high-tech equipment. It's valuable stuff. Valuable enough to be yet another curse on the suffering people of the Congo.

So you'd imagine they'd have been happy to see the clear sky blue color of the UN coming to their aid. Instead, these poor refugees were subject to more abuse, as ten thousand troops from fifty nations in the MONUC (United Nations Mission in the Democratic Republic of the Congo) force proved to be just another curse on the displaced and vulnerable people of the country. The Moroccan troops had apparently been at the forefront of the sexual abuse, but they were not alone.

Vulnerable women and children wanting food, shelter, and protection found themselves having to pay for it in a currency that the UN and international experts termed *survival sex.* That's literally what it is: They are forced to have sex if they are to survive. What a disgusting concept and what a filthy disease the UN peacekeeping force has turned out to be.

One or two officials whose rampant sexual excesses could not be ignored were removed and tried, but hundreds of allegations were swept under the carpet. A terrible situation, you'll agree, but hang on; there's more. You see, it's not just the Congo where such practices occur. For decades, the UN peacekeeping forces have been arriving in stricken countries, where people need their help, like a plague of sexual locusts.

There are around seventy thousand UN troops serving in sixteen peacekeeping missions in sixteen countries around the globe. In Liberia, Sierra Leone, Ivory Coast, and Burundi, there are similar allegations of the peacekeepers turning into sexual predators.

In Cambodia during the 1990s, the presence of UN peacekeepers saw an explosion in the number of Thai brothels opening up in the country and, with them, the arrival of HIV and AIDS. The UN's top official in Cambodia at the time, a Japanese diplomat, shrugged off the depravity with this unforgettably cynical phrase: "Oh well, boys will be boys."

In East Timor, there was a similar phenomenon, with Thai prostitutes flocking into the country and bringing AIDS with them. The hookers didn't have any problems with scheduled flights into the war-torn country. They were flown in courtesy of UN pilots on transit planes meant to be carrying humanitarian relief.

In Africa, the UN maxim is "The younger, the better." After all, a ten-year-old girl is less likely to be carrying the HIV virus than her mother. The legacy of misery this cynical abuse leaves in its wake is obvious, but there's another effect that makes me want to spit.

In another corner of Africa, the Sudanese government is actively encouraging and probably sponsoring militia attacks on refugee camps. It's an overtly racist, ethnic cleansing carried out by Arab militia members, who often travel on camels over tracts of desert to attack the black refugees cowering in camps in Darfur.

Once again, the UN has sat on its hands and allowed this to go on. When the subject of a peacekeeping force to protect the camps was raised, the Sudanese government threw its hands up in horror and declared, "No! The UN soldiers will bring AIDS into the country."

Well, they had a point, didn't they, and the propaganda victory was handed to them on a plate by the tarnished history of the United Nations.

LARGE-SCALE and serious sex crimes are one part of the equation. The second is the totally ineffective nature of the UN's military capability.

Once again, the examples are too many to list here, but the paralysis of Dutch troops during the massacre at Srebrenica, in Bosnia, is one of the most shocking, because they were not useless troops. Those Dutch lads were well trained and tough. I suspect it was a virus of political dithering sent down the line from their bosses in the Hague that paralyzed the Dutch troops. We'll probably never know the cause of it, but sadly, we do know the effect.

Rwanda is another example. Half a million people were murdered there and the UN couldn't even muster a decent reconnaissance force to let the world know what was going on. Kofi Annan was in charge of the UN in Rwanda, and at one point he advocated a last-ditch solution. Hire PMCs, he urged his bosses in New York. Not a chance was the reply.

Kofi Annan then sat as the UN's secretary-general, and after impotently watching over the Rwanda genocide, he helped set up what I call the Iraq oil for cash policy, which handed Saddam and his Ba'athists the billions of dollars that are now funding the insurgency. So the people of Iraq were twice robbed by the UN— once by the corrupt UN officials who made millions helping Saddam nick the cash, then a second time when the money robbed them of the chance for peace. Nice one, Kofi.

To my mind, there are fundamental problems with the concepts of UN peacekeeping forces, and I have closely watched them working on a number of occasions around the world. The first problem is the quality of the troops, which ranges from the top quality troops provided by countries like Britain and Norway right down to the dregs of illiterate Moroccan conscripts in the Congo. Don't get me wrong. The developing nations have some crack troops, but do you think the king of Morocco, faced with an Islamic revolution, is going to send his best lads to the Congo? Not a chance.

Look at India and Pakistan. They have some of the best soldiers on the planet, thanks, I'd suggest, to the way they are organized and trained along British lines. Are they likely to make these guys available for UN duties when on one side they have Sikh separatists and on the other Pakistanis are chasing Al Qaeda around the tribal territories?

On top of that, India and Pakistan are in a tense standoff with each other in the mountains of the Hindu Kush and Kashmir. We know what their best men are going to be doing, and it isn't UN peacekeeping.

The second problem is politics. It would take a cleverer man than I to unravel the tangled bird's nest of international collaborations, trade interests, and treaties that seem to introduce inertia into the responses of UN troops. Often countries just won't send help if it doesn't suit their alliances. Sometimes they do, but they seem to want to place troops only in a particular trouble spot to throw a spanner in the works.

The third problem I've already spoken about, and that's accountability. Virtually no one has been held accountable for the sex crimes of UN peacekeepers, yet academics who object to PMCs constantly bat on about the lack of accountability of military corporations.

Back to Africa and Sierra Leone in 1995, when a rebel army was roasting innocent people alive and had begun the hand chopping of innocent victims that was to be their hallmark for nearly a decade. The country's rulers were desperate to restore order, and as no one else was helping, they hired the South African PMC Company Executive Outcomes. The company brought in 250 crack soldiers and a small wing of helicopter gunships for air support, and within eleven days they'd pushed the rebels into the jungle, away from the Koidu diamond mines and away from vulnerable civilians. Interestingly, the Sierra Leone government was broke at the time, so they just paid Executive Outcomes with a diamond-mining concession, which gave the company even more cash and influence.

In 1998, the PMCs were back again after another coup by rebels and the company Sandline, run by Tim Spicer, regained the country once more for the legitimate government. International dithering and a shoddy UN peacekeeping force let the rebels get a foothold again and it was left to official UK troops and 1 Para to end it in the Operation Barras attack on the West Side Boys.

The point is that PMCs had quickly and efficiently sorted out a horrific situation and restored a lawful government to power with main force, well applied by fine troops. The UN, on the other hand, has proved time and time again that it has neither the quality of troops nor the political will to be decisive. Not only that; such troops are more expensive than PMCs, largely because that lack of drive and will on the part of the UN means that the troops on the ground do not get the job done quickly enough. Neither are they well controlled or attended to; they waste and steal at an astonishing rate. When I was in Bosnia, for instance, I saw that the main preoccupation of some of the UN troops seemed to be the theft and export of UN Land Rovers for resale in their home countries.

Let's apply this to the Darfur genocide in Sudan. Indiscriminate rapes and killings at refugee camps are met with a total lack of action. Strong words of condemnation issue from the UN headquarters in New York, but no action. Isn't it just possible that if the UN didn't have to send its own troops and could mandate for a PMC force to do the job instead, then things would happen?

Once there was a UN resolution put in place to protect these camps, the big companies would tender for the contract within hours and within days a complete force would be in place to do the job. PMCs wouldn't be standing there guarding camp perimeters. They'd be out in the scrubland hunting down these Arab militias and then they'd hit them so hard, these people would be scared shitless about even contemplating another rape or murder of an unarmed refugee. Job done.

What stands in the way of this is the International Convention Against the Recruitment, Use, Financing and Training of Mercenaries, passed by the UN General Assembly in 1989. Typically, Angola and Zaire signed this agreement but they still regularly employ mercenaries to further their aims.

The British government would seem to rather like the idea of a pool of registered, vetted PMCs, working under strict international laws, available for UN operations. The Americans, who for years have patiently paid most of the UN's bills, would like it, too, and I suspect that once the awful truth about UN peacekeeping missions was made public, U.S. taxpayers would probably insist upon it.

In his hour of need, Kofi Annan asked for PMCs to help staunch the bloodletting in Rwanda and said they could save hundreds of thousands of lives. But he conveniently forgot that when he had the chance to act in Darfur. I'm glad he's gone, but the man who replaced him as UN secretary-general seems to have been quickly bogged down in the morass, too.

For my part, I believe that the world's leaders should just get on with it and recognize that there is a reservoir of skilled PMC soldiers and what these soldiers are capable of doing to help the people in the world who are in the most danger.

Remember that SAS colleague of mine who called in an air strike on his own coordinates to stop a genocide in Kosovo? Well, another mate, an ex-Blade, was working as a PMC in Ghana when he came across thirty or so children all tied together on the back of a truck by a blue nylon rope that went from one child's neck to another's.

The slave trade is alive and well in Africa, and he knew these kids would be working as slaves in the fields or a factory within hours. The driver was taking a piss, so this PMC just battered the armed guard left in charge of the children and drove the kids off in the truck to an aid agency down the road, while his sidekick followed in their 4 x 4.

Both those colleagues now run PMC companies hiring out top guns in Iraq, and they're likely to stay as management in the business for years to come.

Now I ask you. Who would you rather have fighting for the oppressed under the UN flag? Those two guys, or some ragtag rapist from a conscript army who couldn't fight his own shadow?

14. Blackwater!

A FRIEND OF MINE CALLED CHAS WAS sitting cross-legged in front of a village elder when the old man pulled up the folds of his *shemag* headdress to cover half his face and keep the dust out of his nose. Chas was trying hard to keep a road open for his call-signs. They'd been using it for a couple of months as a way of avoiding another route that was constantly being dicked by the insurgents. But the elder was in no mood to talk about safe passage. He told Chas that trouble had swept through the village three days earlier and left one of his village clan lying smashed and dying in the roadside dust. The elder said she'd been a two-year-old girl and though her life chances in the fractured, blood-soaked region of Iraq where she lived had been bleak, at least she'd had a life. That's until the big tough men came riding through town in their gunned-up 4 x 4's.

The girl had done what the kids on the Iraq Highway often do: She'd hidden in the bushes when she saw the scary convoy heading toward the village. But this time, one of the trucks bounced off the track and crushed her under its wheels. It was an accident—at least I fucking hope it was—but the driver didn't bother to stop at the scene.

The account Chas was given is that the driver paused for a few seconds after the impact, someone looked down from the gun turret at the broken doll of a child below, called out an instruction, and then they drove on like a bat out of hell. No attempt to give the child first aid. No apology to the parents. No explanation to the village headman. No recompense for the terrible loss. They didn't even have the guts to stand there and take a mother's screams of anger. Seemingly no trace of humanity.

Chas says it was a hell of a job trying to placate the old man's fury and the grief of the villagers, whose mouthpiece he was. How do you explain how a group of men can have so little compassion that not even the sight of a little girl dying on the roadside could move any of them to stop?

The situation wasn't made any easier by the fact that my friend Chas had absolutely nothing to do with the company that employed the call-sign group responsible; he worked for a different company and lived by a different ethic. But even though it was not his responsibility, he and the other members of his call-sign group felt obliged to offer some words of apology and regret to the villagers.

Why? Well, there's the obvious reason: a little girl lying cold in the ground. But those men also felt a professional obligation to explain the difference between them and the perpetrators, however limp that might sound to the villagers. They'd always stopped to speak to the villagers and occasionally they'd give them a case of bottled water, a few dollars, and, poignantly, considering what eventually happened, even a few toys and teddies for the kids. The reason they'd offered those gifts was to acknowledge the simple truth that they were rolling through the villagers' backyard; they were paying their respects to the men and women whose turf they were using. It was simple courtesy and it made strategic sense. Drinkable water is at a premium in Iraq; a few dollars always helps; and those courtesies allowed the headman to act indulgently and keep the young hotheads in check.

The elder and the rest of the village pointed the finger firmly at Blackwater. He told Chas he knew it was them because of their distinctive convoy style and paramilitary style dress code.

Chas only had the word of the villagers but he believed their account. "I tell you something, Johnny, the most interesting thing to come out of that meeting was the absolute recognition by the villagers of those men's Blackwater identity and the absolute loathing they hold them in. It's the same all over the country; Iraqis know Blackwater and they hold those who work for the company in special contempt.

"That's not to say that we'd be on the village Christmas card list if they had one, but at least they recognized the humanity in us. The truth is that Blackwater employees are the real bogeymen of Baghdad and the locals consciously differentiate between them and other PMC call-sign groups."

But let's be utterly fair to Blackwater and not just take the word of one village elder about their behavior on the roads of Iraq. His words might perhaps be easily dismissed but there's independent and weighty evidence about Blackwater's conduct on the roads of Iraq and it comes from no less a body than the Congressional Committee on Oversight and Government Reform in a majority staff report presented on October 1, 2007. And even this report, cleaned up for Congress and the American people, gives us a shocking indication about Blackwater's general attitude toward road safety. The report states:

On November 28, 2005, a Blackwater motorcade traveling to and from the Ministry of Oil for official meetings collided with 18 dif-

ferent vehicles during the round-trip journey (6 vehicles on the way to the ministry and 12 vehicles on the return trip). The written statements taken from the team members after the incident were determined by Blackwater to be "invalid, inaccurate, and at best, dishonest reporting."

According to a Blackwater contractor who was on the mission, the tactical commander of the mission "openly admitted giving clear direction to the primary driver to conduct these acts of random negligence for no apparent reason." The only apparent sanction resulting from this incident was the termination of two of the employees.

But back to Chas and his problems with the headman. Whoever did this lost an opportunity and made everyone else's work a lot harder. And of course, most tragically, killed a child.

"You just can't understand what makes those guys tick. I've no doubt a few of the guys in that call-sign group had kids of their own back home in the States, but maybe they thought that an Iraqi kid was of a lower order. A child in peril needs the help of strong hands, but they weren't on offer. Those guys were real bad Samaritans. All it needed was a few minutes to pay respect, some water, or even a few simple painkillers or some ringworm lotion to keep the peace."

Chas's meeting with the headman was a nightmare, but it had to be done. All the same, the road was off-limits from then on, and it wasn't long before a Blackwater call-sign group got whacked by an ambush in the vicinity and had to run for their lives.

Chas is right about one thing. Those working for Blackwater are held to be odious, and not just by Iraqis but by a tremendous number of other PMC companies, both American and international. I didn't need Chas to tell me that, either. I found that the bad feeling against Blackwater employees was one of the few points of common ground for people on all sides. Ordinary Iraqi citizens who want to get on with their lives, insurgents of all types, and other PMCs, all are united in their condemnation of Blackwater's actions, but of course the Iraqis tend to express that disdain with RPGs and AK-47s and they don't reserve their venom for Blackwater alone.

It's even become common ground for the U.S. military and I've personally heard many U.S. commanders on the ground characterize Blackwater as a pain in the butt, and worse. But don't take my word for that. Let's turn to the oversight committee again and their written evidence.

> In recent days, U.S. military commanders have reported that Blackwater guards "have very quick trigger fingers," "shoot first and ask questions later," and "act like cowboys." A senior U.S. military official has asserted that the impact of Blackwater's actions on Iraqi attitudes toward U.S. forces "is going to hurt us badly" and "may be worse than Abu Ghraib."

Worse than Abu Ghraib? It doesn't get much worse than that, but there's more to come.

THERE'S THE INCIDENT WITNESSED by another PMC mate, called Darren, in Karbala in June of 2005. The gates of a private compound on the edge of the ancient city were flung open and a high-profile, five-truck PMC convoy roared out onto the street and swung a hard right.

They were all gunned up with Minimis and .50-caliber weapons in the turrets of the Humvee gun wagons compassing the road with wide sweeps. Oh no! Here we go! A family sedan had made the terrible error of entering the same road, its occupants going about their lawful business, when the car fell within the invisible security bubble of the convoy.

No fucking about now. These were Blackwater boys. No one fucks with them. Were they under threat? According to Darren, they were not, but apparently they wanted to make sure. First, the Minimi eyeballed the vehicle and hammered burst after burst into the ancient old soft-skin car, and like a wolf pack, the other guns took a bite, too. *Whack! Whack! Whack!* The sickening sound of rounds pounding into the innocent echoed around the street. It was over in a few seconds and as the sedan bumped out of control over the pavement and hit the wall of a building with a grinding of metal, the all-American heroes of Blackwater bowled off down the road and into the sunset.

They left the people in the car behind them for dead, blood mingled with shattered flesh and bone, human beings unrecognizable, and the scene sharing the sickly sweet stench of a slaughterhouse. They were people who'd done absolutely nothing to merit the attention of a trio of machine guns except to commit the cardinal sin of entering the invisible force field around a Blackwater convoy. They couldn't see that force field; they didn't know it was there, but it killed them all the same.

Darren was there because he was working in a call-sign group for a British company protecting a media crew at the time and it was his compound that the Blackwater team had been visiting.

He told me about it. "We'd set it up nicely, John. We had our TV people established and comfortably settled in this private compound on the edge of the town. We were low profile and we'd been so careful and so discreet that the neighbors really didn't know we were there.

"It was all going really nicely until the correspondent jacked up an interview with a coalition high ranker, which was to take place at our compound. We assumed that he would arrive the way we came and went—low profile, disguised, and discreet. Wrong! Rule one is never to assume anything, and we had assumed. What actually happened is that we heard some buzzing in the distance and then we saw two baby birds in the sky heading straight toward us. They were Blackwater's birds and the only thing they didn't have was advertisement streamers trailing behind them.

"The birds were top cover for a convoy, which soon appeared and roared into our compound like they were arriving for a rodeo. Well, you can imagine how we felt. Our cover was well and truly fucking blown. The interview went ahead as scheduled, but I could see the correspondent was pissed and could barely conceal his rage.

"When it was over, they left, all drums, bugles, and bullshit, again drawing attention to themselves and our front gate. Not that it mattered anymore, as we were already packing our bags and getting ready to move pronto.

"That's when it happened. I was watching them leave and they pulled a tight right and tore off down the road. I saw the rounds tearing into the car. We didn't hang around to find out any more, else we'd have been toasted by the locals. These people had a right to life and a right to drive down a street in their own neighborhood in their own country. They were human beings, John, but they were treated like worthless vermin."

And by Blackwater's own account in figures rendered to the oversight committee they're a pretty trigger-happy bunch. The committee says:

Incident reports compiled by Blackwater reveal that Blackwater has been involved in at least 195 "escalation of force" incidents in Iraq since 2005 that involved the firing of shots by Blackwater forces. This is an average of 1.4 shooting incidents per week. Blackwater's contract to provide protective services to the State

Department provides that Blackwater can engage in only defensive use of force. In over 80% of the shooting incidents, however, Blackwater reports that its forces fired the first shots.

In the vast majority of instances in which Blackwater fires shots, Blackwater is firing from a moving vehicle and does not remain at the scene to determine if the shots resulted in casualties. Even so, Blackwater's own incident reports document 16 Iraqi casualties and 162 incidents with property damage, primarily to vehicles owned by Iraqis. In over 80% of the escalation of force incidents since 2005, Blackwater's own reports document either casualties or property damage.

The reports describe multiple Blackwater incidents involving Iraqi casualties that have not previously been reported. In one of these incidents, Blackwater forces shot a civilian bystander in the head. In another, State Department officials report that Blackwater sought to cover up a shooting that killed an apparently innocent bystander. In a third, Blackwater provided no assistance after a traffic accident caused by its "counter-flow" driving left an Iraqi vehicle in "a ball of flames."

Blackwater also reports engaging in tactical military operations with U.S. forces. In addition to Blackwater, two other private military contractors, DynCorp International and Triple Canopy, provide protective services to the State Department. Blackwater reports more shooting incidents than the other two contractors combined. Blackwater also has the highest incidence of shooting first, although all three companies shoot first in more than half of all escalation of forces incidents.

There you have it. They shoot first and don't stop to see who they've killed or injured and then they try to cover up incidents. I personally don't believe Blackwater's figures because I know from my days on the Highway that they send bursts into every junction ahead of them like they are spraying disinfectant onto bugs. How do I know? Because I've watched them do it. The whole of Iraq has watched them do it.

The fact is that these tactics appear to be the central plank of Blackwater's standard operating procedures, and once again I have been told by a couple of their own team leaders that they are taught these tactics in simulations back home in North Carolina on the range before they jet off to Iraq. If that isn't the case then Blackwater should be open and tell us how they actually train their men because if they are not instructing them in those tactics then something is going badly wrong between company training and live operations. I won't hold my breath, though, as Blackwater is steeped in a culture of secrecy, refuses interviews, and has been known to sack any of their operators who talk to the press; four by the company's account in evidence to the oversight committee.

Blackwater isn't the only high-profile operator behaving in that way, but in my opinion, it is the wildest and most undisciplined of the companies as witnessed in the oversight committee report. The official record is bad enough, but from what I've seen, they have opened fire on civilians day after day and it seems to me that most of those shots have been unnecessary and inflammatory.

Imagine the unthinkable. Your country has been invaded by a foreign power that wants to topple a warmongering president who condones the use of torture. You might tolerate the invader, but not if he hung around for too long. After all, it's your country. But if the fucker sent hired guns down your street and they started whacking you and your neighbors for no good reason as you went about your business, then you'd reach for your gun and shoot the bastard to shit if you could. Why should the Iraqis be any different?

Blackwater has created insurgents where before there were shell-shocked civilians who were simply anxious to see the back of the coalition and their friends but not willing to pick up a rifle to speed them on their way. Friends and family shot at on their own turf? That's a kick right in the nuts for the Iraqi clan honor system and they have no choice but to reply with violence.

It's particularly galling as I write this, because the U.S. military, thanks to its 2007 "surge," at last got a handle on the realities of hearts and minds in the particular culture of Iraq. The troops are doing fantastic work, but I know they often feel undermined by the high-handed, thoughtless violence. These incidents can set their work back by years and there's more.

I T WAS IN AL NAJAF. Chas was there. His team had been installed in a compound for two years. They'd paid respect to the locals in those small ways that count when you've just moved into a neighborhood—small acts of kindness, like slowing down when a mother and child are crossing a street, offering first aid to a kid with a cut on his leg. Things like that matter. It's about concern for the human condition. Then the Blackwater guys arrived. I'll let Chas tell the rest. He was there.

> I spoke to the Blackwater guys now and then. Like people in any other organization, a lot of them were fine; there's always good and bad. They all tend to have the same look, though. Weird individualistic haircuts, strange beards with lines cut into them, and they like to wear tight T-shirts to show their muscles. To be honest, a lot of them would look more at home posing on the sidewalk in Venice Beach, California. It's all very macho and it looks like a lot of steroids are in play, but the ethic they seem to have and the way they speak shows they put Arab life low on the scale of things.
>
> They hadn't been there long when there was a wedding in the district. Usual rules apply at Arab weddings, and at one point after the happy couple had tied the knot, the male relatives began

dancing, with their AKs held aloft, and inevitably they started firing celebratory shots in the air. I mean, these are people who shoot into the air if the national soccer team wins.

As bad luck would have it a Blackwater call-sign group was passing close by and heard the gunfire. Instead of returning to their base, they actually diverted to seek out the source of the gunfire and laid down bursts on the wedding party. It was unbelievable. They brassed up a wedding and turned a festive occasion into a bloodbath. A lot of people were hurt, but I don't know if there were any fatalities, simply because we bugged out as soon as it happened, figuring the whole of Najaf would bear down on our location when the news got out. To be honest, I'd be very surprised if anyone hadn't died.

What can you say, John. We look down our noses at those Middle Eastern crowds firing wildly into the air when they are celebrating something. It's bad weapons discipline, a waste of ammo; no way would we do that. But guess what? I've seen a Western group with even less weapons discipline than a crowd of Arabs, and it's the boys from Blackwater.

T HOSE INCIDENTS ARE by no means isolated, and if federal investigators turned over a few not-so-magic carpets in Iraq, they'd find plenty more. For years, Blackwater managed to avoid any official flack over numerous incidents on the Highway. That ended abruptly in a bloodbath on September 16, 2007, when a Blackwater call-sign group sparked off a gun battle in a Baghdad square, which resulted in the deaths of seventeen innocent civilians. This was one that Blackwater couldn't bullshit or busk their way out of; the numbers were simply too big and a cursory look at the facts had FBI agents pointing the finger right at Blackwater. Those people were innocent, the agents clearly stated.

That started a sequence of events that has seen the role of private military contractors propelled to the center stage of U.S. politics, with Blackwater's tactics, ethics, and links to President Bush's administration brought into stark relief.

More of that later, but first I'd ask you to pause a moment and think of that little girl crushed under the wheel of a Humvee, the family who turned down the wrong street at the wrong moment, a wedding celebration turned into a ghastly dance of death. They all took place in the months and years before September 16, 2007.

No one's asking a PMC to go soft on insurgents, and no one's saying anyone should roll over and take it, but that's no argument for creating a charnel house and shooting up innocent civilians.

15. On the Road Again

MAY DAY 2003. I WAS A PRISONER OF the Nigerian Secret Service at the moment when President George W. Bush strode across the deck of the aircraft carrier USS *Abraham Lincoln*, stood in front of a microphone, and made the most controversial statement of his life. Not an easy feat for the man, I'll admit.

"My fellow Americans, major combat operations in Iraq have ended. In the battle of Iraq, the United States and our allies have prevailed."

Well, that's what he said, and he was at least five years premature in his announcement. It's a shame I missed it, because it's not every day that you get to hear a monumental "Peace in our time" clanger being dropped, but that's the way it was.

Anyway, there I was, the prisoner of the Nigerian Secret Service and with more than enough on my plate to worry about. It all began when Mike Curtis asked me to lead a team out to Nigeria to review the security of a well-known opposition politician in a country where people die in quite large numbers for the sake of the party they support.

I had three ex-army types with me and an expert in electronic countersurveillance. Things had been going fine, and the job was progressing well, but the guys got cheesed off with staying in the client's security compound and decided to bug out to the local hotel four or five miles away.

I decided to stay at the compound with the client's own Nigerian security guys. After all, I reasoned, we were unarmed and they were tooled up with automatic weapons of every shape and size. Better safe than sorry; after all, you never know what's around the corner in a hardball African democracy like Nigeria. If there was going to be an attack, then I wanted to be near a gun, and I told the others they ought to be, too.

They thought otherwise and went to the hotel anyway. The bugging expert—we called him "Bug Man"—was white and obviously stood out like a sore thumb down in the town. The three ex-army guys were black; somebody had the bright idea that, based purely on the color of their skin, they wouldn't look conspicuous in an African environment. Wrong. Dead wrong. With their Cockney accents and English mannerisms, they were marked out as pure John Bull. They were as much sore thumbs as the Bug Man.

It wasn't long before the local state governor's henchmen network got to know about their presence in town. Soon after, we were arrested by a posse of security service heavies in the hotel lobby when I went to give the boys their instructions for our next move.

Bug Man and I were pushed around a bit, nothing too rough, but I witnessed a nasty bit of inverted racism when my three black mates, Neville, Vince, and Rich, were given a battering. To be honest, the six or seven blokes bashing them got off very lightly, because two of the lads were experts in a high-powered martial-arts style called "steel-wire kung fu." Don't ask me what that is; I'm just a champion in bog-standard karate. But I've seen them scrapping and it's devastating stuff. Anyway, Nev and Vince were showing remarkable restraint; otherwise, those Nigerian so-called tough guys might easily have been ripped limb from limb and had their guns rammed up their skinny arses.

We were taken to the local police station and put through forty-eight hours of sleep deprivation and constantly repeated questioning. It's tedious hearing the same questions over and over when you haven't had a snooze. "Who are you? Why are you here?" On and on it went, but I wasn't too bothered. It was pretty standard stuff as interrogations go, and if they wanted to waste their time asking me shit, I was quite happy to sit there, at least for a while.

Then I was taken back to the interview room. I was expecting more of the same, when a new face came in and introduced himself as a captain from Secret Service headquarters in Lagos. Once he'd arrived on the scene, he told us we were being moved.

We were put in a people carrier with three armed guards in the back, who were carrying old U.S. Army machine guns, World War II grease guns. The backup car carried two more Secret Service men. The driver set off down a road through the bush. We didn't like it. What was going on? Were they going to take us deeper into the bush and rub us out?

The guards were really tense, too, as the journey began and the whole business had a nasty feel about it. You could cut the atmosphere in that vehicle with a knife. I put down the really agitated mood of the guards to the fact that they may have been told to mallet us.

I wasn't having that, so I began a conversation with the kung fu guys in my regional Geordie accent from the northeast of

England, which I knew they'd both understand, because in the army you have to get to know all the regional accents. They replied in Jamaican patois, which I just about had a handle on, but only just. I was smiling as I spoke to make the guards think we were just having a friendly chat, and it was obvious that they didn't have the foggiest idea of what was going on.

The guys didn't like the feel of things, either, and so we agreed on a strategy that was a bit radical. But then, if you think there's a chance you're going to be shot like a dog, you're obviously going to think about biting back.

"If they turn off this road into the bush, we take these three muppets out, then deal with the driver. And then we make our way cross-country to the High Commission in Lagos. Okay?" I said.

"No problem, Johnny. We'll snap their necks," said Nev in a very matter-of-fact voice.

"Okay, Nev," I said in my singsong Geordie accent, "you take the one opposite. Vince, you take the one alongside you. I'll take the one with the pencil neck. And Rich, you get the driver. Grab the weapons and we take on the backup vehicle. Do it on my word and at the same time."

I could see Vince and Neville were really itching to have a go. I think they were still a bit cross about having had to put up with a battering when they were arrested and I wasn't sure they were going to wait for my word before snapping the guards. One suspicious move on the part of those Secret Service men and they would have been killed by my mates in the blink of an eye; I'm certain of that.

I was beginning to think that we should just do it anyway to end the tension that was building up in the back of the vehicle, which was turning a Japanese people carrier into a pressure cooker. Then suddenly, the guards looked around them as if recognizing where they were, laid their guns down, and started beaming with smiles of relief. The driver even started singing.

What the fuck was happening? They spoke some English, so I asked the guy in charge.

"We've been through a very, very bad area. Very bad. We had to be on alert for an attack. The captain said that no harm must come to you."

Fuck me. We'd nearly totaled those poor bastards and all they were doing was looking after us. Nev nearly pissed himself laughing at the irony of it.

"Fucking hell, John, what a laugh," said Nev, who was back to his Cockney English. "Another few minutes and I wouldn't have been able to hold back. I was going to give that fucker my best move."

The guards looked at Nev quizzically, as though he were some sort of a nutcase. Perhaps they thought he was laughing with relief at knowing he was out of danger. If they'd twigged the real reason why he was wetting himself, they'd have known just who was in danger, and it wasn't Nev.

We were held for another day and went through the same mind-drilling interrogation routine at their Lagos headquarters. The Bug Man had gotten a text message out to Mike Curtis, who rode to the rescue and moved on the problem in double-quick time. Mike informed the Foreign and Commonwealth Office and they quickly negotiated with the Nigerian authorities, assuring them we were doing genuine security work.

Then suddenly, during my last grilling, the chief interrogator took a phone call. He was sort of standing to attention while he was on the phone, a sure giveaway that he was talking to a superior. There was a lot of nodding and shaking of the head as he spoke; then when he'd put the phone down, he looked up and smiled.

"Mr. Geddes, you and your friends are free to go. Thank you for your cooperation and please make sure that you account for every piece of your personal belongings."

I collected my kit and signed for it, very glad to be on my way and free from the tedious interrogation. We were soon at the airport and then got straight onto the first flight back to Britain. I've still got Nev's and Vince's numbers; after all, you never know when you might need some steel-wire work done.

Although I don't keep a diary and my perception of time had been a bit fucked around by the interrogations, I reckon it was at the time of that road journey to Lagos that President Bush was making his statement on the USS *Abraham Lincoln*.

Funny, the last world leader to make such a historic cock-up had also stepped off an aircraft to address the microphones. That was in 1938, and the British prime minister, Neville Chamberlain, was fresh back from talks with Hitler in Munich when he uttered the fateful words "Peace for our time," to the newsreel cameras of the day.

Fair play to George: He'd arrived in a spectacular landing on the *Abraham Lincoln*, on board a four-seat navy jet that had been stopped by a cable brake across the deck. Christ, I bet that was the newest, best-greased length of cable in the entire U.S. Navy, and the blokes who'd laid it must have been in a real sweat. Well, in the end history tells us that George Bush didn't crash, just his predictions.

THE PRESIDENT'S BRAVURA ANNOUNCEMENT that the war had been won came several hours after his historic landing on the aircraft carrier. I think it's worth looking at some of his words, because that speech actually heralded the creation of an environment in Iraq where PMCs could flourish.

My fellow Americans, major combat operations in Iraq have ended. In the battle of Iraq, the United States and our allies have prevailed.

And now our coalition is engaged in securing and reconstructing that country.

In this battle, we have fought for the cause of liberty and for the peace of the world. Our nation and our coalition are proud of this accomplishment, yet it is you, the members of the United States military, who achieved it. Your courage, your willingness to face danger for your country and for each other made this day possible.

Because of you our nation is more secure. Because of you the tyrant has fallen and Iraq is free.

Operation Iraqi Freedom was carried out with a combination of precision and speed and boldness the enemy did not expect and the world had not seen before. . . .

When Iraqi civilians looked into the faces of our service men and women, they saw strength and kindness and good will. . . .

Today we have the greater power to free a nation by breaking a dangerous and aggressive regime.

With new tactics and precision weapons, we can achieve military objectives without directing violence against civilians.

No device of man can remove the tragedy from war, yet it is a great advance when the guilty have far more to fear from war than the innocent. . . .

We have difficult work to do in Iraq. We're bringing order to parts of that country that remain dangerous. We're pursuing and finding leaders of the old regime who will be held to account for their crimes. . . .

The battle of Iraq is one victory in a war on terror that began on September the 11th, 2001 and still goes on. . . .

The liberation of Iraq is a crucial advance in the campaign against terror. We have removed an ally of Al Qaeda and cut off a source of terrorist funding.

Just think about what has happened since President Bush made that speech. From May 2003 to Christmas 2005, the U.S. government had spent $200 billion dollars on the continuing war in Iraq. Around thirty thousand Iraqi civilians had been killed by both sides in the conflict and the cost of reconstruction was estimated by the World Bank to be a staggering $6.5 billion. Two hundred and fifty-one foreign civilian workers had been kidnapped, an average of about five a month, and 76 journalists had been killed, which adds up to a media bloodbath. Altogether, 2,399 coalition troops had been killed, including 98 British soldiers by December 2005. And although there are no firm figures, it's reckoned that around three hundred PMCs had been killed and scores more wounded.

Most of those PMC casualties, I reckon about 60 percent of them, can be put down to roadside IEDs and suicide bombs, with one call-sign group being wiped out by a bomber who had two young boys traveling with him. That's as ruthless and barbaric a camouflage to get his deadly cargo waved through checkpoints as you can imagine.

PMCs think those casualty figures are too high, but look at the official U.S. estimate of the number of insurgents who had been slotted during the same period of time: 53,470. That's a huge bloodletting by any reckoning, and although he's been subjected to a barrage of criticism, I suspect that's the one figure that George Bush will be pleased about whatever the cost.

His critics say he was wrong to go to war against Saddam, and to be fair, the arguments appear to show he was wrong on many counts. Or was he? We know quite well that far from Al Qaeda's being stamped out in Iraq, the organization's fighters and suicide bombers flooded into the country, causing mayhem and a huge loss of life under the direction of Musab al-Zarqawi.

But I have a soldier's hunch that the Pentagon and the CIA wanted it that way. They wanted Al Qaeda to have a focus for their jihad and deliberately set one up. If its fighters flocked to Iraq, then the CIA would know where they were. In effect, a killing ground had been created to suck the enemy in. Better bombs in the street markets of Baghdad than in the shopping malls of the USA. It suited the U.S. government to fight the war against terror on the streets of Ramadi rather than in the center of New York. It also suited that government to see a PMC army developing there, honing its skills, and fine-tuning its operations in Iraq.

It's those Al Qaeda activities and the actions of the Sunni insurgents allied to them that have made PMCs in Iraq an essential element of the coalition game plan. The U.S. companies in particular are well meshed into the military strategy, embedded, if you like, with the U.S. Army, and often travel in convoy with U.S. Marines or Rangers.

During this time, the PMCs of all nations have shown themselves, with a very few but notable exceptions, to be well regulated and to be carrying out their responsibilities with integrity and due diligence to the law. In many ways, they are self-regulating, and it is to the credit of the companies for which they work that anyone stepping over the line is dealt with swiftly and booted out, with little chance of getting another job.

In December 2005, election officials in Fallujah ran out of ballot papers as the inhabitants of the City of Insurgents rushed to polling booths to engage in the democratic process. That was a sign that the Sunnis were beginning to believe they had to engage in the political process, and there were signs of a growing contempt for the activities of Al Qaeda, which, when all was said and done, was killing more Iraqis than Americans.

Only time will tell whether the insurgency will die away or whether Sunni politics will just be a cloak for the insurgency as Republican politics were in Northern Ireland.

But it was PMCs who were given the heavy responsibility of supervising the delivery of ballot papers around Iraq during the elections and referendums of 2005. It was PMCs who distributed the new Iraqi currency across the country as the economy was being revived. And it was PMCs who continued to protect the lives of the thousands of contractors rebuilding the country.

They are, for the most part, lightly armed and they do not represent a cohesive offensive force, but they acquitted these high-risk tasks with style and professionalism. If democracy and the will of the people do eventually prevail in Iraq, it will be in no small part due to the presence of PMCs in the country.

IN MY OWN SMALL way, I tried to make a difference whenever I could. I remember one day I was with a media crew in the north of the Marsh Arab territory.

It's worth remembering that the marshes of southern Iraq were once a great floodplain with reed-covered islands where deer and wild boar ran. Between them were channels of clear water filled with fish, home to huge flocks of ducks and wading birds. All around, the marshes were surrounded by baking desert regions. No wonder some people thought this place was the Garden of Eden written about in the Bible.

The people of the marshes are called the Ma'dan and they were unique, too. They lived close to nature, making fantastic reed buildings and living off the harvest of fish and wildfowl provided by their environment. They were a tribal people and deeply independent. Saddam loathed them.

After the Gulf War, he killed the Marsh Arabs by the tens of thousands and then built a canal to divert the Tigris and the Euphrates and drain hundreds of square miles of marshland in one of the greatest pieces of environmental vandalism of all time.

The crew I was with was filming in a small village not far from the Saddam Canal, which had brought desolation to the Marsh Arabs' land. The first thing the few Marsh Arabs who were left had done was to breach the canal and let the waters take their natural course again. Watercourses and lagoons were beginning to reappear, and one of the villagers took me out onto a lake in a traditional dugout boat. It was the most tranquil place I'd ever found in Iraq.

What usually happened when I visited such villages was that I would get my medical kit out of the vehicle and ask if anyone needed help. Invariably, children were brought to me for help, and it was no different this time. I got talking to an old man through the interpreter. He was wearing a pinstripe jacket over his long robe and he wore the traditional trailing turban. He treated me as an honored guest, offering me a meal of dates and milk.

"I had a son who should be your age," he told me. "But the army took him away and I never saw him again. It was when Saddam made war with our brothers from Iran. Why would my son want to fight Iran? It is a terrible thing."

I told him about Kurt and how I had feared for my own son's life and how I was truly sorry for his loss. Then they brought me his granddaughter, who had a nasty gash on her leg, which I cleaned and sutured. I remember her big brown eyes looking up at me with complete trust and I thought of my own daughter. I felt an overwhelming wish to protect those people who'd suffered so much.

I stitched another kid, gave one some eye lotion, and then I treated about fifteen of them for scabies. I was always sorting out the mites that afflicted the village kids and I always made a point of having a bottle of the right lotion with me.

When I left the village, the old man embraced me and gave me a blessing. I took that blessing back onto the Highway. I had unfinished business there.

T HE TWO GUYS SITTING in the car were completely comfortable with the weapons on their laps and they were pretty much at ease and relaxed as their Iraqi driver sped them along the Highway. The relentless rock and sand of the desert spun past them as they headed down the Highway toward Baghdad.

They had an RV to make at about midday at a grid reference just before they ran the gauntlet of the Fallujah bypass. For some unfathomable reason, they decided to drive past the RV and carry on down the road. No sweat. They were on time and all was well with the world, but they were a bit too relaxed for a pair of crows, because this was their first trip into Iraq. They'd been well briefed on the severe nature of the lethal environment they were about to go into, but perhaps they'd had one warning too many. Perhaps they believed nothing could be as bad as the picture that had been painted.

Well, one thing was for sure: They were on the Highway to Hell and they were just at entry level. Things were going to get a lot messier before the day was over, and it began when the amber warning light on their fuel gauge flashed on. Their Iraqi driver pointed it out to them. They needed fuel and knew they'd better get some, so they asked the driver if he knew where there was a service station. He did, he said.

Five minutes later, after going up a bullet-pocked slip road off the Highway, they turned into the suburbs of a large town. They drove straight past the signpost announcing the name of the city they were entering. Fallujah. Twinned with Armageddon.

Still no alarm bells were ringing in their minds, and yet they should have been deafening them. These guys were not new to the security game. One was ex–Grenadier Guards; the other had been a soldier in the specialist unit 14 Intelligence and had done a huge amount of time undercover in Northern Ireland. He was well versed in tactical awareness from his spook days on the streets of Belfast, but even he hadn't twigged that it was all going wrong.

The driver just kept going. For some strange reason, he wasn't bothered about ferrying two white eyes into the heart of the insurgency. There was no evidence that he was connected to the insurgency. Perhaps he was just having a thick day, too.

They found their gas station and the two of them got out and had a stretch while the driver filled the tank. One of them lighted a cigarette and relaxed a bit more and they both stood around in blissful ignorance, as if someone had erected a force field around them. Then the 14 Intelligence guy woke up and began to smell the funeral flowers. The same car had come around the block for the third time and his undercover instincts were now screaming at him, That's a fucking dicker!

His instincts were right. *Dicker* is the old army term for an IRA spotter in Northern Ireland. The sharks were circling and they'd smelled easy blood, but at that very moment his mobile phone began ringing and a voice snarled down the line. It was my old mate Mike Curtis calling.

"Where the fuck are you! You should be at the RV."

"We're in Fallujah," came the extremely limp-dick reply.

"For fuck sake! Stay where you are. We're on our way!" said Mike.

That call saved their bacon, because it's certain that the dickers must have been making a call at the very same time that mirrored the one with Mike. They must have phoned for the heavy brigade, their gunned-up comrades, to come and mallet the European madmen who, incredibly, were queuing up for an orange boiler suit at a fuel stop in Fallujah. And so it was that the two sets of opposing cavalry met on the way to the service station.

I was in a vehicle behind Mike with a South African guy and a Jordanian driver, following him up the slip road on our way to stop the guys from getting intimate with al-Zarqawi's blade. Suddenly, two flatbed Toyotas pulled out of a junction at the top of the slip road and attempted to block Mike's vehicle. They tried to ram his car off the top of the slip road and roll it down the embankment and back onto the Highway.

I heard Mike on the headset. "Front! Front! Front!"

He managed to swerve around them and keep going, but then the first of the Toyotas ran alongside his car, smashing into the side of it. Sparks and chunks of metal flew as Mike, who was driving, rammed them back.

Suddenly, the window of his 4 x 4 rocked as Stu, Mike's call-sign group partner, opened up on the nearest Toyota with his weapon. Two of the insurgents in the back of the truck were hit and thrown onto the road like rag dolls as the life was slammed out of them. The Toyota ran off the road as Mike screamed to a halt and leapt out to deploy across the hood, while Stu continued pasting the Toyota, which still had three fighting insurgents returning rounds.

Mike began firing from his side of the vehicle, hammering rounds into the second vehicle with absolute disregard for the incoming rounds chewing lumps out of the car frame around him.

VOOSH! The first Toyota burst into flames just as I and the white South African "Yarpee" deployed on the trunk and hood of our vehicle, firing burst after burst into the second truck as we supported Stu's withering fire. They were well fucked-up. How many? Don't know. We didn't stop to count, but I'd hit one of them as he tried a long triple jump into the ditch alongside the road to escape the hail of lead. I got him in the thigh and then a second round whacked him in the torso, doubling him up, midway through his jump.

Minutes later, Mike rocked up at the fuel station and bollocked the two crows as he anointed them "fucking donkeys." It was over and there was no time for long inquests as we sped off. But one thing's for sure: If we hadn't been close at hand, those two would have been killed or taken hostage. We'd just happened to bump into their nemesis on the Highway before they'd met at the petrol station. Simple fate, really.

The 14 Intelligence guy went on to prove that his lapse on the forecourt had been a onetime occurrence. I doubt whether he could ever explain how he'd been so lax, but he ended up as a top player. The other guy vanished after a negligent discharge—that's official jargon for firing his weapon when he shouldn't have—but he then resurfaced in Baghdad, and he's doing a great job, too.

For Mike and Stu, it had been a hot action. For me, it had been the contact that I needed to confirm that I was as sharp as ever, no luck involved. And it had been a success on my own terms. I was over the worst of it. I'd survived my own nightmare of booze and insurgents and the never-ending stress of the Highway.

What of the men we'd left dead on the road? As we drove off, I looked into the ditch and saw the body of the man I'd just killed. Who was he? What was he? Bandit, Ba'athist, or fighter for Al Qaeda? For sure, he was some Iraqi mother's son. But am I haunted by the ghosts of the dead men left on the Highway? No, I'm not, because as I glanced at his body, I asked myself what he would have felt if it had been me lying lifeless in the ditch. I knew in my heart that he would have been glad.

You see, the Highway to Hell is a toll road. Someone has to pay. And guess what? It ain't gonna be me.

About the Author

Based in London, John Geddes is a principal at Ronin Concepts, Ltd., a private security company. His military career spans more than two decades, including distinguished tours around the world with the Special Air Service.